INTERNATIONAL DEVELOPMENT IN FOCUS

Mobilizing Finance for Local Infrastructure Development in Vietnam

A City Infrastructure Financing Facility

Alessandra Campanaro and Cuong Duc Dang

WORLD BANK GROUP

1 2 3 4 21 20 19 18

ISBN: 978-1-4648-1287-3
DOI: 10.1596/978-1-4648-1287-3

Contents

Boxes

Figures

Map

Tables

Foreword

Since the decentralization and liberalization reforms in the 1990s, Vietnam has experienced rapid urbanization and remarkable economic growth. By 2025, more than half of the population will live in cities. The country is at a critical juncture now. Decentralization has delegated significant responsibilities to provincial governments while the affordability of local infrastructure investments has become a fundamental challenge for the provinces. The provinces need to leverage their balance sheets and use debt financing to fund their infrastructure needs. This transition will require enhanced capacity by the provinces to leverage private finance, as well as an enabling regulatory and legal environment for subnational borrowing.

Apart from the primary cities of Hanoi and Ho Chi Minh City, which already have demonstrated capacity and experience in tapping capital markets on their own, a group of secondary provinces (net contributors to the central government budget) have shown strong demand for local infrastructure financing and potential creditworthiness for leveraging private capital. These provinces will need to enhance their capacity to obtain private capital in the market; standardize provincial budgeting, accounting, and financial reporting procedures; and ensure better quality of financial disclosure.

Prepared with the cooperation and support from the Ministry of Finance, the State Bank of Vietnam, as well as selected subnational governments and commercial banks, this book explores the potential development of a city infrastructure financing facility (CIFF) in Vietnam, which aims to catalyze subnational borrowing for local infrastructure development in the context of the abovementioned opportunities and challenges. Global experience has shown that because public funding resources are increasingly scarce, moving toward a more market-driven local infrastructure financing model is a critical step for subnational governments. This book's findings can offer some implications for policy makers in other developing countries, especially those transitioning from a centralized to a decentralized system, and those transitioning from a low-income to middle-income group.

The book confirms that there is broad interest among commercial banks in Vietnam to lend to provincial governments. The banking sector has been gradually recovering from the global financial crisis and has substantial untapped capital available for new funding opportunities. Yet, unfamiliarity with the subnational budget process, and the overall perception of high risk, still limits the willingness of commercial banks to provide financing to local governments. Overcoming the existing technical and operational challenges will require capacity building, including standardization and disclosure of provincial financial reporting, and improvement to the banks' expertise in analyzing and pricing provincial credit risks. Maturity mismatches that exist between the short-term deposits and the long-term tenors needed for infrastructure loans indicate that it is still important to explore other longer-term financing for infrastructure investments in the long run.

There remain significant challenges in the reform of the legal and regulatory framework that constrain the development of the provincial debt market in Vietnam, such as (a) lack of legal clarity in provincial authority to borrow from commercial banks, (b) restrictions on maturities, (c) unspecified debt security, (d) moral hazard resulting from the implicit guarantee of the central government, (e) inadequate standards of disclosure, and (f) inappropriate standards of default and insolvency. To effectively stimulate provincial borrowing from the capital markets, further policy reforms must address these issues.

Many countries have set up financing facilities to catalyze the market, enhance the capacity of both the demand side (subnational governments) and the supply side (capital markets or commercial banks), and help identify future necessary reforms for furthering subnational borrowing based on implementation experience. Informed by both local and international experience, the proposed City Infrastructure Finance Facility (CIFF) could provide incentives for medium- to long-term lending in the provinces, while fostering a credit culture among provincial governments. In turn, this will enhance the governments' capacity to finance themselves in the markets in the longer term. Such experience will also enable provinces to productively use the untapped liquidity of commercial banks in the short to medium term, while familiarizing commercial banks with provincial government practices. In the long term, the CIFF could be expected to pool risks and tap the capital market.

Ultimately, a well-functioning subnational borrowing market would help provinces to finance their infrastructure needs in a decentralized system and would pave the way for inclusive and sustainable urbanization and growth of Vietnam.

Ousmane Dione
Country Director for Vietnam
The World Bank

Ede Ijjasz-Vasquez
Senior Director for Social, Urban, Rural & Resilience Global Practice
The World Bank

Acknowledgments

This book is the final product of Vietnam City Infrastructure Financing Facility Advisory Services and Analytics activity. The lead authors and co-task managers of this book are Alessandra Campanaro (Senior Urban Specialist; Social, Urban, Rural, and Resilience Global Practice) and Cuong Duc Dang (Senior Urban Specialist; Social, Urban, Rural, and Resilience Global Practice), with support from Roland White (Lead Urban Specialist; Social, Urban, Rural, and Resilience Global Practice), Richard Torkelson (Consultant), Johan Kruger (Consultant), Hung Tran (Consultant), Pham Nghiem Xuan Bac (Consultant), and Vision & Associates Co., Ltd. The book was produced under the overall guidance of Abhas K. Jha (Practice Manager; Social, Urban, Rural, and Resilience Global Practice), Victoria Kwakwa (Regional Vice President, East Asia and Pacific Region), and Ousmane Dione (Country Director, Vietnam).

Peer review comments from Bjorn Philip (Program Leader, West Bank and Gaza), Kalpana Seethepalli (Senior Economist; Finance, Competitiveness, and Innovation) and Alwaleed Fareed Alatabani (Lead Financial Sector Specialist; Finance, Competitiveness, and Innovation) are gratefully acknowledged. Administrative assistance has been provided by Inneke Herawati Ross (Senior Program Assistant) and Giang Thi Huong Nguyen (Senior Program Assistant). The book benefitted from editorial support provided by Publications Professionals, LLC. Additional research and editorial support has been provided by Lawrence Tang (Public Finance Analyst, Consultant) and Taotao Luo (Urban Analyst, Consultant).

The team would also like to thank Public-Private Infrastructure Advisory Facility (PPIAF) for co-financing this publication. Established in 1999, PPIAF is a multi-donor technical assistance facility housed inside the World Bank Group. PPIAF is a global facility dedicated to strengthening the policy, regulatory, and institutional underpinnings of private-sector investment in infrastructure in emerging markets and developing countries. PPIAF catalyzes private participation through public-private partnerships (PPPs); market-based financing of subnational entities; and by supporting the generation, capture, and dissemination of best practices relating to private-sector involvement in infrastructure. For more information, visit www.ppiaf.org.

Abbreviations

ADB	Asian Development Bank
AfD	*Agence Française de Développement*
ASEAN+3	Association of Southeast Asian Nations + China, Japan, and Korea
BIDV	Bank for Investment and Development of Vietnam
BOT	build-operate-transfer
CEF	credit enhancement facility
CGIF	Credit Guarantee and Investment Facility Ltd.
CIFF	city infrastructure financing facility
CJSB	commercial joint-stock bank
DAF	development assistance fund
DBP	Development Bank of the Philippines
DDMEF	Department of Debt Management and External Finance
DSA	debt sustainability analysis
EVN	Vietnam Electricity Company
FCF	free cash flow
FDI	foreign direct investment
GDP	gross domestic product
GMB	group management board
GRDP	gross regional domestic product
IFC	International Finance Corporation
IMF	International Monetary Fund
JICA	Japan International Cooperation Agency
JSCB	joint-stock commercial bank
LLC	limited liability company
LDIF	local development investment fund
LGU	local government unit
LGUGC	LGU Guarantee Corporation
LVPB	Lien Viet Post Bank
MDF	municipal development fund
MOF	Ministry of Finance
MPI	Ministry of Planning and Investment
MSB	Maritime Bank
MUFIS	Czech Republic's Municipal Infrastructure Financing Company

NPL	nonperforming loans
ODA	official development assistance
PFI	private financing institution
PFM	public finance management
PMU	project management unit
PPC	provincial People's Committee
PPCo	provincial People's Council
PPP	private-public partnership
PWRF	Philippine Water Revolving Fund
RFF	retail financing facility
SBL	State Budget Law
SBV	State Bank of Vietnam
SEDP	Socio-Economic Development Plan
SME	small and medium enterprises
SOE	state-owned enterprise
SOCB	state-owned commercial bank
SPE	special purpose entity
SRF	state revolving fund
ULB	urban local body
UNDP	United Nations Development Programme
USAID	U.S. Agency for International Development
VAT	value-added tax
VDB	Vietnam Development Bank
WFF	wholesale financing facility
WSPF	water and sanitation pooled financing entity

21,500 Vietnamese dong = 1 US$

1 Overview of a City Infrastructure Financing Facility

INTRODUCTION

Over the period of 1994 to 2016, Vietnam has witnessed significant economic development, with gross domestic product (GDP) growth rate averaging at around 7 percent per year and yielding more than a threefold increase in income per capita overall. The economic expansion has been accompanied by rapid urbanization and steady decentralization of responsibilities to provincial governments. Currently, 35 percent of the population lives in urban areas and this rate is expected to increase to 50 percent by 2025, reinforcing the positive effects of agglomeration on the growth, prosperity, and liability of its cities. Such transformation also sees significant financial challenges for governments at different levels. As seen in many countries, most of the urban infrastructure can hardly be funded on a pay-as-you-go basis from scarce public budgets. Governments need to leverage their balance sheets and use debt financing to fund their infrastructure investment needs.

This juncture also presents an opportunity for Vietnam because a significant part of the investment needs could likely be met by a more efficient use of available resources. The increased efficiency is particularly important because the flow of concessional Official Development Assistance (ODA) funds, which have served as a major source of subnational infrastructure financing, is expected to slow down as Vietnam emerges into a middle-income country. The debt limit of the government of Vietnam has also started to constrain the capacity of the central government to expand its ODA portfolio and channel funds to subnational governments. Moving toward a more market-driven basis is becoming an urgent issue for subnational infrastructure financing in the country.

The Vietnamese government has been making gradual progress improving provincial government access to credit financing. In the early 2000s, the government established a Local Development Investment Fund (LDIF) financing framework for provinces to borrow for cost-recovery infrastructure projects. LDIFs have achieved modest successes in some provinces. Meanwhile, the government has passed several laws and issued many regulations authorizing provincial government borrowing since the 2000s. The recent State Budget Law (SBL) of 2015 reflects the shift toward a more enabling framework for subnational borrowing, including a substantial increase in the statutory debt limit compared with the previous regulation. However, regulatory policy reforms need to be further pursued on several aspects to effectively stimulate provincial borrowing from the capital markets and commercial banks.

Recognizing the potential and challenges for mobilizing private capital available to finance the emerging demand for municipal infrastructure investments among provinces, the government of Vietnam has engaged the World Bank since 2013 to identify a financing instrument that can be piloted to catalyze the subnational debt market. In particular, the government has been exploring the creation of a municipal development fund (MDF) to catalyze the development of a subnational debt market. The Ministry of Finance (MOF) engaged the World Bank to undertake analytical work to develop the concept and explore the possibility of developing such a pilot mechanism—a city infrastructure financing facility (CIFF).

This book presents the findings of three assessments that focused on (a) the borrowing capacity and creditworthiness of selected provincial governments, (b) the capacity of the commercial banking sector to invest in provincial governments, and (c) the current status of Vietnam's regulatory framework.

The pilot CIFF in Vietnam would help develop a steadily expanding provincial government debt market in which financial risk is appropriately allocated and properly priced. In Vietnam, provincial government financial risk is not clearly and legally distinguished from central government financial risk. Commercial banks and the capital market cannot properly price provincial debt on the basis of each province's credit strength. Thus, a key development goal of this book is to inform the design of a CIFF to ensure its objectives of stimulating private sector debt financing for provincial infrastructure. If a financing facility were structured to require private investors to lend their own capital to finance provincial government infrastructure—hence placing their money at risk—the facility would create a significant leveraging effect and would expand private sector financing on a more sustainable basis.

DEMAND-SIDE ANALYSIS

Like many other developing countries, Vietnam faces a demand for infrastructure funding that exceeds the abilities of the public and the donor community to provide. Vietnam needs an annual investment of approximately US$25 billion (D 537.5 trillion) for infrastructure development. To meet that demand, existing public and private sources are able to contribute only an estimated US$16 billion (D 344 trillion) per year. Thus, a shortfall of US$9 billion (D 193.5 trillion) is unfunded each year (World Bank 2013). To finance this shortfall, policy makers must create an enabling environment for the enhanced participation and leveraging of private resources for infrastructure funding at the provincial level. This environment can be achieved by removing impediments that prevent the private sector from participating fully in lending to the provinces at appropriate terms.

The level of overall government debt is approaching 64 percent of the GDP—almost at the maximum level of 65 percent set by Vietnam's National Assembly. Because Vietnam has a unitary financial system, provincial government debt is counted as part of the national debt figures. Provincial debt at the end of 2012 amounted to 1.3 percent of GDP, mostly incurred by the five largest cities: Hanoi (the capital), Ho Chi Minh City, Da Nang, Can Tho, and Hai Phong. The situation has not been changed considerably since 2012, and provincial borrowing remains at a relatively insignificant level.

Provincial government borrowing

Provincial governments can supplement their ability to undertake capital projects by borrowing and they have the authority to borrow for projects contained in the state budget. Provinces can tap the following sources to borrow: (a) the State Treasury for short-term loans not exceeding one year, (b) on-lending from the central government of ODA funding, (c) the Vietnam Development Bank (VDB), (d) state-owned and commercial banks, and (e) bond issues to tap the capital markets.

The bulk of provincial borrowing is sourced from the VDB, from the State Treasury, and from on-lending by the central government, with a small percentage (27 percent) supplied through the issue of municipal bonds and other sources (World Bank 2014). Commercial bank lending is practically nonexistent in the current environment.

Provincial governments will have to finance a major portion of the infrastructure gap because more than 75 percent of government spending for infrastructure is now the responsibility of the provinces (World Bank 2013). This large gap cannot be managed on a pay-as-you-go basis from each province's budget. Therefore, the provinces will need to leverage their balance sheets to borrow more from private sector investors to fund their infrastructure needs.

Although provinces are not prevented from borrowing from the commercial banking sector legally, commercial bank lending to provincial governments in Vietnam has been very limited. As detailed in the section "Supply-Side Analysis," commercial banks are reluctant to finance local authorities, and they view lending for local development as very risky, particularly in the absence of a clear recourse collateral mechanism and multiyear budgeting. Most banks' lending experiences with provincial governments have been as a servicing agent for the central government's program of on-lending funds from ODA sources for infrastructure. In such cases, the banks conduct little or no technical risk assessment and therefore do not develop the capacity to evaluate, price, and monitor provincial government projects according to commercial principles. The repayment capacity of projects and borrowers is rarely considered because of the banks' assumption that the provincial government had the implicit guarantee of the central government. On the demand side, many provincial governments are not motivated to seek commercial financing for their own investment projects because commercial rates are relatively high compared with the favorable rates of the VDB or the state treasury.

Provinces may also legally borrow from the local currency bond market. However, only a few provincial governments have gained access to financing in the capital markets through bond issues—namely, the provincial governments of Hanoi, Ho Chi Minh City, Da Nang, Dong Nai, Quang Ninh, and Bac Ninh—totaling approximately US$853 million (D 18.35 trillion). Although the Vietnam MOF and the World Bank have been working toward a market-based borrowing system, at present this effort is constrained because the amount of local borrowing and the interest rates for such borrowing are controlled by the MOF. Furthermore, issuing municipal bonds is time consuming and cumbersome and entails relatively high fixed costs (that is, the costs of documentation, advertisement, payment to securities companies, and so on). As a result, issuing municipal bonds has been very limited and is considered worthwhile only for relatively large projects.

The effective demand for each province is collectively determined (a) by the legal caps set by the SBL on the amount of debt each province can incur, (b) by the overall governmental debt ceiling of 65 percent of GDP set by the National Assembly for the country, and (c) by the fiscal condition of each province. The previous SBL (passed in 2002) established a cap on the amount of capital that provinces can mobilize, which must not exceed 30 percent (with an exception of 100 percent for Hanoi and 150 percent for Ho Chi Minh City) of the annual capital expenditures for construction in the provincial budget. The effect of this cap is that total borrowing, assuming recurrent costs average 70 percent of the budget, is limited to approximately 9 percent of a province's total own revenues in a given year, irrespective of what could be afforded on a sustainable basis. As elaborated in the section "Legal Framework," the new SBL of 2015, which became effective in the state budget year of 2017, increases the legal caps for the provinces, thus creating more fiscal space for borrowing. The new law will also require more financial discipline and better budgeting at the provincial level to ensure that debt incurred remains sustainable.

For potential borrowing volumes, an assessment—detailed in chapter 2—identified the potential provincial effective demand by focusing on the debt capacity of a sample of 3 out of the 11 second-tier provinces that are net contributors of revenue to the central government budget.[1] These provinces are Quang Ninh, near the China border and the port city of Hai Phong; Dong Nai, in the south near Ho Chi Minh City; and Bac Ninh, in the north near Hanoi. The assessment was based on the new SBL's statutory debt ceiling limit for net contributing provinces, namely 30 percent of provincial revenues. The assessment gives a good indication of debt levels that are affordable and sustainable, and it complies with the new statutory debt ceiling.

The financial data provided by those three provinces were analyzed through a free cash flow method and a debt sustainability analysis. According to available data, the three provinces are preliminarily assessed to be financially healthy and able to absorb substantial amounts of additional debt (chapter 2) within the new SBL debt cap. That cap limits their total debt stock at 30 percent of the previous year's revenue, assuming loan tenors are extended. The analysis of the three provinces indicated considerable fiscal space for borrowing before the debt ceiling is reached or the ability to service debt becomes an issue. The initial realistic aggregated borrowing demand of 11 provinces is estimated to be D 6.6 trillion (US$307 million) and remain around D 6.45 trillion (US$300 million) per year over the next five years.

Weaknesses that may inhibit provincial borrowing

If the private sector is expected to take the full risk when lending to provincial governments, it will do so only after conducting a credit assessment on the province's financial data to ensure that it meets the need of the individual bank. Although the new SBL of 2015 substantially increased the limit for the provinces to borrow, several weaknesses can affect a provincial government's borrowing ability:

- Lack of timely availability and integrity of information. Financial data must be collected from multiple sources and are often inconsistent, raising fundamental integrity concerns. The budget cycle is long, and final audited figures do not have to be available until 18–20 months after the end of the financial year. That system renders the actual figures virtually useless as a management tool or as a base to assess financial creditworthiness.
- Incomplete financial statements. Provincial budget information often lacks details needed for banks to make a decision because, for example, (a) ODA loans are regarded as off budget, (b) debt is not accounted for, (c) the activities of state-owned enterprises with varying degrees of autonomy are not shown, (d) carryovers are not formally reflected, and (e) contingent liabilities are not transparent.
- Substantial year-to-year swings in projected provincial data. These swings inhibit predictability and make credit assessments with any degree of integrity impossible.
- Significant underestimation of revenue and consistent overspending on capital. The tendencies are to underspend or overspend against budget, which indicates a weakness in financial management and a lack of management information systems.
- Low revenue collection in provinces. Collection in provinces averages about 60 percent of potential revenue (World Bank 2015).
- An unclear regulatory framework. Banks prefer clarity in regard to the relationship between a provincial borrower and a lender, especially as far as default and recourse measures are concerned, and they need to see provincial credit risk legally differentiate from central government debt repayment responsibility.

Benefits to provinces from a city infrastructure financing facility

Because of the issues described, there is potentially a substantial level of demand from the provinces for access to and support from a new facility to promote more provincial borrowing. However, regulatory constraints and the financial attractiveness of the terms offered by the financing facility—particularly in comparison with the two current primary sources of provincial government credit (VDB and the state treasury)—will have a significant influence on the ultimate effective demand. In particular, effective demand for provincial borrowing will be dependent on the degree to which reforms are implemented to extend debt tenors, promote more autonomy, enhance revenues, and improve financial management capacity. The efforts to facilitate the creation of a long-term debt market for provincial infrastructure financing will also have to be accompanied by substantial interventions to make a clear legal distinction between central government and provincial debt and to build financial-management capacity at the provincial level. Finally, efforts to stimulate stronger demand for provincial borrowing will have to be managed in the context of a macro-environment in which national government debt (which includes provincial debt) is already approaching the statutory limit set by the National Assembly.

SUPPLY-SIDE ANALYSIS

Vietnam's banking sector has shown impressive growth in both loans and deposits since 2000. The fastest growth rate took place from 2002 to 2007, when total loans and deposits grew at a compounded annual growth rate of 35.8 percent and 37.5 percent, respectively. This growth rate peaked in 2007, when loans grew by 53.9 percent and deposits grew by 51.5 percent. The slowdown in loan growth has largely been the result of a high level of bad debts or nonperforming loans (NPL) on the balance sheets of Vietnam's banking sector. Overall, the banking sector is gradually recovering from the global financial crisis and only recently addressed the substantial NPL overhang.

In a period of low investment demand and low individual consumption, commercial banks are looking for new funding opportunities. It is estimated that the whole commercial banking system had about D 200 trillion, equivalent to US$9.3 billion, of untapped capital. Having commercial banks lend to provincial governments on a market basis would represent a new frontier for the Vietnamese banking industry. Historically, commercial banks had loans for government infrastructure projects at both the central and provincial levels secured with central government guarantees. Hence such loans were essentially riskless. However, in the rare instances in which short-term direct loans were made to provincial governments by commercial banks, they were not provided with proper collateral or a guarantee. In the absence of a recourse mechanism, the lender banks have been exposed to greater credit risks.

Commercial banks in Vietnam have shown some experience in providing loans at longer tenors. On average, the banks used approximately 31 percent of their assets to make loans at tenors greater than five years. This suggests that the banks have the ability to lend at longer tenors and could possibly do so for provincial governments, if the appropriate regulations were put in place to authorize it. However, commercial banks would need to balance any expansion of long-term lending to provincial governments with the potential increase in liquidity risk, given that extensive mismatches already exist between long-term assets and long-term liabilities. Hence, the availability of a refinancing window through which the banks could obtain longer-term capital to fund long-term loans to provincial governments would potentially serve as a key market stimulant for commercial banks.

Although commercial banks are interested in diversifying their portfolios, they would approach lending to provincial governments with caution, because of the following operational as well as legal and regulatory constraints:

- Commercial banks have limited expertise in analyzing provincial government books, records, and management and thus have no internal credit assessment process for identifying and evaluating the risks of lending to provincial governments.
- Commercial banks would prefer to depend on their own internal credit review of each province to help them assess the risks of lending to provincial governments.
- Commercial banks generally assume that all provincial government debt is merely an extension of the national debt and ultimately guaranteed. However, because there is uncertainty about this assumption, banks prefer to buy central government bonds. Central government bonds are viewed as more valuable and trusted assets that insulate banks from having to deal with myriad

provincial government issuers and interpretations of an ambiguous provincial government regulatory system.
- Commercial banks perceive that direct loans to provincial governments pose a high risk of nonpayment and are concerned that they have no clear, legal right to protect themselves and their investors in the event of a default.
- Commercial banks want their investments to have security, which could be achieved with credit enhancements, a recourse mechanism, or government guarantees.
- Commercial banks need liquidity because there is no market for trading bank loans to provincial governments or rediscounting them to the state treasury.
- Commercial banks are concerned with deal size, frequency, and credit quality.
- Commercial banks need clear, timely, regular, frequent, and comprehensive disclosure about the financial condition of their borrowers.
- Commercial banks want regular communication with their borrowers, not just when they are about to request a loan or a debt issuance.

LEGAL FRAMEWORK

The three main laws that control borrowing by provincial governments in Vietnam are the SBL of 2002, revised in 2015; the Law on Public Debt Management; and the Law on Credit Institutions. At present, there is no legal prohibition for commercial banks or the capital markets to provide loans to provincial governments. However, provinces are forbidden to borrow from offshore financing entities. The authority for provincial borrowing is not unfettered, and there are certain legal limits on how much provinces may borrow.

State Budget Law

Under SBL 2015, effective since January 2017, provinces may borrow to offset their local budget deficit (which should be used only for investment in projects that are included in medium-term public investment plans already decided by the provincial People's Council) and to repay the principal of debts. The law specifies the limits of local budget borrowing on the basis of the revenue that provinces are entitled to retain, instead of on the investment spending for capital construction as stipulated under the SBL 2002 previously. Such limits are different for groups of provinces, broken down by the difference between the provinces' retained revenues and its current expenditures, as follows:

- Hanoi and Ho Chi Minh City can borrow up to 60 percent of the provincial revenue they are entitled to.
- Provinces entitled to revenue that exceeds their recurrent expenditure amount can borrow up to 30 percent of that revenue.
- Provinces entitled to revenue equal to or lower than their recurrent expenditure amount can borrow up to 20 percent of that revenue.

The financial capacity of the provincial budgets in the estimation year must be below financing needs generated by the investment plan for the year. In addition, provinces are required to meet the ceiling of the local budget deficit annually allocated for each province by the central government because the local budget deficit is included in the state budget deficit and decided by the

National Assembly. The government of Vietnam prescribes in detail when a local budget deficit is permitted to ensure the debt repayment capacity of localities and to fit the total deficit of the state budget.

Under SBL 2015, provincial governments can borrow in the form of bond issuance, on-lending from the government's foreign loan, or other legitimate sources allowed by law. Generally, in the annual budgeting process of local governments, each provincial People's Congress prepares a budget estimate on local deficit, borrowing, and repayment of debt based on the balancing capacity of local budget, borrowing balance limit, and demand for development investment capital; submits it to the provincial People's Council for approval; and then submits it to the central government for approval.

The 2015 SBL, including all its guiding legislation, is silent on recourse to ensure that, in the case of provincial government default on borrowings from other sources (such as commercial banks or capital markets), the lenders or financiers could recover the funds from the provincial budget. Nonetheless, MOF budget officials reported that the MOF has an informal recourse mechanism when a provincial government fails to repay advances from the state treasury,[2] which is to deduct the amount of arrearages from the provincial government's future budget allocations. It should be noted that advances from the state treasury are not legally regarded as borrowing or loans provided by the central government (that is, the MOF) to the provincial government.

Law on public debt management

The Law on Public Debt Management (29/2009/QH12; June 17, 2009) authorizes provinces to issue bonds or borrow from "legitimate domestic financial sources."[3] The law authorizes provinces to enter into loan agreements and stipulates that the source for payment shall be "guaranteed" by the provincial budget and revenue from investment projects by the provinces. This language could be interpreted to provide lenders with some comfort, although if a default were to happen, there is no clear, explicit recourse for a lender under this law.

The Law on Public Debt Management does not specify that provincial governments can actually borrow from commercial banks because the definition of "other legitimate financial sources" does not explicitly include commercial banks. Guidance included in Decree 79/2010/ND-CP (issued July 14, 2010) also does not clarify the definition to include commercial banks. However, this has not inhibited provincial government borrowing, because commercial banks are commonly understood to be a "legitimate financial source." Nevertheless, the Prime Minister's Instruction 25 in 2014, which prevented provinces from borrowing from commercial banks to cover the expenditures of the local budgets (including investment in infrastructure development) for the purpose of state budget management for the last months of 2014, is still perceived as in effect because no document yet says that Instruction 25 is no longer applicable. This continues commercial banks' perception that lending to provinces is not fully legally supported, and it needs to be clarified clearly in a legal document to change this perception.

The Law on Public Debt Management also authorizes the MOF to directly provide or authorize a financial or credit institution to make available on-lending of the government's foreign loans to provincial governments. On-lending beneficiaries include (a) financial and credit institutions taking loans for further lending to users under credit programs or credit components of programs and projects using foreign loans, (b) enterprises taking loans for investment in programs and projects capable of recovering part or all of the loans, and (c) provincial governments taking loans for investment in socioeconomic development within the provincial budget spending task.

Decree 78/2010/ND-CP (issued July 14, 2010) provides further guidance and clarifies that the MOF shall authorize financial and credit institutions to act as on-lending agencies in the following cases: (a) on-lending to enterprises for execution of specific investment programs or projects and (b) implementation of credit limits or programs subject to conditions on borrowers, areas, sectors, on-lending interest rates, and other relevant conditions. In cases of on-lending of a government foreign loan to a provincial government, the MOF is responsible for evaluating the debt repayment capacity of the provincial government and ensuring that the on-lending interest rate is the same as the foreign loan interest.

Law on credit institutions

The Law on Credit Institutions (47/2010/QH12; June 16, 2010) is the underlying legal framework for credit activities in Vietnam. The law contains general regulations about permitted activities for commercial banks, which are regulated by the SBV. The law is silent about lending to provincial governments.

To clarify the Law on Credit Institutions, SBV issued Document 1354/NHNN-CSTT, dated April 12, 2002, and, at the request of the MOF, Document 576/NHNN-CSTT, dated June 10, 2005, to commercial banks providing guidelines related to making loans to provincial budgets for infrastructure projects. The provisions of Document 576 state that commercial banks are responsible for their loans to provincial budgets for infrastructure development and for complying with the laws on bank credit and the state budget, as well as the guidance of the State Bank of Vietnam. One of the most limiting provisions of the issuance is that commercial banks may only issue loans with a maximum duration of 24 months.

From a legal perspective, such documents have only guiding power—not binding power. However, commercial banks that have made loans to provincial governments seem to be strictly following the SBV's guidance in Official Letter 576/NHNN-CSTT dated June 10, 2005 so as to avoid any subsequent legal consequences. To resolve uncertainties, SBV should issue future guidance related to commercial bank lending to provincial governments in the form of a circular that has binding power in order to open up more commercial bank loan activity with provincial governments and to provide more protection for the banks.

In 2015, a new SBL was enacted by the National Assembly that became effective in budget year 2017. Among other things and as mentioned in the section on the SBL, this law changes the provincial debt caps (a) for Hanoi and Ho Chi Minh City to 60 percent of the provincial revenue; (b) for provinces that have revenue that exceeds the recurrent expenditure amount to 30 percent of the provincial revenue; and (c) for provinces that have revenue equal to or lower than the recurrent expenditure amount to 20 percent of the provincial revenue. This is a positive change, because it will allow the 11 provinces that are net contributors of revenue to the central government to increase their debt caps by 21 percent over the old law, assuming recurrent costs average 70 percent of the budget.

The MOF has also drafted a new circular that will replace Circular 86/2004/TT-BTT (issued August 25, 2004), which would guide the management of capital from provincial government budgets for infrastructure development. The new circular would provide more detailed guidelines related to provincial governments' borrowing from credit institutions. This draft circular contains important reforms, including requirements that (a) provincial governments have to comply with the SBL, the Public Debt Management Law, and the new circular; (b) loans are to be a part of the annual capital mobilization plan approved by the provincial People's Council; (c) the dong is to serve as the currency for loans to provincial governments; (d) interest rates will be determined by the market; (e) the loan terms must be suitable to the implementation time of the project; and (f) loans are disbursed to the provincial government's account at the state treasury.

These changes in laws and regulations demonstrate that the government is moving to improve provincial government access to credit institution funding, and at a greater amount than previously allowed. However, to implement a CIFF with a capability to stimulate more provincial government borrowing, additional regulatory reforms will be necessary from the MOF and SBV to address fundamental issues that have been identified. These issues include the following:

- The absence of clear stipulations on a recourse mechanism, including its detailed procedures, that could ensure that in the case of provincial government's default, lenders and financiers could recover funds from the provincial budget
- The absence of specific guidance or regulations regarding the assessment of credit risks relating to the loans to be provided by commercial banks to the provincial governments, which is critical given the dearth of experience among commercial banks for assessing loans to provincial governments
- The current maximum allowable loan term of 24 months for loans provided by the commercial banks to provincial governments, which is grossly inappropriate given the financing needs of infrastructure investments

Finally, if the government is successful at stimulating more provincial government borrowing, it will add to the stock of national debt and thereby be required to either raise the debt ceiling or adjust overall levels of national government debt.

LOCAL AND INTERNATIONAL EXPERIENCES WITH INFRASTRUCTURE FUNDS

Vietnam has authorized several financing programs supported by major donor investments that are focused on either a specific source of repayment, for example project revenues, or a specific sector, such as water. Two of these programs—Local Development Infrastructure Funds (LDIF) and the Asian Development Bank's (ADB) Water Sector Investment Program—are still evolving and are briefly described here.

Local development infrastructure funds

LDIFs are special subnational finance institutions created at the provincial level to mobilize capital and invest it in the municipal infrastructure projects of each province. LDIFs were first piloted in Ho Chi Minh City in 1997, and the legal framework supporting this municipal financing vehicle has continuously been updated, most recently in 2013 (via Decree 37/2013/ND-CP) to clarify the sectors that LDIFs can invest in, to delegate business decision making to provincial People's Committees, and to allow cofinancing between LDIFs.

LDIFs are expected to operate as commercial-oriented entities, raising medium- and long-term capital from domestic and foreign sources and investing in municipal infrastructure projects that will generate a sufficient financial return on investment. LDIFs are statutorily restricted to financing revenue-generating municipal infrastructure in their respective provinces.

The LDIF model has expanded to 36 of the 63 provinces, mobilizing capital for infrastructure investment. Funding commitments have grown from US$40 million to approximately US$144 million as of February 2015. According to World Bank Implementation Support Reports (IEG Review Team 2017; World Bank 2014), each dollar invested from LDIF had leveraged US$1.73 in investment from the private sector as of March 2015.

LDIFs have proven to be an important financing channel in Vietnam, but there are limits to their effectiveness as a broad-based municipal-infrastructure financing vehicle. LDIFs are statutorily restricted to financing revenue-generating municipal infrastructure, which leaves a major gap for infrastructure investments that do not have explicit revenue streams. LDIF professionals have developed new and better technical and financial-management skills, which could be used to help provinces obtain loans from commercial banks to finance provinces' non–revenue-generating infrastructure projects.

Asian Development Bank's water sector investment program

The ADB financing facility was established in 2010 with a fund commitment up to US$1 billion for the water-supply needs of Vietnam identified in its Socio-Economic Development Plan 2011–2015. The program expects to leverage more than US$1.7 billion from private investors in the water sector. The program terms are flexible and can be tailored to individual project needs. The program terminates in 2020, unless extended.

Progress is very slow because loans get bogged down in the provincial government approval process. The local standing committees, which need to approve everything, meet only two times a year, so getting variances is time consuming. Some variances may need central government approval, in some cases from the prime minister. Provincial governments are also reluctant to establish and approve water tariffs at proper levels to pay for operations, maintenance, and debt service. The result is that applicants for funding from the ADB facility that cannot demonstrate they have the ability to pay a loan back from system tariffs are forced to try to get other financial support from the provincial budgets to finance the project.

ADB staff members agreed that investors, including the ADB, would welcome the legal establishment of a recourse mechanism. The ADB was encouraged to learn about the CIFF feasibility study but had no reaction to the wholesale or retail options.

Internationally, countries have successfully met their subnational infrastructure development challenge by using other financing mechanisms. Some countries have activated borrowing by setting up second-tier financing using their commercial banks. Others have used intermediaries to provide access to local currency capital markets, and many regularly use credit enhancement techniques to strengthen their credit profile to initiate access to capital markets. Examples of each of these models are provided here to help inform the Vietnamese government as it considers establishing a broader intervention to provide provincial governments access to private sector investments.

International experience of infrastructure funds

Infrastructure wholesale financing funds

Colombia and the Czech Republic formed local development finance companies as second-tier (wholesale) lenders to their countries' commercial banks. These banks then handled the review, credit assessment, and loan approval process for local government borrowing. Colombia's Findeter (Financial Territorial Development SA), a public financial institution, was capitalized frequently by international donors until it had issued enough loans to enable the company to recycle repayment streams and gain access to the local capital market for funds to make new loans. The Czech Republic's Municipal Infrastructure Financing Company (MUFIS) provided the capitalization for its commercial bank lenders to make loans to local governments. A key difference is that Findeter discounted the loans to the commercial banks and the Czech Republic did not. As the municipal credit market grew in the Czech Republic, the commercial banks stopped borrowing from MUFIS and started using their own resources. However, Findeter still provides discounted loans to its commercial bank system for on-lending to local governments (World Bank 2013).

Retail financing facility

In 1987 the United States government decided to appropriate capitalization grant funds (nonrepayable) to all 50 states and required that such funds be maintained in perpetuity and be used to provide state revolving fund (SRF) loans for public water and wastewater infrastructure needs. The federal authorizing statutes allowed for leveraging, but many states opted to merely use the first on a direct loan basis. Hence, each state created its own retail-like entities to manage these funds. Several states used their treasury, others used simple bond banks, others formed new types of bond banks (called revolving funds) to leverage their capitalization. From a retail perspective, the capitalization could be used to makes loans from each dollar of SRF federal money received either at zero interest or at some predetermined interest rate. This retail structure is known as the direct loan model, which has been employed by over 20 states. This type of direct loan model works well if the need for financing water or wastewater projects equals or is less than the capital that the bond bank has on hand for providing financial assistance to its municipalities.

A second retail structure is known as the cash flow model and is used by at least 27 states. In this case, a revolving fund makes direct loans first and then leverages the repayment stream of those direct loans by pledging them to pay the debt service of a capital market bond issue. The proceeds of the bond issue are then loaned out in new direct loans to municipalities. This model has the advantage of making money available sooner than it otherwise would be from the loan repayment stream of the original direct loans.

In the second structure, by aggregating or pooling municipal loans to issue debt, municipal bond banks provide market access, particularly for numerous small local municipalities and school districts. These local units often borrow infrequently, and their debt issues are small. By using their respective higher-rated bond banks, each will pay lower debt service and issuance costs (shared pro rata) than would be typical of a local governmental unit trying to obtain debt financing with its own credit profile.

The credit strength of municipal bond banks is based on three criteria: (a) a general obligation loan pledge from each local government that supports its individual debt service repayment obligation or revenue bond pledges from water and sewer utilities backed by the statutory pledge of property taxes by the underlying local government, if enterprise revenues are insufficient; (b) substantial debt service reserves (equal to maximum annual debt service or to 1.25 times average annual debt service) that offer significant default tolerance; and (c) strong oversight and legal protections combined with a history of timely receipt of payments from borrowers.

Bond banks internally screen all loan applications, regularly monitor participants' credit quality once loans are made, and review annual budgets and audits. Most important, payments from borrowers are scheduled to provide sufficient notification of nonpayment and to allow time to cover any shortfalls from the bond bank's substantial debt service reserves. Finally, bond banks also have state deficiency make-up provisions, which have rarely been tested. Credit-rating agencies recognize that a deficiency make-up provides additional credit enhancement if the mechanics are soundly structured to provide timeliness of payment or when a state treasurer serves as a member of the bond bank's governing body, providing incentive for central government cooperation. The strength of the bond banks is also based on their ability to get timely and audited local financial data, to attract private investors in the capital markets, and to enforce payment of provincial government debt obligations using a legally approved recourse regime, if needed.

In India, the state government of Tamil Nadu established a water and sanitation bond bank (Water and Sanitation Pooled Fund [WSPF]) and issued its first pooled financing transaction in December 2002 to enable its small- and medium-size local governments (urban local bodies, ULBs) to obtain financing at market rates for their water and sanitation infrastructure needs. This entity's credit structure followed the general norms articulated earlier for bond banks. By aggregating or pooling municipal loans to issue debt (as a *pooled financing entity*), municipal bond banks provide market access. Moreover, the program added some strong credit features such as requiring the routing of all ULBs revenues (including transfer payments from the state government of Tamil Nadu) to a special no-lien escrow account in a local commercial bank. In that same bank, the ULB was required to establish a different and separate fixed deposit account that would be filled monthly from the aforementioned escrow account to ensure that by the end of the 10th month that fixed deposit account would have enough funds to make the yearly required debt service payment to the trustee bank servicing the WSPF bond debt service for the pooled issue. This fixed deposit provision would enable the staff of WSPF to monitor the ULB account and have time to act if the account was insufficient to make the required debt service payment. Additional credit enhancement mechanisms were put in place for recourse (intercepting direct devolution payments to the defaulting ULB) and for liquidity, each pool financing had a bond service fund (a reserve fund) capitalized in cash by the Tamil Nadu government and a partial guarantee from the US Agency for International Development (USAID) to replenish 50 percent of any principal withdrawn from the bond service fund to meet timely WSPF debt service payments (Fitch Ratings 2003).

The state of Quintana Roo in Mexico created a bond bank to finance local government water and sanitation projects. In an arena in which municipal credit ratings are low compared with domestic investment grade standards, credit enhancement is a necessity for gaining access to debt capital markets. The bond bank was formed as a pooled financing vehicle with a credit structure based solely on intercepting different local government revenue streams and pledging them to pay for local debt obligations to the bank, thereby increasing the credit rating of the borrowing entity. This is a gross revenue pledge credit structure—in which debt is paid first, operations and maintenance second—that results in very high ratings (AA). This approach was used to overcome a number of constraints that prevented the state of Quintana Roo from building a strong, effective, and consistent financing framework for the water and sanitation sector. For example, water utilities, not being federal entities, received no national tax transfers. Water bill collection rates were very low, because Mexico guaranteed water supply to its citizens even if they did not pay for it. Pledging revenue streams from water utilities was not perceived as secure by potential investors.

Credit enhancement facilities

The Philippine Water Revolving Fund (PWRF) is a pooled loan financing facility focused on local water utility infrastructure that was funded by a Japan International Cooperation Agency (JICA) loan to the Development Bank of the Philippines (DBP) and by private financing institutions (PFIs), mainly commercial banks. The financing ratio ranged from a 50 to 75 percent DBP/JICA loan to a 25 to 50 percent PFI loan share. The JICA loan was backed by a sovereign guarantee from the Philippine government and had favorable concessional terms, namely an effective interest rate 100–200 basis points lower than the then prevailing market rate and a 30-year tenor with a 10-year grace period. The PFI loan was lent at market terms for a term of 20 years with a right for the PFIs to exit after the 7th year. Lending decision criteria and due diligence were all based on the PFIs' requirements, so the PWRF catered to only creditworthy water service providers. The PWRF loan security package included an intercept of the internal revenue allotment coming from the national government to local government units (LGUs) in case of default, as well as a debt-service reserve fund. Despite the structure, the PFIs were still concerned about the water-utility default risk and demanded more protection. So, the PWRF obtained a credit risk guarantee that covered up to 85 percent of the PFI loan from a private domestic guarantee corporation, the provincial government, and the LGU Guarantee Corporation (LGUGC), backed up by a coguarantee of the USAID Development Credit Agency for up to 50 percent of the LGUGC's exposure, enabling the program to be implemented (PWRF 2011).

The Philippine financing facility was able to support the policy of the government by shifting the financing of water utilities to market-based sources and mobilizing additional resources by leveraging public funding (ODA and central government funds) with private funds. The PWRF successfully channeled more than ₱4.0 billion (US$91.2 million), of which ₱2.45 billion (US$55.8 million) came from private banks, in financing for 21 water and sanitation projects over a six-year period.

The design of the PWRF created a mechanism whereby local private banks could invest in the sector with low risk. This transformed the way banks assessed and financed projects—moving from collateral-based to project-based lending with guarantees and liquidity coverage credit enhancements that significantly lowered bank financing risks. Training provided by the staff of the financing facility, along with an appraisal guidebook on how to assess water utilities and water projects, enabled several private banks to learn how water utilities operate and how a well-managed utility can make an excellent borrower (PWRF 2011).

What the examples demonstrate

In several of the examples examined, an external credit enhancement or guarantee was required to make a transaction marketable because private sector investors have limited or no experience with subnational governments, their budget practices, or history of borrowing and repayment. Vietnam will undoubtedly need to use credit enhancement techniques to attract private sector investors who will lend their money to provincial governments. Two external financial guarantee entities are briefly profiled here as examples of how such mechanisms work and in what sectors they provide guarantees. The examples validate the need for Vietnam to develop some type of credit enhancement mechanism to stimulate its provincial national debt financing using private sector investments.

LGUGC is a private Philippine financial guarantee corporation, owned 38 percent by the Bankers Association of the Philippines, 37 percent by the DBP, and 25 percent by the ADB. LGUGC was incorporated on March 2, 1998, and guarantees the indebtedness of LGUs, water districts, electric cooperatives, renewable energy technology providers, state universities and colleges, and medium to large enterprises. It facilitates local government access to private sources of financing through credit enhancement, is leveraged 10:1, and does not allow acceleration of debt when a project goes into default.

A new ADB-capitalized guarantee program was approved by the SBV for use in Vietnam for a corporate bond transaction. The guarantee program is offered by Credit Guarantee and Investment Facility Ltd. (CGIF), which was established in 2010 as a trust fund of ADB. It is rated AA by S&P and AAA by three other regional rating agencies. CGIF provides 100 percent guarantees primarily on local currency bonds issued by creditworthy corporations that are domiciled in 13 member countries of ASEAN+3 (Association of Southeast Asian Nations + China, Japan, and the Republic of Korea).

The guarantees issued by CGIF are irrevocable and unconditional commitments to pay bondholders upon nonpayment by issuers throughout the tenor of the bonds. CGIF retains the right to accelerate the principal claim payments prior to the maturity of the debt issuance upon default of the issuer or to maintain the payment schedule of the guaranteed obligations. CGIF's leverage ratio—as measured by the ratio of aggregate outstanding guarantees to total paid-in capital plus retained earnings after deducting loss reserves and illiquid investments—will not exceed 2.5:1. CGIF has a single risk country threshold of US$350 million. On December 5, 2014, CGIF closed its first guarantee for a D 2.1 trillion (US$98.2 million) bond for Masan Consumer Holdings, a subsidiary of Masan Group Corporation, marking the first time a nonbank corporate Vietnamese bond had been issued with a fixed rate, 10-year tenor.

Vietnam should not copy these examples exactly but rather design a financing facility with the best techniques to ensure that Vietnam meets the long-term objective of access to private sector financing for its provincial governments and to make clear who bears the credit risk obligations when provincial governments borrow. The goal is to create a sustainable private sector financing capacity in the country, not a permanent public funding capacity. When infrastructure needs cannot be satisfied solely from central or local budgets, international experience has shown that central governments have stepped in to try to alleviate this problem.

Each government created its own type of mechanism through which local entities could gain access to private sector financing. The critical differences between the mechanisms reflect individual country policy preferences. For example, Colombia chose to subsidize its local governments by discounting loans to commercial banks so that borrowing became more affordable. This option created a lengthy demand for more resources to maintain the subsidies and, therefore, effectively crowded out private sector capital market financing. The Czech Republic's MUFIS, on the other hand, did not subsidize local governments; it merely provided capital to their commercial banks for financing local governments at market rates, preparing local governments to gain access to the capital market once it matured in that country. Other countries created highly rated structures that provide access to the market for a basket of local government loans to achieve savings through that process. Although this crowds out private sector financing for individual localities on their own credit, the mechanism still acquires its funding from the private sector at capital market rates.

To mitigate risk, virtually all these mechanisms used some form of financial structuring (overcollateralization, reserve funds, and so forth), and many acquired public or private financial guarantees as a credit enhancement. Such examples were found in Tamil Nadu and the Philippine Water Fund to provide comfort about debt repayment for private lenders, especially in the initial phases of obtaining private sector debt financing.

FINANCING FACILITY OPTIONS

The 2013 World Bank report, *Assessment of Financing Framework for Municipal Infrastructure* (World Bank 2013), described successful international models that could be applied to Vietnam. These models include MDFs (wholesale option), public funding intermediaries (retail option), market-oriented financial intermediaries, credit enhancement, and land-based infrastructure financing programs. This chapter describes the fundamental workings and risks and mitigations associated with retail finance, credit enhancement finance, and wholesale finance but not land-based financing programs (figure 1.1).

Retail financing

A "retail" financing facility (RFF) provides direct loan financing to provincial governments; the government is required to create a special purpose entity to act as a financial intermediary between the provinces and the facility. The entity invests the monies of the facility (usually capitalization grants from the government or donors); establishes the loan application, review, and approval processes for provincial governments; determines the terms and conditions for loan approval; makes loans and disburses funds to the borrowers; and provides oversight and surveillance of the performance of the provincial governments to ensure that they use the money for allowable capital purposes and repay their loan obligations on time and in full.

FIGURE 1.1
Structuring Options for a City Infrastructure Financing Facility

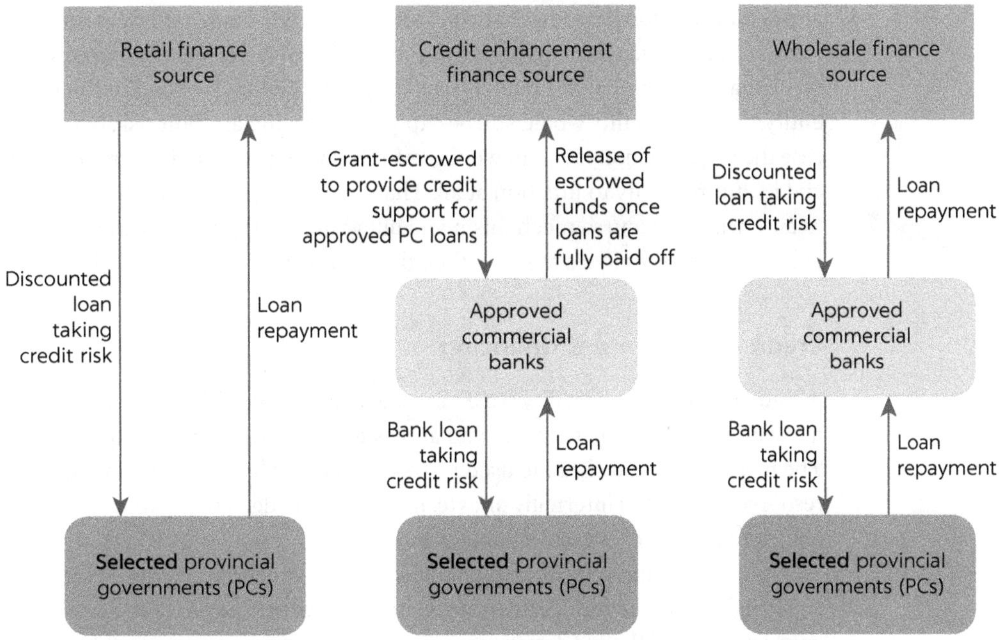

Note: Selected provincial governments are net contributors of revenue to the central government.
PCs = People's Committees.

This type of financing facility does not leverage its equity, nor does it induce private sector financing for provincial governments; properly managed, it should not have any recourse to the central government budget should loan obligations not be repaid. A retail facility takes on the full credit risk of the provincial governments, which means that, if a provincial government fails to repay its direct loans, the facility will have less money in the future to make new loans. There would be no capital market impact.

An RFF would not achieve the government's goal of stimulating private sector lending to provincial governments because it is unlikely to leverage private capital. It also would be under great pressure to provide cheap capital, which would crowd out private sector competition to provide provincial government financing. The creation of a new bureaucracy would take time. If the retail facility provided subsidized financing, it would put pressure on the government to commit to funding it incrementally over time. Consequently, there is little interest in going in this direction from the Vietnam government or the World Bank.

On the positive side, an RFF might be considered in the future as a potential tool to help finance poorer provinces by providing technical help to structure their projects so they could be financed from a variety of governmental, donor, or ODA sources. The RFF then might blend funding from the province's own budget, from grants provided by the central budget, or from ODA loans on-lent through the budget, and possibly from private sector proceeds generated by executing pooled loans financed by commercial banks or the capital markets. There are many managerial benefits that can accrue to even the poorest provinces from the experience of preparing and going through the lending process. This is what motivated the creation of bond banks and ultimately revolving funds in some developed and developing countries.

In the future when the market is more developed, a retail entity could itself become a conduit financing entity (similar to bond banks), obtain its own rating, and obtain additional nondiscounted financing (pooled financing) from the local currency capital markets on behalf of the provincial governments, particularly those that are poorer with smaller issuance needs. Acting as a conduit financing entity, the retail facility would still be exposed to provincial credit risk, but in this case the impact of nonpayment would severely damage the facility's credit rating and its future ability to function at all. That is why the government would need to authorize a recourse mechanism and allow the facility to use various credit enhancement techniques to strengthen the creditworthiness of the facility.

Credit enhancement financing

A credit enhancement facility (CEF) is used to boost the credit of borrowers and mitigate risk to enable them to gain access to external private sector funding. The most common technique used is a *reserve fund,* which is funded with extra resources generated internally or externally and is pledged to repay specific loan obligations in the event of a default (figure 1.2).

The reserve fund type of credit enhancement leverages its equity (which can be as high as 10–1),[4] induces private sector investment, exposes the facility to only a portion of the local government risk, and has no recourse to the central government. The reserve fund needs to be able to be legally pledged to provide security for a specific local government loan and make it available to pay a portion of the debt service on that loan if the local government defaults on its payment obligation.

Credit enhancement makes provincial government debt more attractive for investment. An issuer's financial value is solely in its cash flows. Therefore, mitigating default risk is one of the best ways for a lender to get comfortable about recovering its invested capital. Credit enhancement stabilizes cash flows, thus broadening the investment opportunities for domestic markets. A CEF is established to provide a provincial government a standby source of liquidity over and above the cash flow pledged by the provincial government to repay its debt should it ever be needed.

FIGURE 1.2

Credit Enhancement Facility Reserve Fund

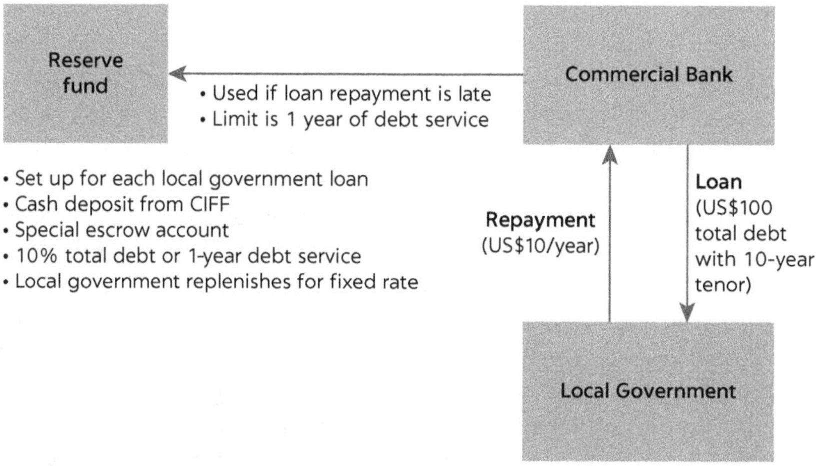

Note: CIFF = city infrastructure financing facility; LG = local government.

Credit enhancement involves using external financial techniques to provide investors with additional security that they will be repaid. The role of external credit enhancement is to bolster (over collateralize) cash flows in support of debt service. When used to finance a government, credit enhancement should be in a form that mitigates default risk rather than enhances recovery value.

A provincial government's agreement to repay its debt is generally considered a type of *general obligation* commitment that does not normally need credit enhancement. This means that the revenues of the provincial government are standing behind its debt obligation and that they are sufficient to repay debt. However, if investors judge provincial governments to be marginally or less than creditworthy or they are first-time issuers of debt or there is no recourse mechanism established in law and regulation to potentially recover their investment upon a default, investors will demand some sort of external credit enhancement be obtained before they will lend.

The main characteristics of external credit enhancement are as follows:

- The issuer (province) remains the sole obligor for the debt.
- The external credit enhancement is legally authorized, if provided by a government or governmental entity, or is contractually valid if provided by a private entity or a bank.
- The external credit enhancement is managed by a trustee-initiated trigger that can be either proactive (when the trigger is activated by the insufficiency of funds within a debt service account some days in advance of a scheduled payment date) or reactive (when the trigger is activated post-default). A proactive trigger, which mitigates default risk, has a higher value to investors than a reactive trigger, which enhances recovery value on a post-default basis.

Credit enhancement techniques will be necessary to provide comfort to private sector lenders, particularly in the early stages of financing provincial government infrastructure needs. The SBV reported that it has regulations covering risk mitigation (credit enhancement) techniques that the commercial banks can use when making loans for corporate clients.[5] These included earmarking and pledging revenues, hard asset pledges, parent company guarantees, among others. As mentioned, the SBV recently gave approval to use a private company's CGIF, credit guarantee, for the first time on a corporate debt issue, which was favorably viewed and priced in the local currency in Vietnam's debt capital market. Therefore, it is reasonable to expect that the SBV could develop risk mitigation regulations specifically tailored to provincial governments, allowing commercial banks and the capital markets to use various risk mitigation techniques to encourage more provincial government financing.

Many credit enhancing techniques can be used by governments to reduce investor concerns about repayment of their investment. Some of the more common ones are briefly presented to give the government a sense of what investors internationally have accepted as risk mitigants to encourage them to finance subnational public infrastructure debt. The techniques are as follows:

- Guarantee: a legally binding commitment by a central government, either 100 percent or partial, to pay debt service of a defaulting subnational government. Guarantees of this type increase a central government's debt burden and count as contingent liabilities on their balance sheet.
- Unlimited full faith and credit pledge: a contractual agreement by the subnational government (backed by clear legal authority) to repay its

debt obligations from the first revenues generated by that subnational government and a commitment that they will raise fees and taxes to ensure such debt is repaid.

- Limited obligation pledge: a contractual agreement by a subnational government in which it requests additional budgetary resources to ensure that its debt obligations are repaid or pledged that it will make best efforts from any resources available to the subnational government to repay its debt obligations (a nonbinding, moral obligation pledge).
- Double barrel pledge: a contractual commitment to use two or more sources of revenue, such as the taxes collected by the subnational government and revenues from a specific user fee, to repay a subnational government debt obligation.
- Recourse: a legally binding authority to intercept central government payments to the subnational government if it doesn't repay its debt. This cash stream is a valuable asset for subnational governments because these revenue streams can be used for credit enhancement, especially if the payment streams are definable, regular, statutorily and formulaically established in law or policy, and are authorized for any subnational governmental purpose.

Credit enhancement mechanisms have not been used for provincial government debt obligations in Vietnam, and there is no current regulation or guidance on using these risk mitigation tools. However, the value of credit enhancement has recently been accepted by the SBV and the debt capital markets for a corporate bond issued by Masan Consumer Holdings. This development and the risk mitigation guidelines used by SBV for corporate debt issuances should enable the MOF and the SBV to move quickly to prepare risk mitigation and credit enhancement guidelines for provincial government debt obligations. The application of a reserve fund is not complex, but it is new to Vietnam officials. The complexity will come from the process of establishing the best coverage levels for the reserve fund and determining the amount of financing it can support. A reserve fund should be sized to help provincial government debt obligations get approval from private investors; it is not a full guarantee, which would only distort any serious effort to perform a true credit analysis of provincial governments.

Wholesale financing

A wholesale financing facility (WFF) provides direct funding to commercial banks, which then on-lend to subnational governments to finance their infrastructure. A wholesale facility's loans, especially if discounted, will crowd out private lending because the proceeds from the loans will become the only source of money that the commercial banks use to provide longer tenor loans to local governments. This would lead to a long-term need to capitalize the wholesale facility, as happened in Colombia, where the Findeter program took over 15 years to evolve and required multiple infusions of capital from the government and donors. The risk of this problem would be lowered if the wholesale facility's loan to the bank is at market rate or if the facility requires the bank to commit a significant portion of its own assets to blend into a single loan to a subnational government and allows the bank to charge normal commercial interest rates for its funds. In the Czech Republic, the WFF (MUFIS) downsized after 10 years once its debt capital market was able to provide financing for provincial government and corporate debt issuances.

A wholesale facility is an attractive, short-term way to stimulate or jump-start private sector financing of a subnational government's infrastructure needs, because the financing from the central government will be used by commercial banks as a long-term deposit, which can then be used to extend subnational government loan tenors. It is also a way to develop risk mitigation or credit enhancement techniques for subnational government borrowing while using commercial bank loan preparation, review, risk mitigation, and approval processes to facilitate financial discipline at the subnational government level. Ultimately this will enable subnational government access to capital market financing on a more sustainable basis with longer terms.

Once started, however, a wholesale facility may become very difficult to terminate. Commercial banks are fundamentally short-term lenders with short-term depositors, whereas financing for infrastructure should be financed on a longer tenor basis to make costs more affordable to the borrower. This asset mismatch makes it unrealistic to expect the commercial banking sector to be the final financing solution for subnational government infrastructure financing in the long run. Ultimately, subnational government financing should be done in the Vietnam capital market. However, its incipient status dictates that interim solutions be sought. In this sense, commercial banks could fill a vacuum in the short term and contribute to building a subnational lending market. Their presence in the market may contribute to developing more discipline about subnational government infrastructure financing with a goal to getting subnational governments ready to gain access to the capital market in the future. This would be a sustainable financing strategy for the country.

A WFF may limit the achievement of the government's goal of properly pricing and stimulating private sector investment in provincial government infrastructure if not designed carefully to safeguard moral hazards and long-term risks. Provincial governments around the world always look for the cheapest sources of funds to carry out their infrastructure programs. Provincial governments will bring intense pressure on the government to use the funds in the wholesale facility like a grant or with deeply subsidized interest rates. If allowed, doing so would prevent the evolution of a credit culture in the provincial governments and crowd out any hope of private sector lending. Also, if the wholesale facility is intended to stimulate private-bank lending, then WFF loans to commercial banks should be conditioned on the bank's cofinancing each loan. The facility should be open to all qualified commercial banks that want to provide provincial government loans. If not, it will crowd out banks that are not on the WFF's preferred list.

A model of a CIFF with a wholesale function, which uses the government's foreign loan ability, may not work without clarification or an appropriate amendment to Decree 78/2010. As mentioned earlier, the on-lending agency for the government's foreign loans to provincial governments is always only the MOF itself. Thus, for a CIFF to be legally established, it is necessary to have (a) a clarification or an appropriate amendment of Decree 78/2010, allowing the establishment of a CIFF with wholesale function or (b) an international loan treaty signed by the government or Finance Ministry and an international donor, such as the World Bank, allowing the establishment of a CIFF with credit enhancement function; or (c) a combination of (a) and (b) that allows the establishment of a CIFF with wholesale function and credit enhancement function.

Potential structure of city infrastructure financing facility

Each option has advantages and disadvantages associated with the government's overall objective of expanding provincial governments' access to private sector resources for their infrastructure programs (table 1.1).

Among all the options explored for Vietnam to accomplish its private sector financing objective, a sound option would be for the national government to establish a WFF to make infrastructure loans to eligible provincial governments and, in addition, to set up a separate facility that would provide credit enhancement for the loans that are financed by the wholesale facility. The former would be structured to provide capital to make loans to qualified commercial banks and require the banks that want to develop a provincial government line of business to cofinance (that is, put their own capital at risk) each provincial government approvable loan. Simultaneously, the government could create a CEF, ex ante capitalized with a smaller amount of funding, to mitigate provincial government risks to the participating banks, thereby providing a subsidy for the provincial government borrower. The credit enhancement mechanism leverages private sector borrowing and revolves back to the facility at the end of the loan term to be used in other loan transactions. Because the government believes that new techniques should be subject to pilot testing before making permanent changes to its system, it would make sense to combine both the wholesale option and the credit enhancement option into a single initiative.

TABLE 1.1 **Comparison of Three Types of Financing Facilities**

ATTRIBUTES	RFF	CEF	WFF
Dedicated entity to manage	Yes	Yes	Yes
Managed by	SPE	Entity established in/outside of MOF	Agency/department/PMU in/outside of MOF
Program focus	Poorer/not fully creditworthy provinces	Creditworthy provinces	Creditworthy provinces
Minimum expected timeline for setup	3 years	2 years	2 years
New start-up capital injection	Yes	Yes	Yes
Leverage of private capital	No	Yes	Yes, if commercial banks required to put in capital
MOF oversight	Yes	Yes, limited	Yes
Credit risk	SPE and provinces	Creditworthy provinces	Commercial banks
Size of exposure	100% to MOF	Creditworthy provinces	100% to banks
Interest rate	Established by SPE (with MOF oversight)	Market rate established by bank	Market rate established by bank
Recycle repayments	Possible, if allowed	Yes	Possible, if allowed
Crowd out private investment	Yes	No	Partial
Encourage capital market lending	No	Yes	Yes, if bank is required to cofinance loans
New legal/regulatory changes	Yes	Yes	Yes
New skills required	Yes	Yes	Yes
Improvement of provincial management	No	Yes	Yes

Note: RFF = retail financing facility; CEF = credit enhancement facility; WFF = wholesale financing authority; MOF = Ministry of Finance; PMU = project management unit; SPE = special purpose entity.

TABLE 1.2 **Financing Options versus Government Objectives**

OBJECTIVE	RFF	CEF	WFF
Attract private-sector debt financing	No	Yes	Maybe[a]
Increase infrastructure financing	Yes	Yes	Yes
Provide sustainable private-sector financing	No	Yes	Maybe[a]
Separate central-government risk from provincial credit risk	No	Yes	Yes

a. "Maybe" becomes "yes" if the central government requires cofinancing from commercial bank funds.

From an institutional perspective, this study's findings indicate that the best solution is for the MOF to set up a CIFF with a wholesale and credit enhancement capability on a five-year pilot basis and to structure it into two separate units or divisions separately providing wholesale financing and credit enhancement. This entity should be established within the MOF (that is, as a department or a project management unit) and would require the CIFF to be authorized under a decision of the MOF or a decision of the prime minister (or a decree of the government). Simultaneously, the MOF could form another separate unit dedicated to legal and regulatory reforms, as well as organize training and education programs to build the financial capacity of the provincial governments and the banks.

In summary, table 1.2 shows how the three financing options measure up against the government's objectives outlined at the beginning of this book. The conclusions assume that all the legal, regulatory, and capacity-building efforts are implemented as recommended. The judgment of "maybe" in the table's wholesale option is based on an uncertainty about whether the government will require cofinancing by the commercial banks. If cofinancing is not required, then it is doubtful that the wholesale option will attract any additional private financing.

CONCLUSION AND RECOMMENDATIONS FOR REFORM

The enabling environment in Vietnam for provincial governments to obtain private sector funding for their infrastructure is weak. The government is perpetually barraged by provincial government officials asking for more funding for their infrastructure needs from the central budget or ODA sources. The government responds to this annual demand by allocating resources from the central budget to help poorer provinces, but there is not enough to meet all the critical provincial demands.

No one solution solves all problems. However, the glue that keeps things together is a strong, clear legal and regulatory framework for lenders and borrowers. The second part of that equation is to employ the expertise of all the people involved in financing so they can use the law and regulations properly, ensuring that they speak the same financial language and know how to prepare and evaluate bankable projects.

A CIFF with a wholesale function and a credit enhancement function would meet the twin objectives of the Vietnamese government to mobilize more funds for provincial governments for infrastructure development and to develop the capacity of the commercial bank and debt markets for financing provincial government infrastructure. For the implementation of the potential CIFF program, weaknesses in the legal and regulatory framework need to be addressed in future reforms, and capacity-building programs are needed for both the governments and the commercial banking industry. Ultimately, those would help lay the foundation for further development of provincial debt market for public infrastructure investments in Vietnam.

Legal and regulatory upgrades

The current legal and regulatory framework must be upgraded to meet the government's financial objective. In general, this will involve a thorough review of the existing legal framework to identify all the rules that are now in place (an ex ante review), determine which inhibit borrowing, and revise them to unlock private sector financing whether or not the government establishes a financing facility. Chapter 4 in this book provides a legal and regulatory summary that is a good starting point for examining the current rules and identifying changes needed in several critical borrowing-related regulations, such as the following:

- Change the debt cap on provincial borrowing, measured now as a percentage of capital spending. This changed in 2017 under the new 2015 SBL to a percentage of provincial revenues.
- Lengthen or remove the two-year limit on tenor for commercial bank loans to local governments.
- Clarify that provincial financial liabilities are not central government liabilities.
- Allow provincial governments to pledge revenues to pay debt service, establish escrow accounts, and enter into overcollateralization agreements, among other capabilities.

A new legal and regulatory framework needs to be developed to govern what happens after provincial-government debt is issued. Vietnam needs to establish a recourse mechanism to deal with the full range of rights and obligations of lenders and borrowers in the event of a default. This sensitive issue requires a great deal of collaboration and coordination within various levels of government, as well as with the private investor community. Commercial banks have made it clear that they need a legal recourse mechanism to get comfortable with provincial-government credit risk. The MOF staff at meetings conducted during the report period acknowledged that an ex post legal system is required. Mature countries like South Africa and the United States have established recourse mechanisms specifically for local governments, because they cannot go out of business. These legal recourse mechanisms have been used in the United States for the last few years because of the 2007–08 financial crisis and have provided an orderly method to handle some very dramatic and large defaults by US municipalities.

The central government has moved directly to make some changes to laws and regulations to facilitate provincial government use of commercial bank financing. However, the typical approach of the government is to use pilot projects to demonstrate new ways of doing things before committing to scale up reforms, as was done with the LDIF and public-private partnerships programs. The government could develop a pilot financing facility to stimulate commercial bank financing of provincial governments and use it to request approval from appropriate governmental authorities for exemptions that would apply only to the approved pilots. For example, this would be the way to get clearance to initiate work on creating a recourse mechanism. Subsequently, the experiences of the pilot programs could be used to guide future changes in law and regulation.

Increased financial management capacity

For the provincial government, needs to commit money and time to extensively develop the financial knowledge and skills of the personnel in various central government and provincial government agencies. If they are to accept long-term credit risk, commercial banks will require high-quality and timely data and other information from provincial officials to enable banks to make informed and prudent credit decisions. Data at the moment are dated, unreliable, and even conflicting. Among the provinces, this study found that annual deviations of up to 50 percent of actual expenditure against budget seem to be the norm rather than the exception. Financial management skills—specifically planning, budgeting, accounting, reporting, and auditing skills—will have to be upgraded to improve provincial governments' financial management capacity.

A capacity-building assistance program would be also needed at commercial banks and at central ministry agencies involved in finance and banking regulation. Bankers and their regulators need more formal education about provincial government finances, as well as different credit enhancement mechanisms and how they can be applied to mitigate risk in provincial government transactions. The banks need to develop a provincial government credit-assessment tool, and regulators and finance agencies need to develop standardized financial reporting requirements to appraise the credit condition of provincial governments.

NOTES

1. The 11 net contributing provinces are Ba Ria Vung Tau, Bac Ninh, Binh Duong, Can Tho, Da Nang, Dong Nai, Hai Phong, Khanh Hoa, Quang Ninh, Quang Ngai, and Vinh Phuc. Overall, there are three tiers of provinces and cities in Vietnam. The top tier comprises special cities with relatively good fiscal conditions and sufficient capacity to borrow from the bond market on their own, such as Hanoi and Ho Chi Minh City. The second tier includes provinces that are net contributors of revenue to the government of Vietnam; however, the provinces have limited access to funding for urban infrastructure. The third-tier provinces depend heavily on the central government's transfers and have very limited creditworthiness.
2. MOF Budget Office meeting with World Bank staff and consultants, March 31, 2015.
3. This book was prepared before the new Law on Public Debt Management (LPDM) 2017, was approved (which goes into effect July 2018); therefore, the main discussion is focused on LPDM 2009. Draft LPDM was reviewed in the preparation of this book and does not substantially affect the discussion on the regulatory framework.
4. In the United States, most revenue bond issuers are required by investors to have a funded cash reserve equal to 10 percent of the par amount raised. To achieve higher credit ratings and to lower the interest rate on debt, some issuers fund reserves at a higher percentage of the par amount of bonds they issue. Reserve funds that exceed 30 percent of par generally are rated in the AA to AAA categories.
5. Briefly discussed in authors' meeting with SBV and MOF on June 10, 2015, although regulations were not provided.

REFERENCES

Fitch Ratings. 2003. "Water and Sanitation Pooled Fund (WSPF)." India Public Finance Credit Analysis. Fitch Rating Services, New York.

IEG Review Team. 2017. *Vietnam-VN-Local Development Investment (LDIFP)*. Washington, DC: World Bank.

Monitor Consulting. 2015. *Assessment of Vietnam Banking Sector*. Report.

Moody's Investor Services. 2014. *Banking System Outlook, Vietnam.*

PWRF (Philippine Water Revolving Fund). 2011. *Philippine Water Revolving Fund (PWRF) Support Program Final Report.* Washington, DC: United States Agency for International Development.

SBV (State Bank of Vietnam). 2014. "Vietnam's New Regulation on Capital Adequacy and Liquidity of Credit Institutions." Circular 36/2014/TT-NHNN. Hanoi: State Bank of Vietnam.

World Bank. 2013. *Assessment of the Financing Framework for Municipal Infrastructure in Vietnam.* Washington, DC: World Bank.

——. 2014. "Ho Chi Minh City Investment Fund for Urban Development Project, 2007–12." Implementation Completion Report Review, World Bank, Washington, DC.

——. 2015. *Making the Whole Greater than the Sum of the Parts: A Review of Fiscal Decentralization in Vietnam.* Summary Report, World Bank, Washington, DC. http://documents.worldbank.org/curated/en/389051468187138185/text/103669-v1-WP-P128790-v1-PUBLIC-FDR-summary-FINAL-Oct6-15.txt.

2 A Demand-Side Analysis of the Provincial Governments

Vietnam has experienced profound changes that have transformed the country in the past two decades. The nation's transition to a market economy has been accompanied by economic growth that averaged around 7 percent annually between 1994 and 2016. Poverty has been drastically reduced as well, from 58.0 percent of the population under the poverty index in 1993 to 14.5 percent in 2008, and further down to 3.0 percent in 2017.[1] Vietnam's transformation also has been marked by rapid urbanization that offers unique opportunities for the country's development. Since 1990s, the government of Vietnam has pursued a path of fiscal decentralization, which has given provincial governments greater responsibilities in public finances and infrastructure development.

A fundamental challenge for maintaining Vietnam's high level of growth is the need to improve the affordability and efficiency of infrastructure investment. A major cause of investment inefficiency is the fragmentation of public infrastructure investment, which results in duplication and waste. In addition, Vietnam's decentralized investment system faces the challenges of uneven administrative capacity at the local levels (provincial governments and smaller), insufficient accountability and transparency, poor coordination, and unpredictable availability of financial resources. Policy makers have an opportunity to correct these inefficiencies in infrastructure investment; that is, they can do more with the same amount of resources.

The government's current framework for municipal infrastructure investment lacks a proper mechanism for providing clear, transparent, and efficient funding allocations from all available sources. Improving that framework would link the investment planning process at national and subnational levels to reduce unnecessary fragmentation and competition among provinces. The World Bank report, "Assessment of the Financing Framework for Municipal Infrastructure in Vietnam" (World Bank 2013) recommends setting up a municipal development fund that could act as a specialized financing facility at the national level to enhance credit, guarantee service, and fund municipal infrastructure. Taking into account relevant international experience, the Vietnamese government and the World Bank also are exploring the establishment of a city infrastructure financing facility (CIFF) as a wholesale market instrument that would evolve into a full-scale entity that can facilitate local government borrowing from the private sector at market-related spreads.

A growing number of provinces in Vietnam have attained the requisite capacity to assume greater fiscal responsibility for financing their municipal infrastructure needs if the enabling environment is put in place to allow them to leverage private sector capital. Eleven so-called second-tier provinces, which are net contributors (excluding the two major cities of Hanoi and Ho Chi Min City) to the central government budget, consistently generate local revenues that exceed their recurrent expenditures. The resulting budget surpluses can be leveraged to fund local infrastructure needs.

This chapter has two objectives. First, it aims to analyze whether the provinces have sufficient effective demand to finance infrastructure by borrowing from a facility such as the CIFF. Three of 11 secondary provinces were selected for a closer assessment: Bac Ninh, Dong Nai, and Quang Ninh Province. The second objective is to (a) review some international practices, approaches, and experiences of municipal governments that have attained subsovereign creditworthiness and (b) draw preliminary conclusions about creditworthiness criteria and debt management.

An assessment of the demand for financing must consider that provinces and cities that report directly to the central government have limited experience in long-term borrowing and are more accustomed to meeting their capital requirements from their own resources: grants and short-term loans. Although some provincial governments have borrowed from commercial banks or the capital markets, for many, such transactions would represent a substantial change in how they operate. This chapter provides a preliminary review of the available pipelines for bankable projects in the three provinces visited, using the project information provided to the study team by the provinces. The projects are some that potentially could be implemented if funding, land, and approvals were in place. The research assessed sustainable debt levels and constraints at both the central and provincial levels, using the three provinces as pilots for the assessment of possible overall demand.

MACROECONOMIC AND DEVELOPMENT CONSIDERATIONS

The International Monetary Fund (IMF) issued a press release in late 2014 with the following description of Vietnam's economic status:

> Economic performance has improved over the last year and the economic recovery is taking hold, although domestic activity remains weak, in part constrained by weak banks and inefficient state-owned enterprises (SOEs). Inflation has declined, the current account remains in large surplus, and international reserves have increased. The authorities place a priority on preserving macroeconomic stability, tackling banking sector vulnerabilities, and reforming SOEs, though implementation has been gradual in some key areas.

Outlook and risks: Growth is projected to recover gradually over the coming years, with the current account returning to a deficit and inflation contained. On current policies, public debt is projected to reach 60 percent of gross domestic product (GDP). Risks include weaker trading partner growth, geopolitical tensions, slow structural reforms, and delayed fiscal consolidation. Early conclusion to key trade negotiations would be growth-positive.

Fiscal policy: Deficits have been sizable and rising public debt requires attention. A medium-term growth-friendly consolidation is recommended, based on enhancing revenue and rationalizing unproductive expenditures while preserving crucial social and capital spending. This would ensure public debt sustainability with space to address contingent liabilities from banking sector and SOE restructuring.

Banking sector reform: Several policy measures have been taken recently, but the overall gradual approach will likely continue constraining credit growth and keep the system susceptible to shocks and significant asset deterioration. A more expeditious recognition of nonperforming loans, bank restructuring and orderly resolution would support robust credit creation and macro-financial stability (IMF 2014, 1).

Vietnam's real GDP growth for 2014 was 5.5 percent with an estimated 5.6 percent for 2015, and the consumer price index was 5.2 percent in 2014 with a projection of 5.0 percent for 2015. Per capita GDP, according to Fitch bond ratings, was D 4,0162,000 (US$1,868), and GDP was D 3,676 trillion (US$171 billion). In 2014, Vietnamese bonds were given ratings of BB- by Standard & Poor's, BB- by Fitch, and B2 by Moody's.

Mirroring the IMF statement, the Fitch rating reports of November 2014 recommended the following measures for improving the state of Vietnam's economy: (a) manage fiscal deficits, (b) make contingent liabilities more transparent, (c) further reform the thinly capitalized banking sector, (d) show estimated SOE debt as aggregated instead of fragmented, (e) pursue SOE reform more vigorously, and (f) focus policy on increasing stability and maintaining stable inflation.

According to the United Nations Development Programme (UNDP) (2013) only 4.2 percent of the population lived in multidimensional poverty, while an additional 7.9 percent were vulnerable to multiple deprivations. The Human Development Index value for 2012 was 0.617—in the medium human development category—positioning Vietnam at 127 out of 187 countries and territories (UNDP 2013).

These statistics point to two factors that could affect the creation of a CIFF. First, if Vietnam continues its economic growth, its status will change from a lower-middle-income country to an upper-middle-income country, probably in the next decade. That change would have a significant effect on official development assistance (ODA), giving the government a limited time to carry out externally supported reforms and to improve institutional arrangements and reforms. Vietnam depends to an extent on ODA, but both the quantity and structure of the assistance are likely to change as the balance between loans and grants changes and becomes predominantly loan based. Second, the level of government debt is estimated by the World Bank to be approaching the maximum level—65 percent of GDP—set by the National Assembly. To manage this debt increase, the government could again curtail capital programs as it did in 2011, which could place a ceiling on borrowing by provincial authorities.

In 2010 the government of Vietnam prepared a Socio-Economic Development Plan (SEDP) for the period 2011–20, which articulated the following growth strategy goals (World Bank 2015): (a) keep average GDP growth at 6.5–7.0 percent, (b) target social investment at 33.5–35.0 percent of GDP, (c) keep the budget deficit below 4.5 percent after 2015, (d) do not allow government and national debt to exceed 50 percent of GDP, (e) keep the consumer price index at 5–7 percent, and (f) keep urban unemployment below 4 percent by 2015.

The following are some of the SEDP strategies the government aimed to apply for the 5 years starting in 2011:

- Restructure public investment, first targeting investments sourced from the state budget and government bonds, by modifying the regulation on management decentralization. The restructuring will maintain the principle that investment should go only to projects that go through the required procedures and only when capital sources, capital level, and capital balancing capacity are clear.
- Without delay, determine the criteria and priority order that will be the basis for approving or rejecting investment projects.
- Restructure the financial market, focusing on the commercial banking system and financial institutions.
- Continuously strengthen the public investment apparatus of the central government and local governments at all levels, and pilot an urban government model without delay.

Unfortunately, the SEDP goals for the 5 years 2016–20 are not yet quantified to the same level of detail and do not provide additional guidance.

The statistics cited earlier indicate that economic growth will continue and that the Human Development Index will show continuous improvement; however, the central debt, which is approaching the maximum target, may slow economic growth. Policy makers should therefore explore other means to address the substantial need for investment and to stimulate the flow of private sector resources for funding infrastructure.

INSTITUTIONAL FRAMEWORK

Assessing the needs, constraints, and challenges of local government infrastructure financing requires an overview of the state administrative structure. Vietnam is a unitary state divided into provinces and cities under the direct control of the central government. It has five tiers of government: the central government; 58 provinces; five cities that fall under the direct control of the central government; about 680 districts; and about 11,000 communes. Each of these entities has both legislative and executive authority. At the central government level, legislative authority rests with the National Assembly, and executive authority rests with line ministries and agencies. At the local level—provincial and below—each tier of government has People's Councils to exercise legislative authority and people's committees and line departments to exercise executive authority. In some instances, the People's Councils are being abolished, and the positions of party secretary (of the council) and chairman of the People's Committee have been merged. Hanoi and Ho Chi Minh City are regarded as special cases, with higher authorities. That is, the cities have a higher degree of independence and decision-making capacity, and because they have some market access already, they are not included in this assessment.

In a strictly legal sense, the provinces and cities are branches of the central government that have budget implementation responsibilities. Provinces are responsible for all municipal trade services, such as water, sanitation, and solid waste removal, as well as public transport, roads, education, health, and economic development. Most provinces have their own water and sanitation utilities (although sanitation is a hugely neglected sector). They have some input into setting tariffs, but they mostly maintain the tariffs well below the centrally authorized national limits. Electricity is provided and distributed by a state-owned company, Vietnam Electricity Company (EVN), and other state-owned entities, but provinces buy some of their electricity from independent suppliers.

BUDGET PROCESS AND FISCAL RELATIONSHIP BETWEEN THE CENTRAL AND PROVINCIAL GOVERNMENTS

Budgets of local authorities are prepared and submitted through a bottom-up process in which local legislatures review and appropriate funds for the local budgets before submitting them to the central government. The national legislature ultimately adopts a state budget for the entire country by consolidating the central and local budgets. Provincial budgets are an integral part of this unitary budget, but they have more decentralized spending (Albrecht, Hocquard, and Papin 2010). The process has been regulated by the State Budget Law (SBL), which regulates the relationships between the different government levels. The 2002 SBL was revised in 2015; the new SBL took effect January 1, 2017.

This nested budget approach is unique to centralized economies, and it creates ambiguity in terms of responsibilities for execution. However, the responsibility for managing budget expenditures is largely decentralized to the provinces, with the provision that the budget as implemented should comply with the approved state budget (although substantial discretion to adapt the budget is generally accepted). The provinces' capacity and ability to develop their own source revenue is very unequal. The SBL incorporates a redistribution system to equalize revenues, with richer provinces contributing more to the central government, which in turn makes grants to the poorer provinces.

Local authorities in Vietnam are responsible for over half of total government spending (table 2.1). Those expenditure shares are executed directly by

TABLE 2.1 **Summary of Budget and Expenditures at Central and Local Levels**

	D, TRILLIONS	US$, BILLIONS
Total state budget	816	38
Total state expenditure	978	46
Total deficit	162	8
Local budget	490	23
Official development assistance	105	5
Recurrent expenditure (central level)	337	16
Recurrent expenditure (local level)	322	15
Capital and development investments (central)	82	4
Capital and development investments (local)	93	4

Source: Ministry of Finance. Vietnam Budget 2012-13. Numbers are rounded.

provincial, district, and communal authorities out of revenues raised and retained within their jurisdictions and out of transfers from the upper levels of government. Therefore, local authorities have played a significant role in providing services that reduce poverty in the country.

The central government is still responsible for large national-level projects, and some of the recent increases reflect stimulus spending to address the effects of the 2008 global economic crisis. The economic stimulus measures adopted after the crisis resulted in overheating of the economy and high inflation and led to the curbing of capital spending in October 2011 (Prime Minister's Instruction 1792/CT-TTg, dated October 5, 2011). Nonetheless, local authorities now have more direct responsibility for capital spending, and the only borrowing that is allowed is for capital spending.

The budget cycle and consolidation process is slow, with final figures not required until 14 months after year-end and financial data not available often 18–20 months after year-end. This deficiency in the budget system renders ineffective the use of actual expenditure as a management tool. Budgeting and performance tracking against the budget do not occur regularly, and the existence of a large number of SOEs and extrabudget funds makes a full assessment difficult.

PROVINCIAL FINANCIAL PERSPECTIVE

Local revenue is divided into two categories: income retained by the provinces and income shared with the central government. Income that is 100 percent retained by the provinces includes land and housing taxes and registration fees on the natural resources tax, licensing, transfer of land use rights, and sale of state property. Income shared with the central government includes value added tax (except value-added tax—VAT—on imports), corporate income tax (except uniform accounting), personal income tax, special consumption tax on domestic goods and services, and environmental protection tax. The sharing ratio established for each 5-year stabilization period defines the proportion of shared revenue that is retained by the province. The central government retains 100 percent of some revenue, including VAT on imports, import and export taxes, revenue from petroleum, consumption tax on imports, and corporate income tax (with uniform accounting). Other sources of provincial funding include intergovernmental transfers from the central government, as a distribution component (not applicable to all provinces); tariff and tax income (own revenue); income from land transactions; borrowing; ODA income; and private-public partnerships (PPPs). Provinces that have a higher level of income contribute to the state budget using a sharing formula. The central government in turn makes unconditional transfers to less affluent provinces and earmarks funds to targeted national programs in provinces.

Provincial authorities can supplement their ability to undertake capital projects by borrowing, and they have borrowing power for projects contained in the state budget. However, the province must maintain a balanced budget. Provinces and their SOEs can currently tap the following sources to borrow: (a) Treasury for short-term loans not exceeding 1 year,

(b) on-lending from central government or ODA funding, (c) the Vietnam Development Bank (VDB), (d) state-owned and commercial banks, and (e) bond issues to tap the capital markets.

Based on the most recent data available, 51 provinces incurred some debt in the period of 2006–12 (World Bank 2014a). The provincial debt financing remains driven by central government financing, with local bond issuance accounting for less than 30 percent of total provincial debt (figure 2.1). Provincial debt amounted to 1.3 percent of GDP, and the share of the five biggest cities was 50 percent. Commercial bank debt has been limited up to now, at least until 2015.

FIGURE 2.1

Sources of Provincial Debt, Year-End, 2012

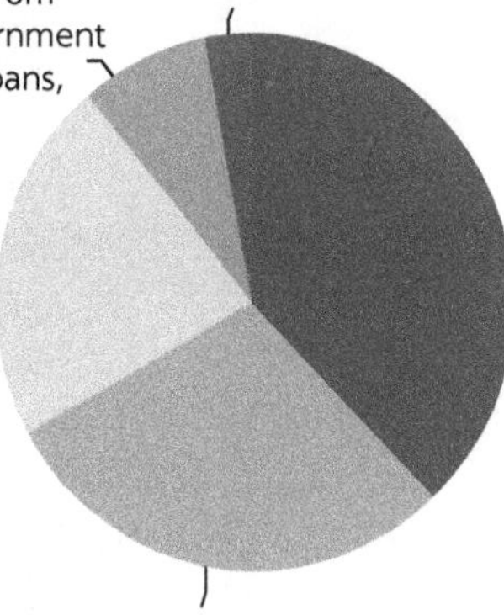

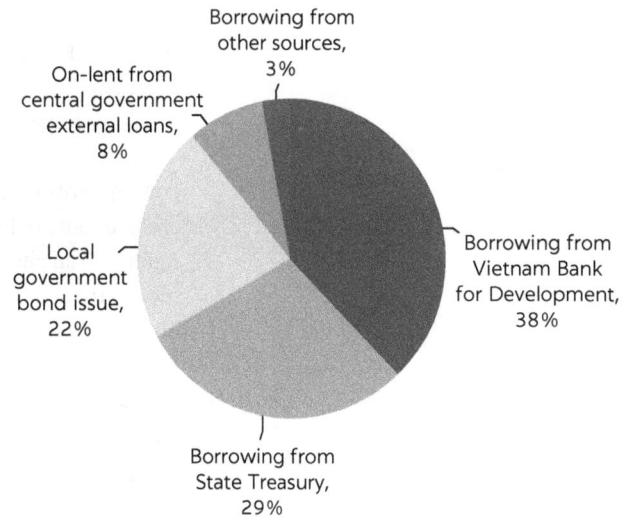

Source: World Bank 2014a.

All provincial borrowing requires approval from the central government, which monitors compliance with the thresholds. Such debts are closely monitored by the Ministry of Finance (MOF) under the SBL ceilings and are usually considered as on-budget borrowing, although that designation is not reflected in the budget. The 2002 SBL placed a ceiling on borrowing by provinces under Clause 26(g), as follows:

> The mobilized capital debit balance at the time of submitting the plans and the debit balance if the plans are approved must not exceed 30 percent of the annual domestic capital construction funding of the provincial-level budget, excluding investment capital supplemented according to objectives of a non-regular stability nature from the central budget to the provincial-level budget.

That rule set the ceiling of total outstanding debt at 30 percent of the capital expenditure in a given year, and a letter from the State Bank of Vietnam (SBV letter 576, May 8, 2015) restricts the borrowing tenor from commercial banks to 2 years. Taken together, these two rules severely limit borrowing by the provinces. In most creditworthy provinces, the debt service ceiling would probably be far below the sustainable level. Short-term debt makes sense for provinces because it allows them to make maximum use of their limited spending flexibility. However, short-term borrowing and bond issues are unsuited for funding infrastructure with an economic life of 15–20 years.

The implication of the current debt ceiling is that total borrowing would be restricted to approximately 9 percent of a province's own total revenue, given that the capital expenditure would account for an average of 30 percent of provincial budgets, regardless of what the province could afford over the long term.

The 2015 SBL recognized this limitation, and the MOF recommended that the National Assembly amend the restrictions in the following ways: (a) total debt must not exceed 60 percent of previous years' revenue in the case of Ho Chi Minh City and Hanoi; (b) total debt must not exceed 30 percent of previous years' revenue for provinces in category 2[2]; and (c) total debt must not exceed 20 percent of previous years' revenue for provinces in category 3.

The amendment will create more spending flexibility but will also require more financial discipline and better budgeting to ensure that incurred debt remains sustainable. Allowable debt stock for category 2 provinces would increase from approximately 9 percent to 30 percent of revenue, depending on the percentage of recurrent expenditure in total revenue. The 2015 SBL provides for the creation of small reserves at both the central and provincial levels. Those reserves are sometimes used as bridging loans.

Given a single central budget, the credit risk of all debt incurred by provincial governments can actually be viewed as central government debt, at least at the credit exposure level. That view was confirmed by this study's consultation with Agence Française de Développement (AfD): according to the Vietnamese constitution, there is only one state and one budget (Albrecht, Hocquard, and Papin 2010). The only exception would be debt from limited recourse projects with ring-fenced income streams. The study found limited evidence that recourse instruments were being used at scale, but this instrument could be used more widely in the future.

METHODOLOGY

Ideal approach

To determine possible effective demand for infrastructure funding and to identify the funding gap, the study team should create a development plan and the associated funding plan. That approach would entail the following:

- Analyze the historical trends in income, expenditure on capital backlogs, expenditure on economic backlogs, and so forth in the province.
- Design a long-term development plan that identifies (a) backlogs in infrastructure, (b) the balance between social and technical infrastructure to promote and support growth, (c) expected urbanization rate, (d) predicted economic growth rate, (e) predicted inflation rate in the construction industry, and (f) poverty-reduction goals and subsequent improvement in the quality of life that enhances the requirement for services.
- Design the long-term capital investment plan in alignment with the financial plan, including identifying multiyear projects.
- Develop a financial plan that is consolidated with the capital investment plan and that articulates (a) predicted economic growth and increases in revenue, (b) revenue increases due to increased rates and taxes, (c) predicted inflation rate, (d) composition of and increases in recurrent costs, (e) prudent liquidity reserves, (f) existing debt, (g) likely market conditions, (h) statutory constraints, and (i) market constraints on borrowing (that is, solvency ratios, debt service cover, and so on).

The financial plan in the last step would then translate into a funding plan that matches projects with the most appropriate instrument and funding source. Those sources might be ODAs, provinces' own resources, or borrowing, and they are used when determining a fund's mobilization plan.

This study did not allocate sufficient resources to undertake primary research to determine the size of provinces' effective demand for infrastructure funding. It therefore accepted the projections provided by the provinces, despite the possibility that the data may be deficient. Because final accounts in provincial governments are available only after 18–20 months, actual data for the period 2012–14 were collected for this study.

Basic research approach as adopted

The methodology used in this study aims to establish a potential range of effective demand for infrastructure funding to assess the need for infrastructure on a national basis. The study first investigates what financial constraints might be imposed by the government of Vietnam's macroeconomic policy, the government's planned actions, or the current public debt levels that would inhibit provincial borrowing more than the statutory restrictions contained in the SBL. Those findings are based on whether public debt is at a level at which the central government could restrict provincial borrowing. Once the study team makes those assessments, the projected sustainable debt levels for the three sample provinces can be analyzed.

The method's analytic approach first assesses the debt capacity and then superimposes other constraints to assess effective demand. Three of eleven provinces for analysis—Quang Ninh, Bac Ninh, and Dong Nai—which would serve as indicators of what the effective demand could be. That demand is determined by using affordability and sustainable debt levels based on the provinces' own projections of their financial position, and not by considering the credit see-through that might result from the unitary budget. Further, the analysis used statutory constraints imposed by the 2015 SBL, which uses a total debt stock ceiling of 30 percent of the previous year's *revenue* for second-tier provinces. The debt capacity for the second-tier provinces under the 2002 SBL was set at 30 percent of capital *expenditure* in a given year, which limited the conditions to less than what is allowable under the new SBL.

Analytic methods

The study used two analytic methods: free cash flow (FCF) and debt sustainability analysis (DSA).

Free cash flow analysis

FCF analysis is often used by commercial lenders to supplement the ratio tests.[3] The methodology is based on at least a 10-year view. The main numeric assumptions used in this study are as follows:

- The analysis period was set at 10 years because it is the minimum that is normally used for infrastructure projects.
- Loan terms were set at 2 years in 2016, with tenor increasing to 7 years by 2020.
- All loans were regarded as amortizing, on the assumption that bonds would be matched with sinking funds.
- An additional 3 percent of the capital program was added annually to the recurrent costs.
- To avoid duplication, debt calculations were based on the capacity of the previous year being used in the following year.

The projected annual operational surplus (revenue minus recurrent expenditure) is viewed as available for discretionary allocation. Discretionary revenue can be used to service debt or can be invested in the capital program. Any unforeseen reduction in revenue or an unexpected increase in operational and maintenance costs can normally be accommodated by a corresponding reduction in the annual direct capital investment (the discretionary component), providing a substantial risk buffer. This protection would pose a challenge only if all capital expenditure covered multiple years, eliminating the flexibility of the discretionary component, or when fixed recurrent expenditure grows to a level at which the risk of having insufficient discretionary funds available becomes real.

The analysis assumed that all discretionary income (after adjusting for the cumulative impact of existing and previous-year borrowing) will be used to borrow annually. Any statutory or regulatory constraints will be superimposed, and the maximum borrowing capacity in any year will be adjusted accordingly. In practice, of course, actual borrowing will be less concentrated and the cash flow managed more circumspectly and smoothly. FCF is a good quick method of determining the maximum debt that can be borrowed sustainably while complying with statutory requirements. The results in practice are tested against the normal ratios applied by lenders to ensure that no breaches of the particular lender's credit conditions occur (normally mostly by a ratio analysis). The tests would include debt coverage ratios, liquidity tests, and other measurement tools. The FCF analysis provides reliable maximum debt absorption capacity if the projections of both the revenue and the recurrent income are reasonable.

Debt sustainability analysis

The second analytic method used in the study, DSA, is based on macroeconomic criteria and ratios. The DSA tests the current and potential financial position against certain criteria to assess the fiscal capacity of the province to take up debt on a sustainable basis. The analysis uses a set of ratios based on gross regional domestic product (GRDP) to assess how the province's current debt and potential future debt will affect its future ability to service its debt.

The first step in such an analysis is to set a baseline scenario on how selected macroeconomic and debt variables might evolve. The indicators and variables normally used are (a) real GRDP growth as a basis, (b) solvency ratio expressed as debt exposure to GRDP (norm of 25 percent), (c) liquidity ratio expressed as debt service to local revenue (norm of 25 percent), (d) fiscal sustainability ratio expressed as interest to recurrent spending (an acceptable norm often is 10–15 percent), (e) primary fiscal deficit, and (f) ratio of local revenue to recurrent expenditure (in excess of 1).

The DSA assesses compliance with these nonabsolute norms, not to calculate quantitative sustainable debt but to form a view of the sustainability of the debt under certain projected scenarios and the degree of fiscal space remaining. As used in this study, the DSA was intended to confirm or adjust the sustainability of the quantified levels as calculated in the FCF approach.

Application of analyses to provincial data

This study applied the FCF and DSA analyses described to the data supplied by the provinces to determine the sustainable levels of debt and trends in the financial data that may affect financial creditworthiness. The most critical components of any province's debt sustainability are its economic base and its projected growth, as well as the projected increase in revenue and the rate at which recurrent expenditures are increasing.

Using the information supplied by the three provinces, the analyses assessed the potential pipeline of infrastructure projects to form a view of the size, sector, and state of readiness of each project. This book discusses the potential that the other provinces would be contributing to the central government using the financing facility, and the potential that they are not contributing to the central government but are receiving transfers from the central government and using the facility. The study also identifies other entities that potentially could use the financing facility.

The final step analyzes the aggregate information of the 11 provinces. The assessment identifies the nonfinancial provincial constraints that could inhibit the provinces' use of the financing facility and estimates the potential range of effective demand from all the factors discussed in this section.

EFFECTIVE DEMAND: NATIONAL PERSPECTIVE ON THE NEED FOR INFRASTRUCTURE

The amount available for infrastructure development from both public and private sources totals only D 344 trillion (US$16 billion) annually, resulting in a shortfall of D 193.5 trillion (US$9 billion) each year (World Bank 2013). Whether inflation, rapid urbanization, economic growth, and provision for rehabilitation and refurbishment are included in these figures is not clear, but at a macro level they represent a huge demand for infrastructure funding. Such findings are not unexpected for a developing economy, and it is clear that the resources of the public sector will be incapable of satisfying this demand, even with substantial ODA.

If the provinces had the capacity to implement infrastructure projects, the annual D 193.5 trillion (US$9 billion) gap in funding might be closed by additional borrowing, for example, at a weighted average of 5 percent annually over a 10-year term. There is concern that public debt is already approaching the maximum level set by the National Assembly. However, the curtailment of provincial borrowing as a result of uncontrolled public debt expansion may not likely occur given the general short tenor of subnational debt (generally within 24 months) and an approximately 6–7 percent GDP annual growth projection through 2019.

Furthermore, not all infrastructure projects are paid for by central or local government, so some of the required funds could come from the private sector through companies created by the provinces. Because provinces are responsible for 75 percent of government spending on infrastructure (World Bank 2014a), funding through the private sector would help in situations in which provincial capital expenditures were severely curtailed, as they were in 2011, when the central government reined in inflation and cooled down the economy by slowing down investment in infrastructure (Prime Minister's Instruction 1792). Repeating such action could negatively affect the effective demand of provinces for infrastructure expenditure.

Quang Ninh province analysis

Quang Ninh is a coastal province bordering on China and the Gulf of Tonkin (map 2.1). The economy is still largely based on agriculture but has a high

MAP 2.1

Vietnamese Provinces

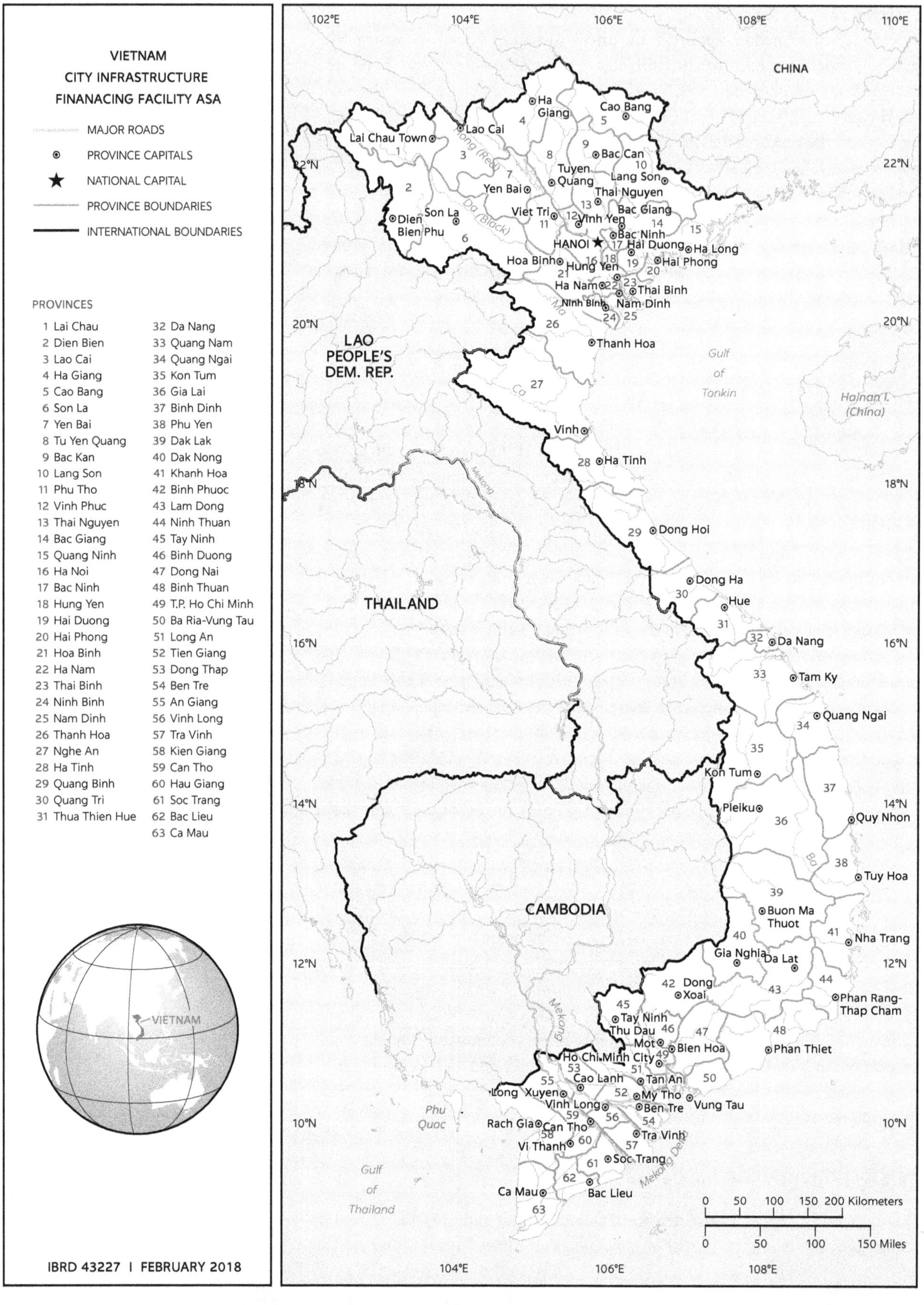

potential growth in the mining, tourism, and industrial sectors. In 2013 the population was estimated at 1,200,000, and GRDP was an estimated D 77.441 trillion (US$3.6 billion). Province officials project population growth to continue at about 1.25 percent per year.

Gross regional domestic product

GRDP is a simple proxy that reflects the strength of the economic base. It is an important indicator because of the implied correlation between GRDP and the potential revenue that can be collected by the province. In this analysis, provincial authorities were optimistic about the province's growth potential, basing their expectations on its growing trade with China and its mining and tourism potential. Quang Ninh officials projected strong provincial growth of around 15 percent, with the exception of 2014–15, when GRDP data as provided by the province indicated lower growth (figure 2.2). That drop was apparently caused by the conversion to a different base year and not by an economic decline. The predicted growth rates were used in the assessment of sustainable debt; however, debt may not increase given the national average GRDP growth rate of 6–7 percent annually.

Revenues

The ratio of revenue to GRDP is important because it indicates the extent to which revenue is optimized. The ratio normally would follow the GRDP trend (figure 2.3). The projected economic growth rate exceeds the annual population growth rate, which averages 1.25 percent. That growth again implies a relatively sharp rise in GDP per capita and will probably result in an increase in the quality of services demanded as disposal income increases.

The estimates provided by Quang Ninh, however, show the proportion of revenue collected declining relative to GRDP and do not reflect the strong GRDP growth. Revenue growth as shown in figure 2.4 remains relatively flat around

FIGURE 2.2

Projected Gross Regional Domestic Product Growth, Quang Ninh Province

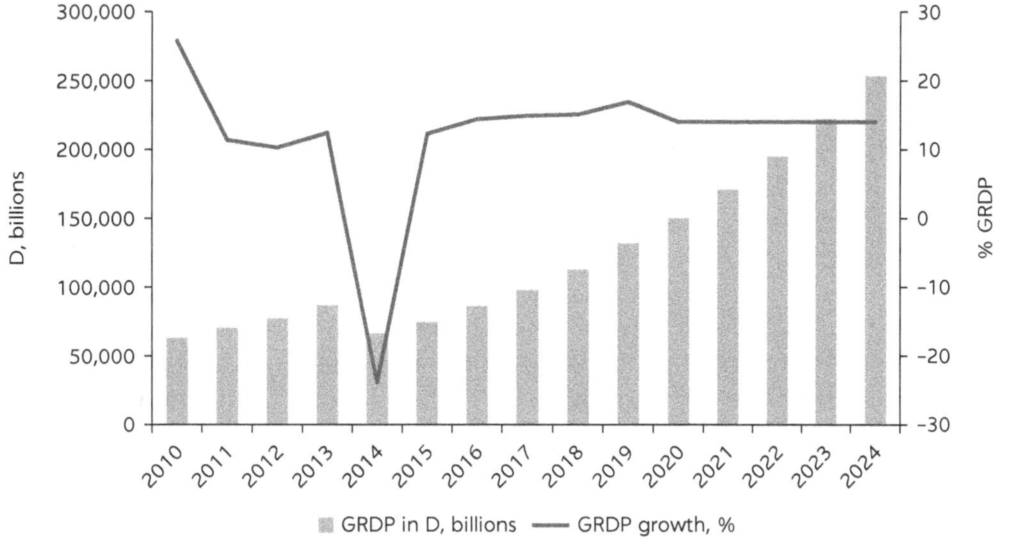

Source: Quang Ninh Province.

FIGURE 2.3
Ratio of Actual and Projected Revenue to Gross Regional Domestic Product, Quang Ninh

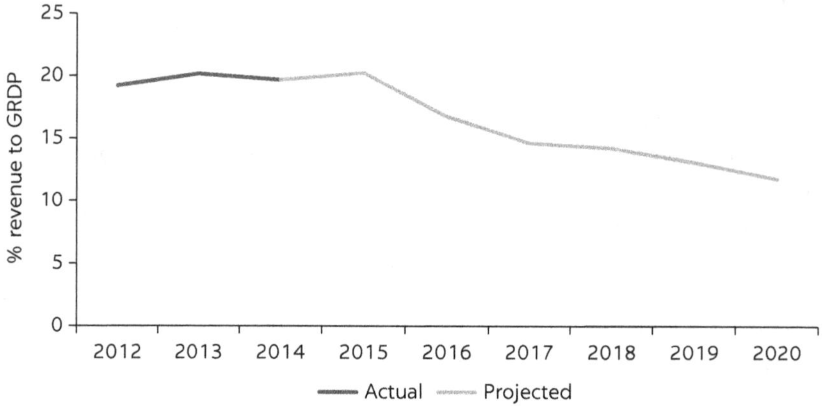

Source: Quang Ninh Province.

FIGURE 2.4
Actual and Projected Revenue, Quang Ninh

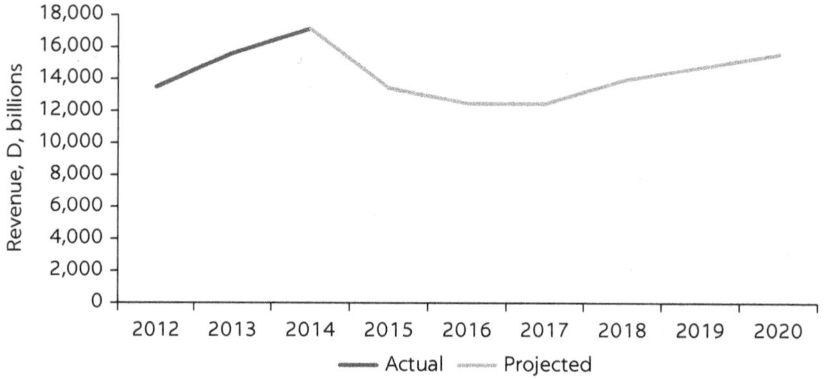

Source: Quang Ninh Province.

5 percent, compared with the strong 15 percent GRDP growth shown in figure 2.2. If the estimates are correct, they would indicate either that tax rates have decreased or efficiency has increased or that the fiscal approach adopted is very conservative. In addition, the sharp drop in GRDP observed in 2015–16 does not affect the revenue. Figure 2.3 shows a conservative approach to estimating revenue.

Recurrent expenditure

Recurrent expenditure is an important dimension because it determines the proportions of revenue that are committed and those that are discretionary (figure 2.5). Increases in recurrent expenditure are a normal occurrence as local governments mature and aging infrastructure requires more maintenance. The decrease in actual recurrent expenditure from 2012 to 2014 reflects the rise in revenue, with the expenditure remaining relatively steady. However, the sharp rise in the percentage of recurrent expenditure in later years is disturbing and will negatively affect the province's creditworthiness. When recurrent expenditures reach 80 percent of GDP, the potential for new borrowing will be lowest.

Budgeted capital program

The projected capital expenditure indicates a decline after 2015. This estimate may be a function of the province's underdeveloped future planning capacity,

FIGURE 2.5

Ratio Recurrent Expenditure to Revenue, Quang Ninh

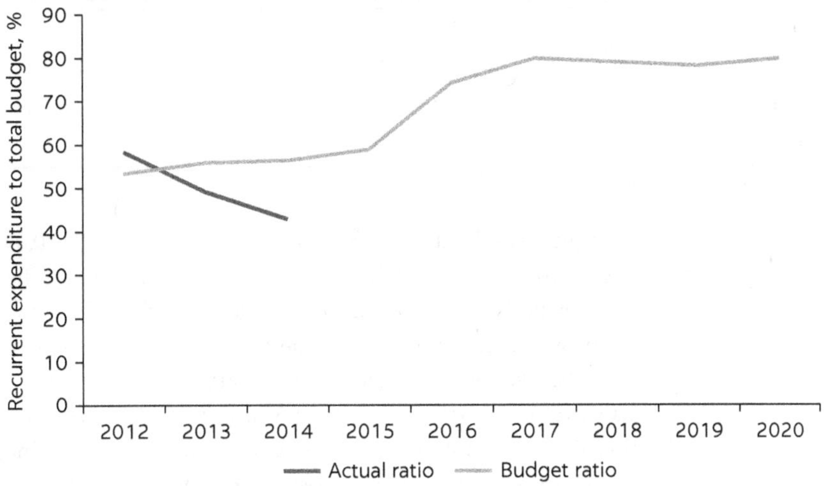

Source: Quang Ninh Province.

FIGURE 2.6

Actual and Budgeted Capital Expenditures, Quang Ninh

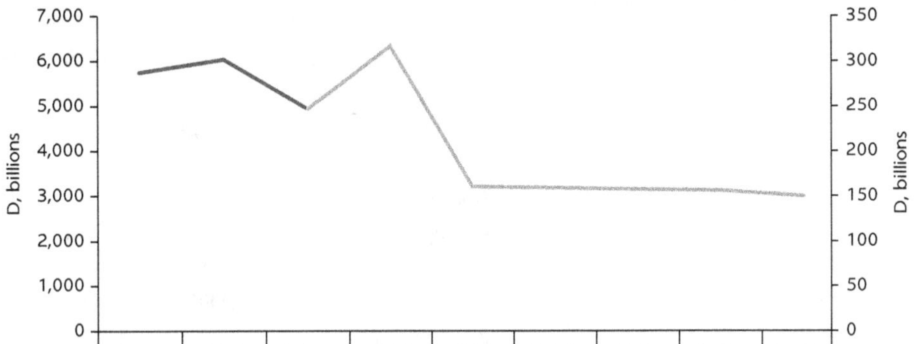

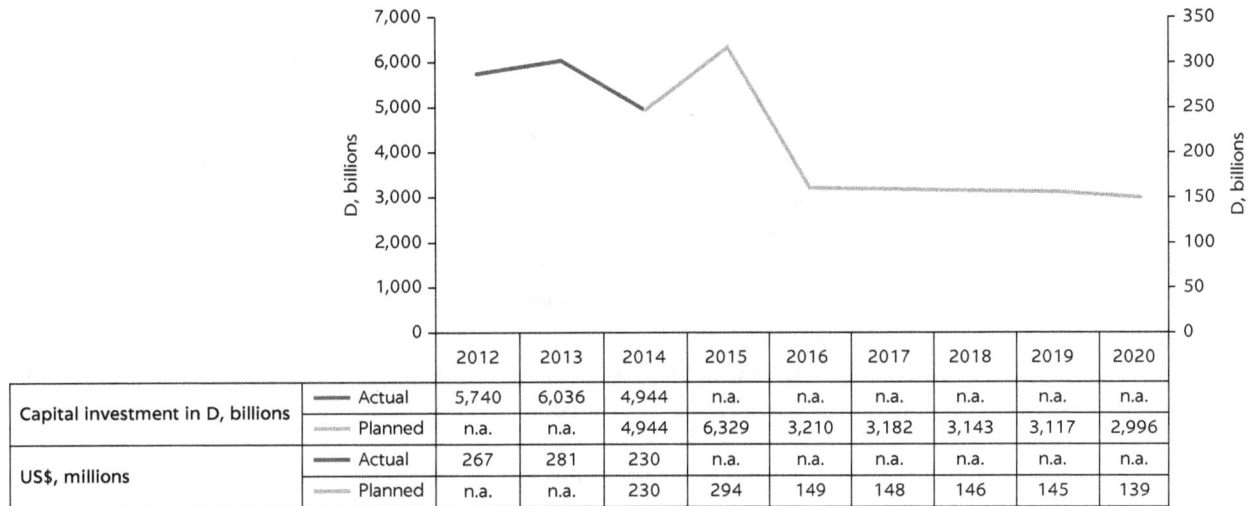

		2012	2013	2014	2015	2016	2017	2018	2019	2020
Capital investment in D, billions	Actual	5,740	6,036	4,944	n.a.	n.a.	n.a.	n.a.	n.a.	n.a.
	Planned	n.a.	n.a.	4,944	6,329	3,210	3,182	3,143	3,117	2,996
US$, millions	Actual	267	281	230	n.a.	n.a.	n.a.	n.a.	n.a.	n.a.
	Planned	n.a.	n.a.	230	294	149	148	146	145	139

Source: Quang Ninh Province.
Note: n.a. = not applicable.

its wait-and-see attitude, or a decreasing capital budget due to the increasing recurrent expenditure (figure 2.6).

The planned investments program is estimated at D 21.977 trillion (US$1.022 billion). It is based on the master plan prepared by McKinsey, consultants who generated a list of priority projects that have a total value of D 227.505 trillion (US$10.5 billion), or 10 times the value of the planned investment program. The master plan includes 69 economic projects (casinos, golf courses, a commercial complex, and industrial parks) of D 158.140 trillion (US$7.3 billion) that would generate income. Those income-generating projects would be funded through PPPs, a local development investment fund, SOEs, and private developers, which together would reduce the capital expenditure needed to D 69.365 trillion (US$3.2 billion).

TABLE 2.2 **Capital Expenditures for 204 Infrastructure Projects, Quang Ninh**

PROJECT EXPENDITURES	D, MILLIONS	US$, MILLIONS
Total	20,370,143	964
Average	103,139	4.97
Maximum	1,198,128	55
Minimum	1,316	0.06

Source: Quang Ninh Province.

FIGURE 2.7

Composition of Capital Program, Quang Ninh

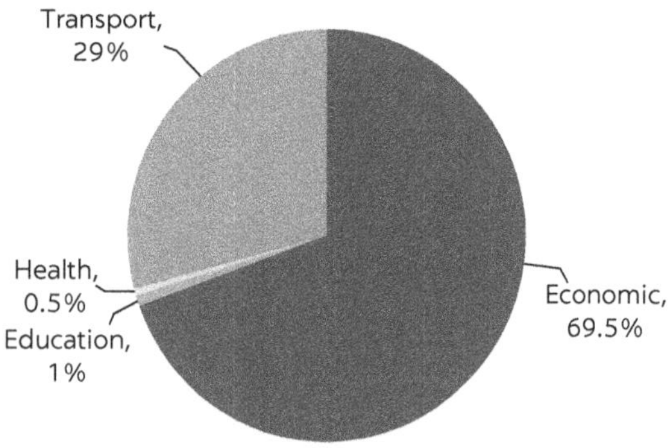

Source: Quang Ninh Province.

The project list submitted by the province still amounts to D 20.37 billion (US$964 million), and the plan is to fund that amount mostly from the province's own resources, with some borrowing. The province's emphasis on economic projects probably implies that some of them will also eventually be undertaken as PPPs or by developers. The analysis also notes that the province's projected decline and stabilization of expenditure after 2016 are also not realistic for a growing province. However, the lack of more realistic estimates is ascribed to the fact that planning probably has not progressed to a level at which detail could be recorded in the budgets.

Unfortunately, the information submitted gave no indication of longer-term planning incorporating all services. Also, details of the services to be delivered by the SOEs could not be obtained. The provincial authorities indicated that projects in housing and municipal infrastructure would be done by developers, with no estimate of an impact on the province's financial situation. The characteristics of the projects are shown in table 2.2. and figure 2.7.

Borrowing history

Quang Ninh's experience borrowing for capital projects includes borrowing from the VDB for rural infrastructure. The province has also issued bonds for highway construction of D 800 billion (US$37 million), with a 3-year maturity to 2016, and for the construction of a hospital of D 150 billion (US$7 million). The bond issuance shows that the province has some experience dealing with banks and bond issues. Quang Ninh has also planned further debt and bond issues as shown in table 2.3.

Quang Ninh authorities indicated that they requested the central government to provide a guarantee to the water utility but that the central government will not provide subsidies.[4] That condition should have created a contingent liability that will affect the province's creditworthiness and debt absorption capacity. However, it was not possible for the analysis to establish the extent of the contingent liabilities, and they have not been considered in the quantification of debt absorption capacity. However, the central government indicated that the contingent liability rests with the central government and not with Quang Ninh province.

Projected debt absorption according to the free cash flow approach

Using the FCF approach, the analysis calculated the debt and capital program for Quang Ninh province as shown in figure 2.8. The initial variations are largely due to existing loan redemptions. The total cumulative sustainable debt amounts to D 57.168 trillion (US$2.658 billion) with capacity of D 4 trillion (US$186 million) in 2016.

The debt in the case of Quang Ninh is restricted by the statutory ceiling and not by affordability. The revenue projections show an initial decrease in revenue and then a relatively slow growth of 5 percent that materially affects the borrowing capacity, especially in later years.

Additional criteria used by the commercial banks and capital market investors to assess credit exposure include (a) debt coverage ratio of revenue

TABLE 2.3 **Planned Borrowing by Quang Ninh, D, billions**

	YEAR	2011	2012	2013	2014	2015	2016	2017	2018	2019	2020
Vietnam Development Bank	Borrowing by facility	20	40	250	60	100	100	100	100	100	100
	Actual withdrawals	20	40	210	100	n.a.	n.a.	n.a.	n.a.	n.a.	n.a.
	Repayment	18	20	30	83	83	83	83	83	83	83
	Outstanding balance (planned)	55	75	255	273	290	308	325	343	360	378
State Treasury	Loan facility (planned)	300	400	200	300	300	300	300	300	300	300
	Actual withdrawals	300	400	200	300	n.a.	n.a.	n.a.	n.a.	n.a.	n.a.
	Repayment	51	256	259	355	n.a.	n.a.	n.a.	n.a.	n.a.	n.a.
	Outstanding balance (planned)	250	400	350	300	300	300	300	300	300	300
Issue of Bonds	Planned issues	n.a.	n.a.	950	0	0	1,000	0	0	1,000	0
	Interest repayment	n.a.	n.a.	n.a.	82	82	1,032	100	100	1,100	100
	Capital repayment	n.a.	n.a.	n.a.	n.a.	n.a.	950	0	0	1,000	0
	Planned outstanding balance	n.a.	n.a.	950	950	950	1,000	1,000	1,000	1,000	1,000

Source: Quang Ninh Province.
Note: n.a. = not applicable. Numbers are rounded.

FIGURE 2.8
Debt Profile, Quang Ninh

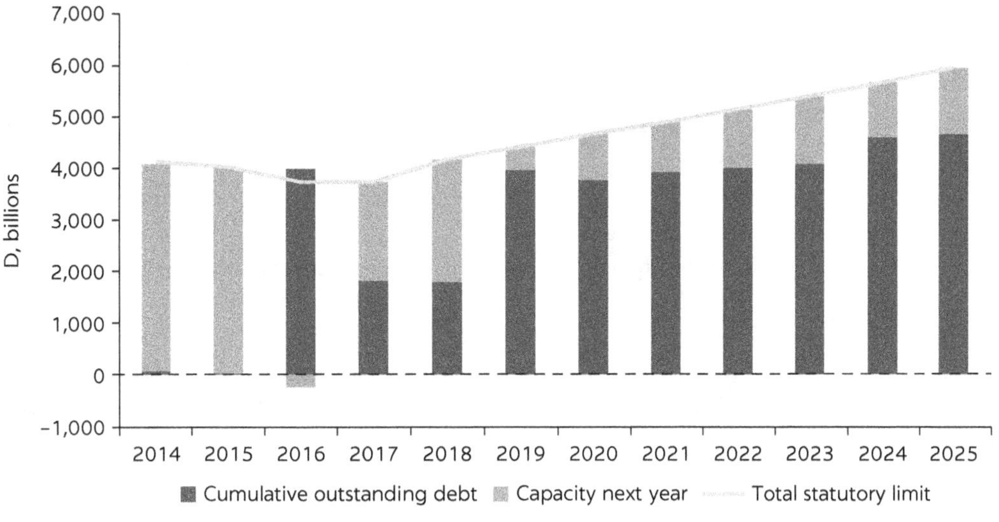

Source: World Bank calculations.

to debt servicing, (b) liquidity ratio, (c) working ratio, and (d) solvency ratio. The debt coverage ratio remains in acceptable limits (minimum 1.2) and never gets below 6. The other ratios are tested using the DSA.

The capital program and sustainable debt capacity is defined by the statutory limitations imposed by the SBL, conditions set by the SBV on commercial banks, real economic growth, inflation, the collection of all potential revenue, the right balance between income-generating and socially orientated programs, and the ability to curtail recurrent expenditure.

The provision of infrastructure can be accelerated by borrowing instead of using only the province's own resources to directly invest in infrastructure. However, it is important to note that repayments will have to be generated using the province's own resources. Borrowing accelerates the creation of infrastructure but does not create new resources. Creation of new resources can be done only by increasing rates and taxes, decreasing operational costs, or using resources more efficiently.

Projected debt capacity using the debt sustainability analysis approach

In applying the DSA approach, the analysis assumes that the requirement of the balanced budget approach will still apply, and in the testing of the fiscal space it makes no provision for borrowing for operational purposes to achieve a balanced budget (no budget deficits or surpluses). In practice, however, such provisions are not always the case, with substantial carryovers or shortfalls being the norm.

Like the FCF methodology, the DSA approach aims to establish sustainable debt levels by developing a baseline scenario using macroeconomic indicators and acceptable ratios. Similar to the FCF analysis, the DSA does not take into account short-term bridging loans from the central government and ODA. It was assumed that cash flow management challenges would be bridged by short-term borrowing from the central treasury.

The macro debt indicators used in the Ho Chi Minh City analysis (World Bank 2014b) are also used in this analysis to ensure a degree of consistency in the setting of sustainable debt levels. The indicators and ratios are mainly used to test the assumptions and confirm the FCF model. The indicators include (a) the solvency ratio, with debt to GRDP not to exceed 25 percent; (b) debt service to local revenue, preferably not to exceed 25 percent; (c) statutory limitations, with the SBL 2015 requirement such that total debt stock may not exceed 30 percent of the previous year's revenue; (d) a liquidity test, with interest payments as a percentage of recurrent expenditure, preferably not to exceed 25 percent; (e) a budget deficit of 0 percent (no deficit); and (f) existing debt similar to the FCF, short term and expected to be redeemed by the time new debt is considered

Quang Ninh remains comfortably within the financial norms but breaches the preferred solvency ratio in 2016 and 2019 (figures 2.9–2.11). The total debt was not adjusted to bring the ratio to the recommended levels because, over time, it returns to an acceptable level, and the substantial breach occurs in the period when there is considerable doubt about the integrity of the GRDP and revenue data. The projected 2019 breach can be managed by good cash management.

According to the provisions of the SBV, the recommended acceptable debt level for the province should be 30 percent of revenue, indicating a maximum

FIGURE 2.9
Debt Sustainability Analysis Indicators: Liquidity Ratio, Quang Ninh

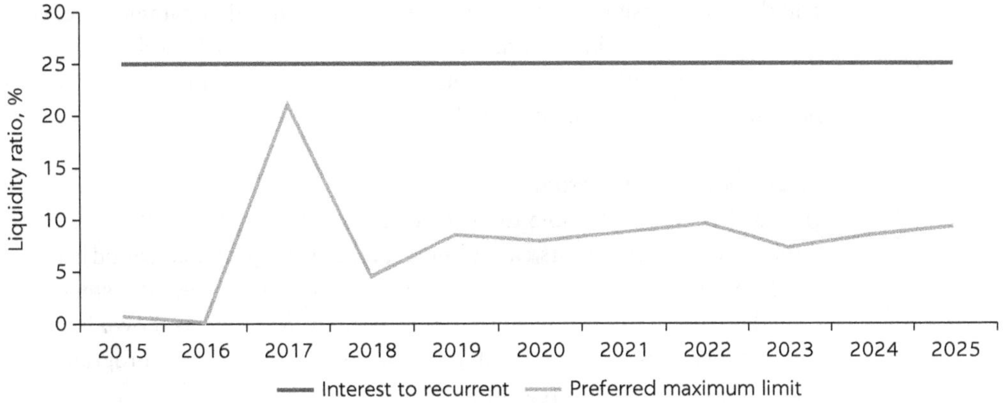

Source: World Bank calculations.

FIGURE 2.10
Debt Sustainability Analysis Indicators: Solvency Ratio, Quang Ninh

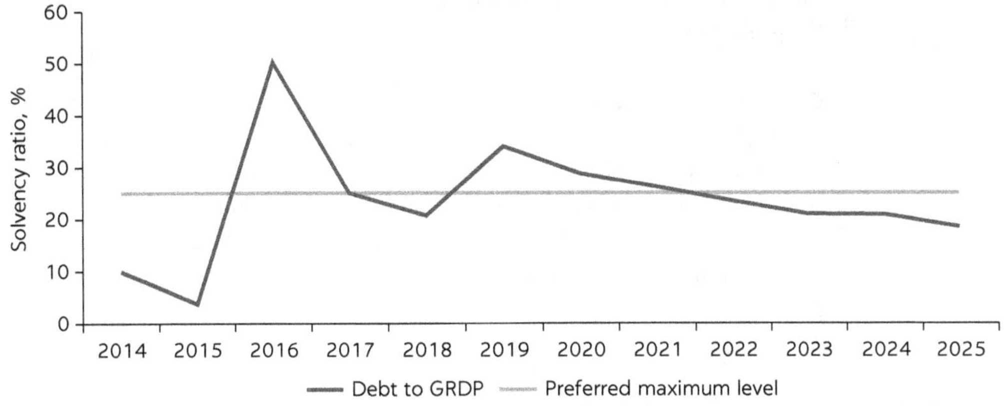

Source: World Bank calculations.

FIGURE 2.11
Debt Sustainability Analysis Indicators: Debt Service to Revenue, Quang Ninh

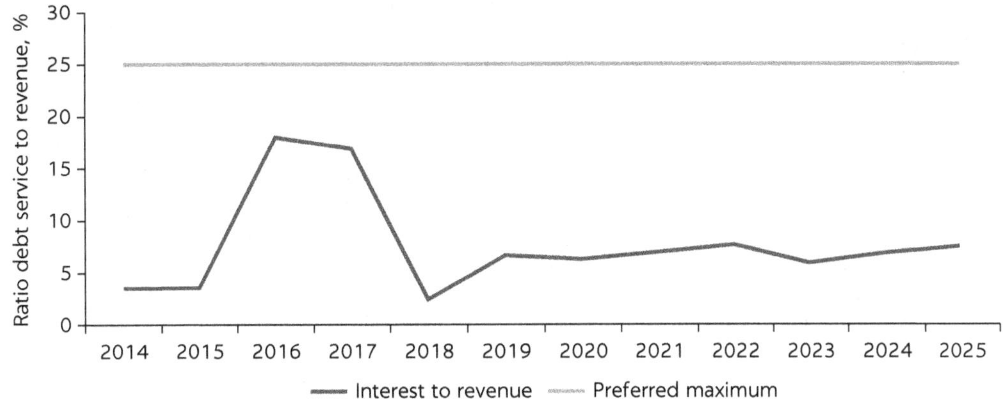

Source: World Bank calculations.

initial debt level of D 4 trillion (US$186 million), rising to D 6 trillion (US$279 million). Higher realized levels of revenue will increase this substantially because considerable fiscal space exists on all the other parameters except the solvency test. In this regard, the ratio of revenue to GRDP levels is relatively high compared with the other provinces, and the increase in revenue also will have to be based on an increase in the GRDP.

Potential capital program

Quang Ninh would be able to borrow on the order of D 4 trillion (US$186 million) and accelerate its capital program, but the province would have to carefully monitor the allowable total debt stock. A more realistic smoothed capital program conforming to the expected statutory norm is shown in figure 2.12, in which it is compared with the projected planned capital program. The lumpiness of the capital program budgeted in 2016 will have to be smoothed by combining the resources available in 2016 and 2017. The ceiling is derived from the revenue estimates, which were conservative relative to GRDP growth, although reducing the percentage of revenue to GRDP would assist in a better credit profile and compliance with solvency criteria. According to the provincial authorities, the entire projected capital program can be funded and some further capital programs accelerated (though this assessment does not refer to the project list).

Constraints and summary

Quang Ninh is in a healthy financial position and, from a financial perspective, is able to borrow. The ability to borrow is probably understated as a result of a very conservative revenue growth projection compared with the predicted GRDP growth. Borrowing capacity in 2016 is indicated as D 4 trillion (US$186 million). Quang Ninh also has a borrowing plan as well as a detailed list of priority projects.

FIGURE 2.12

Capital Program with and without Borrowing, Quang Ninh

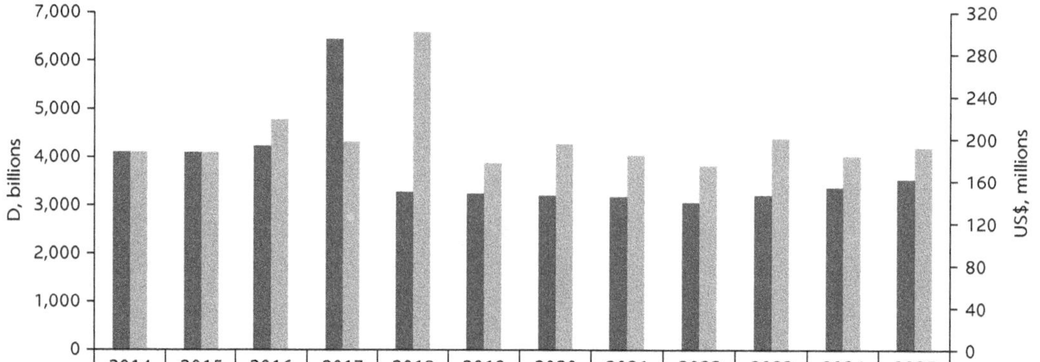

	2014	2015	2016	2017	2018	2019	2020	2021	2022	2023	2024	2025
Budgeted capital program, D, billions	4,028	4,020	4,156	6,329	3,210	3,182	3,143	3,117	2,996	3,146	3,303	3,468
Capital program with borrowing, D, billions	4,028	4,020	4,692	4,239	6,464	3,804	4,197	3,969	3,754	4,312	3,952	4,121
Budgeted capital program, US$, millions	187	187	193	294	149	148	146	145	139	146	154	161
Capital program with borrowing, US$, millions	187	187	218	197	301	177	195	185	175	201	184	192

Source: World Bank calculations.

In conclusion, the province has the ability to borrow and the need and the willingness to borrow, and it has the knowledge that the effective demand will be a function of the terms of any financing facility. The increase in size of the capital program is such that insufficient capacity is unlikely to be a factor. It is also clear that a substantial amount of preparation has been undertaken.

A long-term concern is whether recurrent expenditure will increase faster than revenue, which in the long term will inhibit borrowing. However, this potential has to be viewed against the conservative predictions about revenue increases.

Dong Nai province analysis

Dong Nai is adjacent to Ho Chi Minh City (map 2.1) and enjoys a spillover from the economic growth of that city into its thriving industrial and construction sectors. The province aimed for a GRDP on the order of D 57 trillion (US$2.6 billion) in 2014, and it aims to grow this by 10–11 percent per year (World Bank 2015). Currently it is also the preferred destination of foreign direct investment (FDI) in Vietnam, attracting over D 36 trillion (US$1.66 billion) in 2014 (Smetts 2014). A substantial project to construct an airport as a regional hub is also being considered by the National Assembly. The approval of this project could have a substantial positive economic impact on Dong Nai. However, it also would put additional strain on the infrastructure to support such a hub, despite the indications that the regional airport itself would be funded by national funds.

Gross regional domestic product

Provincial authorities were optimistic about the province's growth potential, basing their expectations on the high level of foreign fixed investment and the historic economic performance (figure 2.13). Dong Nai projects a strong annual GRDP growth of around 15 percent, compared with a national target of around

FIGURE 2.13
Gross Regional Domestic Product Growth, Dong Nai

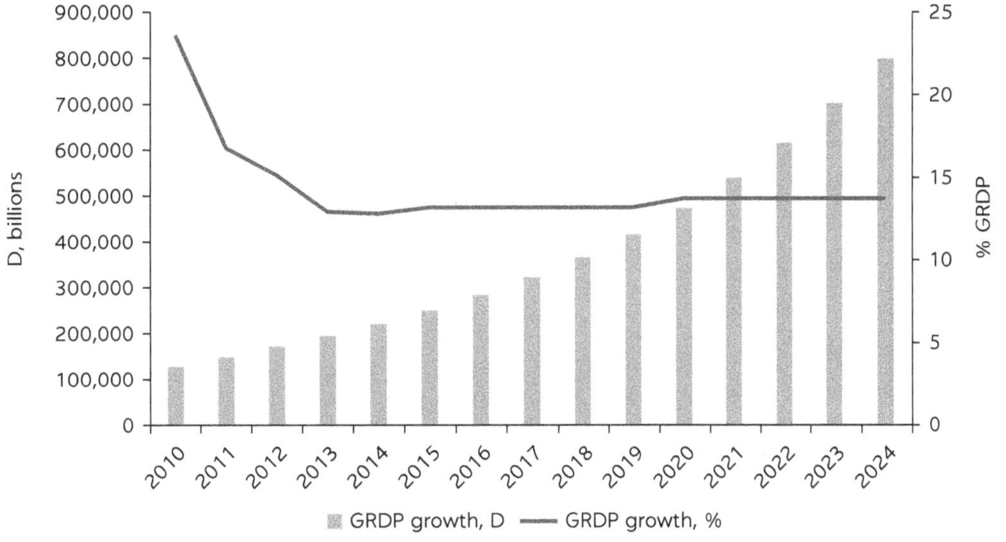

Source: Dong Nai Province.

6–7 percent. In light of the historic performance, this projection seems to be realistic; however, it should be noted that, as the overall economic base expands, the maintenance of high growth rates becomes more challenging.

Revenue

The ratio of revenue to GRDP is important because it indicates the extent to which revenue is optimized, which would normally follow the GRDP trend. The estimates provided by Dong Nai, however, show the revenue collected declining relative to GRDP (figure 2.14). The province's revenue, which is growing at an average 10 percent per year, is more realistic for future planning, although lower than the GRDP growth (figure 2.15).

FIGURE 2.14

Actual and Projected Revenue to Gross Regional Domestic Product, Dong Nai

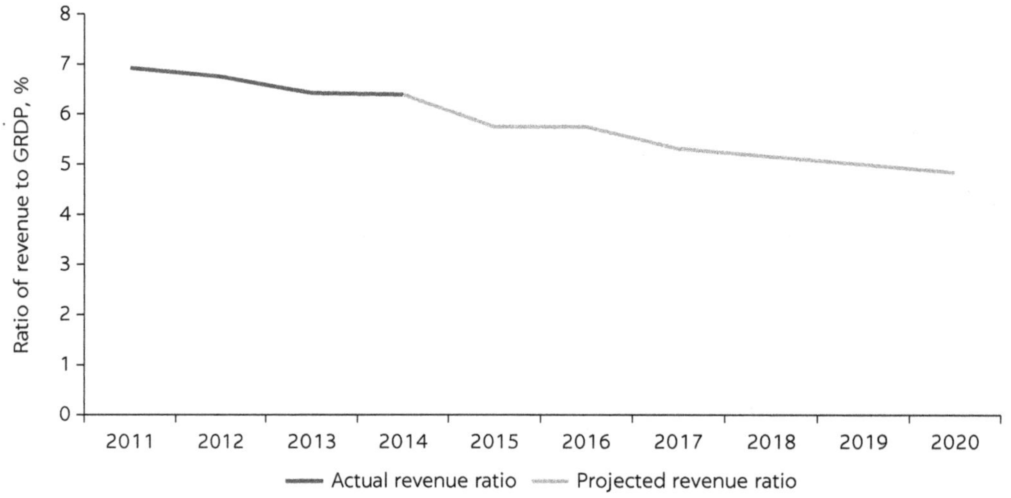

Source: Dong Nai Province.

FIGURE 2.15

Actual and Projected Revenue, Dong Nai

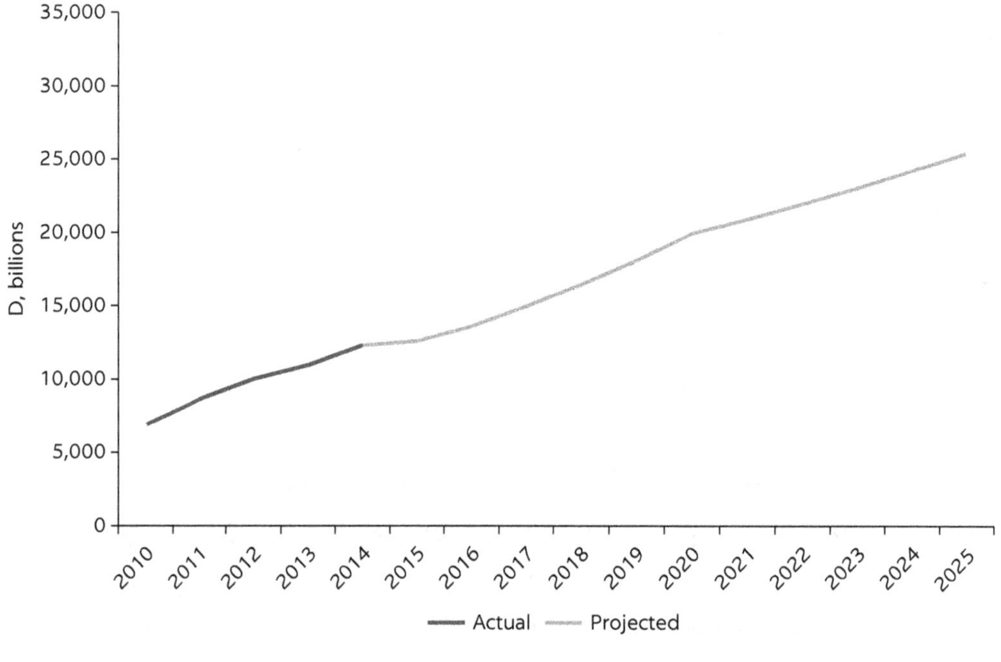

Source: Dong Nai Province.

Recurrent expenditure

Recurrent expenditure is an important dimension because it determines the proportions of revenue that are committed and those that are discretionary (figure 2.16). Increases in recurrent expenditure are a normal occurrence as local governments mature and aging infrastructure requires more maintenance. However, the sharp rise in percentage of recurrent expenditure in the case of Dong Nai is disturbing and will negatively affect its creditworthiness. Despite the predicted revenue growth of 10 percent and strong GRDP growth, the level of recurrent expenditure relative to revenue is predicted to reach 95 percent, a level which not only will affect future borrowing ability but also will be seen as a risky area in credit assessments. Future revenue increases could remove this concern if recurrent expenditure does not also increase.

Budgeted capital program

The projections show a smooth rise in capital expenditure (figure 2.17). The province's capital investment program amounts to D 9,213,945 million

FIGURE 2.16

Recurrent Expenditure to Revenue, Dong Nai

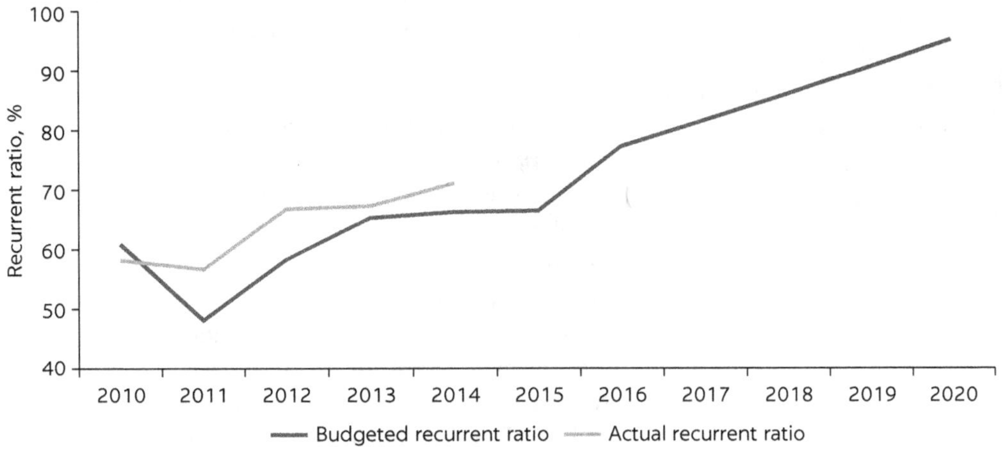

Source: Dong Nai Province.

FIGURE 2.17

Actual and Budgeted Capital Expenditure, Dong Nai

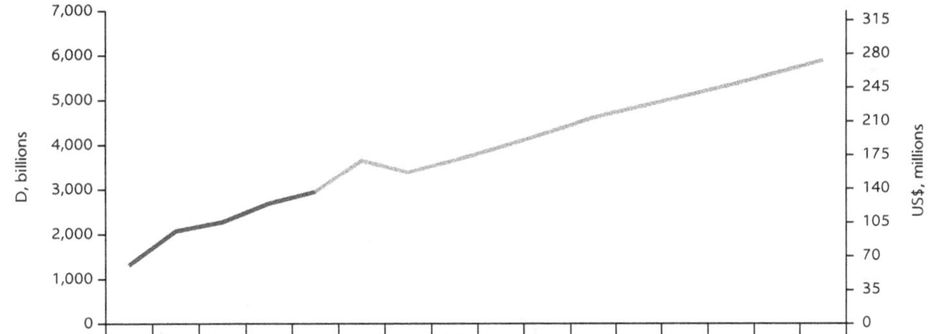

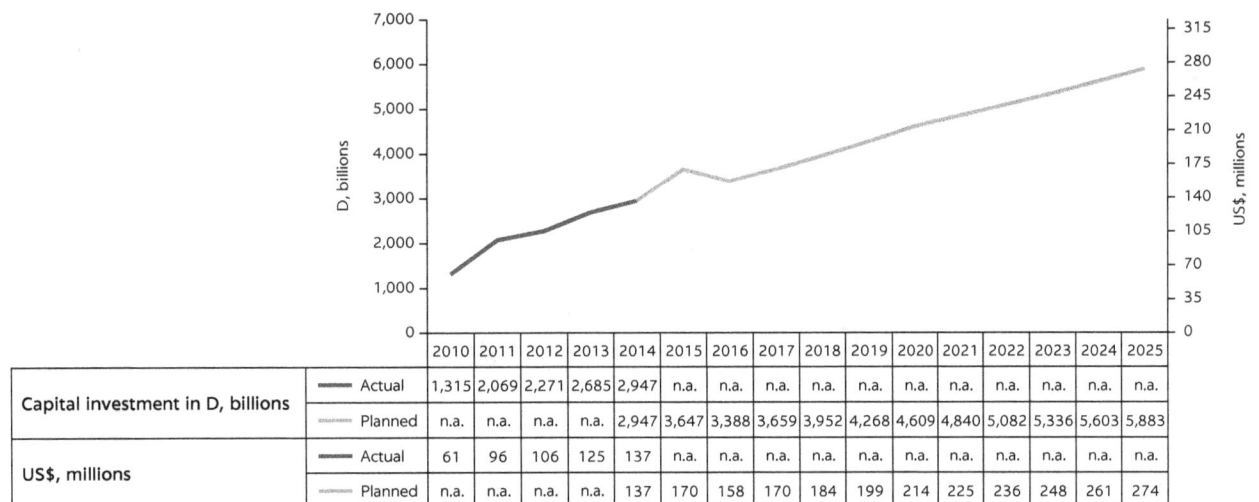

		2010	2011	2012	2013	2014	2015	2016	2017	2018	2019	2020	2021	2022	2023	2024	2025
Capital investment in D, billions	Actual	1,315	2,069	2,271	2,685	2,947	n.a.	n.a.	n.a.	n.a.	n.a.	n.a.	n.a.	n.a.	n.a.	n.a.	n.a.
	Planned	n.a.	n.a.	n.a.	n.a.	2,947	3,647	3,388	3,659	3,952	4,268	4,609	4,840	5,082	5,336	5,603	5,883
US$, millions	Actual	61	96	106	125	137	n.a.	n.a.	n.a.	n.a.	n.a.	n.a.	n.a.	n.a.	n.a.	n.a.	n.a.
	Planned	n.a.	n.a.	n.a.	n.a.	137	170	158	170	184	199	214	225	236	248	261	274

Source: Dong Nai Province.
Note: n.a. = not applicable.

(US$428 million) over 5 years, with plans to fund it from the province's own resources. Given the need to address the already severe congestion on the transport routes and the need to expand, this estimate seems conservative. Unfortunately, this analysis could not obtain any indication of longer-term planning that incorporates all services and the services to be delivered by the SOEs. The relative amounts committed to capital program areas are shown in figure 2.18.

Borrowing history

Dong Nai has both borrowed from banks and issued bonds. Dong Nai officials concluded two loans with VietinBank of D 200 billion (US$9 million) and D 1 trillion (US$46.5 million) in 2014. Both have an interest rate of 7 percent. In addition, they have a loan of D 400 billion (US$18.6 million) from the Bank for Investment and Development of Vietnam (BIDV) with an interest rate at 6 percent and a tenor of 2 years. It is interesting to note that the loans were used for nonincome-generating infrastructure projects and that no collateral was provided. In addition to these loans, the province previously used a bond that has since matured and been repaid. The debt profile of Dong Nai over the next 10 years is shown in figure 2.19.

FIGURE 2.18

Composition of Capital Program, Dong Nai

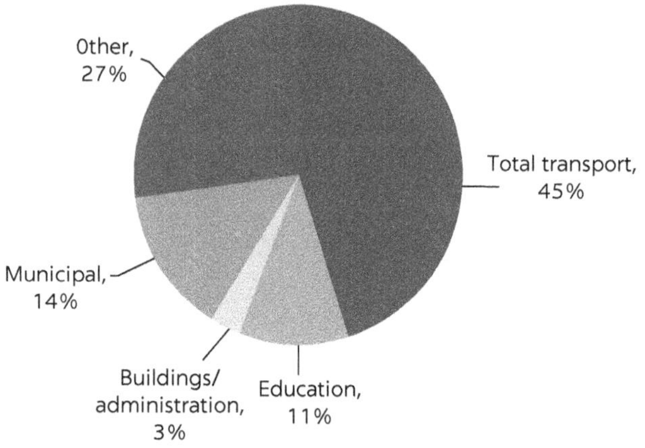

Source: Dong Nai Province.

Projected debt capacity according to the free cash flow approach

The debt coverage ratio remains in acceptable limits (minimum 1.2) and never gets below 7. (The other ratios are tested in the DSA.) To a large degree the capital program and sustainable debt level will be defined by the statutory limitations imposed by the SBL, conditions set by the SBV, real economic growth, inflation, the collection of all potential revenue, the right balance between income-generating and socially orientated programs, and the ability to curtail

FIGURE 2.19

Debt Profile, Dong Nai

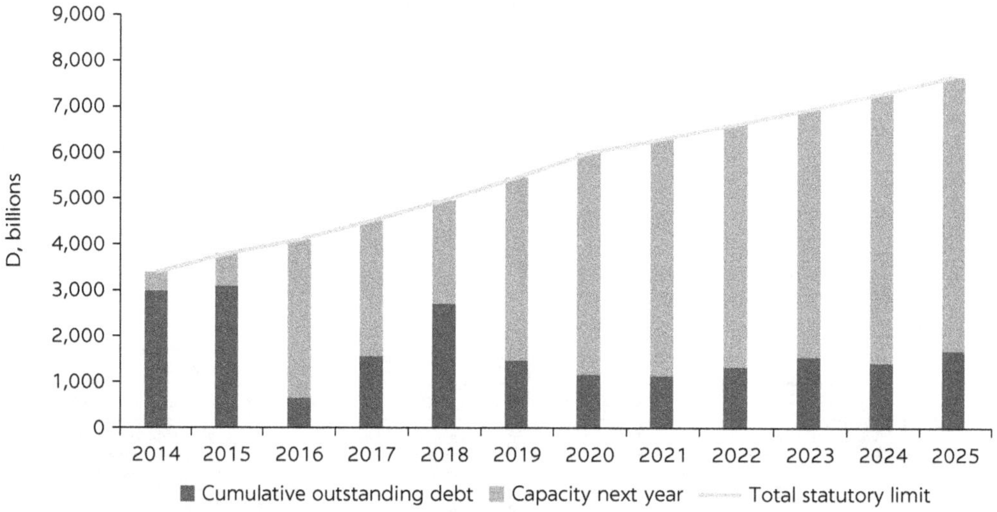

Source: World Bank calculations.

recurrent expenditure. The provision of infrastructure can be accelerated by borrowing instead of using only provincial resources to directly invest in infrastructure.

Projected debt capacity using the debt sustainability analysis approach

In the DSA approach, the analysis assumes that the requirements of the balanced budget approach will still apply. When testing the fiscal space, no provision is made for borrowing for operational purposes to achieve a balanced budget (no budget deficits or surpluses). In practice, however, that approach is not always the case; instead, substantial carryovers or shortfalls are the norm.

Like the FCF methodology, the DSA approach aims to establish sustainable debt levels by developing a baseline scenario using macroeconomic indicators and acceptable ratios. Similar to the FCF analysis, the DSA has not taken into account short-term bridging loans from treasury and ODA. It was assumed that cash flow management challenges would be bridged by short-term borrowing from the central treasury.

Dong Nai remains comfortably within all the financial ratios of the DSA approach (figures 2.20–2.22). Therefore, it is recommended that the acceptable

FIGURE 2.20

Debt Sustainability Analysis Indicators: Liquidity Ratio, Dong Nai

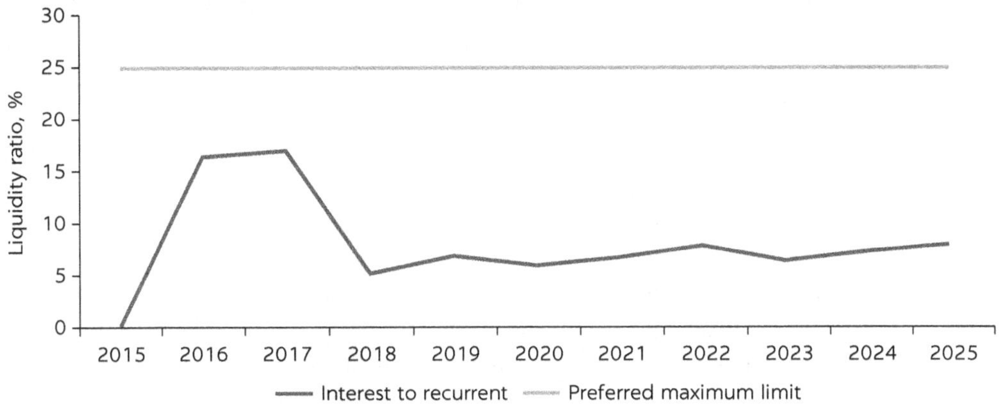

Source: World Bank calculations.

FIGURE 2.21

Debt Sustainability Analysis Indicators: Solvency Ratio, Dong Nai

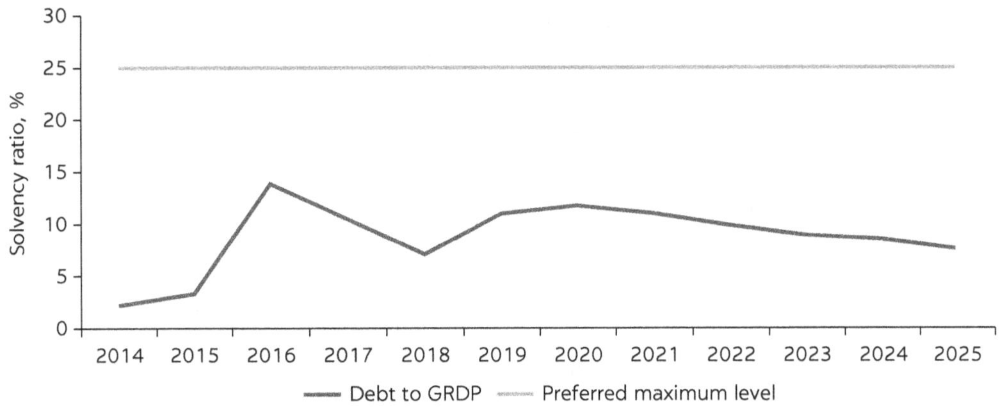

Source: World Bank calculations.

FIGURE 2.22
Debt Sustainability Analysis Indicators: Debt Service to Revenue, Dong Nai

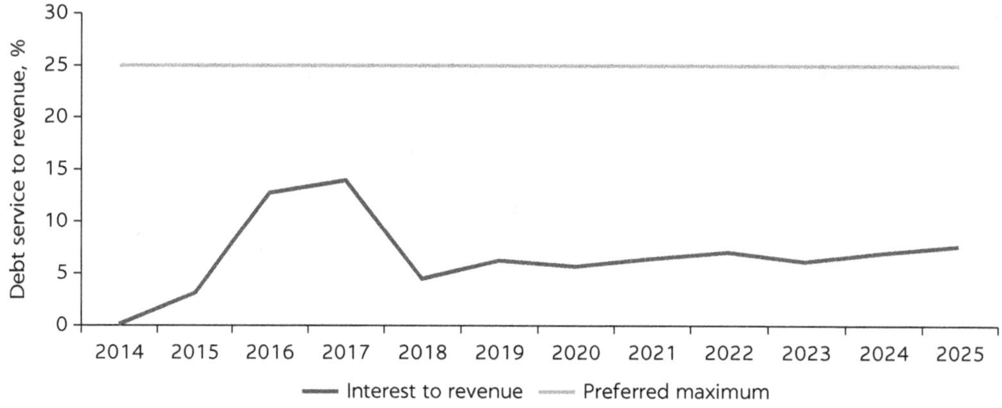

Source: World Bank calculations.

debt level for the province be accepted as 30 percent of revenue, indicating a maximum initial level of debt capacity of D 4.94 trillion (US$230 million), rising to D 7.65 trillion (US$356 million), and a cumulative level of total debt of D 59.772 trillion (US$2.78 billion).

Potential capital program

Dong Nai would be able to borrow on the order of D 3.347 trillion (US$155 million) in 2016 after accounting for existing debt. The province can accelerate its capital program but would have to carefully monitor the allowable total debt stock. A realistic smoothed capital program conforming to the expected statutory norm is shown in figure 2.23. The comparison with the budgeted projected capital program indicates that the budgeted capital program plus some additional projects can be undertaken. The ceiling is determined by the revenue and, as discussed, the projections indicate a very conservative estimate of future revenue despite the high projected GRDP growth rate. In reality, the actual revenue and the consequential debt cap are expected to be higher.

Constraints and summary

Dong Nai is in a healthy financial position and, from a financial perspective, is able to borrow. The ability to borrow is probably slightly understated as a result of a conservative revenue growth projection compared with the predicted GRDP growth. Borrowing capacity in 2016 is indicated as D 4.94 trillion (US$230 million), but new debt will be restricted to D 3.347 trillion (US$155 million).

In summary, the province has the ability, experience, and willingness to borrow. Effective demand is most likely to be constrained by the terms of any potential additional borrowing. Although factors such as access to land and other planning issues may present short-term constraints, the increase of the annual capital program with borrowing is not so great as

FIGURE 2.23
Budgeted versus Potential Capital Program with Borrowing, Dong Nai

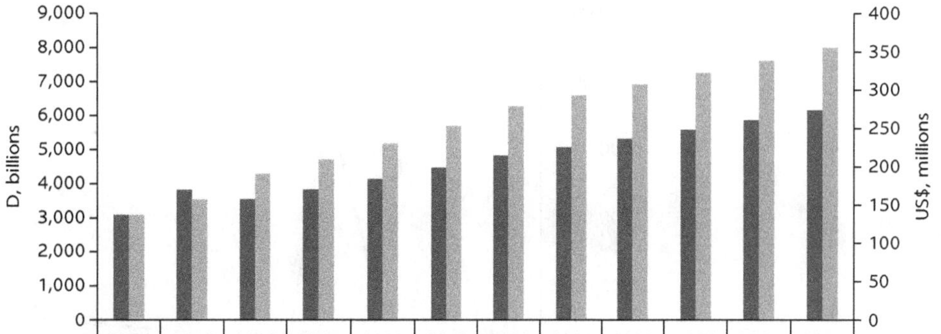

	2014	2015	2016	2017	2018	2019	2020	2021	2022	2023	2024	2025
Budgeted capital program in D, billions	2,947	3,647	3,388	3,659	3,952	4,268	4,609	4,840	5,082	5,336	5,603	5,883
Capital program with borrowing in D, billions	2,947	3,385	4,094	4,503	4,954	5,449	5,994	6,294	6,609	6,939	7,286	7,650
Budgeted capital program in US$, millions	137	170	158	170	184	198	214	225	236	248	260	273
Capital program with borrowing in US$, millions	137	157	190	209	230	253	279	293	307	323	339	356

Source: World Bank calculations.

to be substantial, and it is likely that the full capacity could be used. Therefore, Dong Nai is likely to have a total debt capacity of D 4.94 trillion (US$230 million).

Bac Ninh province analysis

Bac Ninh is next to Hanoi in the Red River valley and as such enjoys an overspill from the economic growth of Hanoi (map 2.1). It has thriving industrial and construction sectors based on virtual export harbors and export credit zones. It is a fairly recently formed province that is rapidly converting from a rural economy to an industrial economy. Currently industrial activity is dominated by Samsung and its dependent suppliers, which provide some 60 percent of the province's GRDP, posing a serious systemic risk for the province.

Gross regional domestic product

The provincial authorities were optimistic about the growth potential of the Bac Ninh economy, basing their expectations on the historical growth, the projected growth of 14 percent per year, and the fact that Bac Ninh lies on a number of transport corridors. The impact of Samsung's activities is illustrated by the drop in GRDP growth when it reached production capacity in 2013 (figure 2.24). It is notable that the high increases in 2010–13 were from a relatively low base.

Revenue

The important ratio of revenue to GRDP indicates the extent to which revenue is optimized and would normally follow the GRDP trend. As in the two other provinces, the revenue shows a declining trend in GRDP that is contrary to intuitive expectations and indicates a conservative approach was taken in estimating future revenue growth (figure 2.25).

FIGURE 2.24
Gross Regional Domestic Product Growth, Bac Ninh

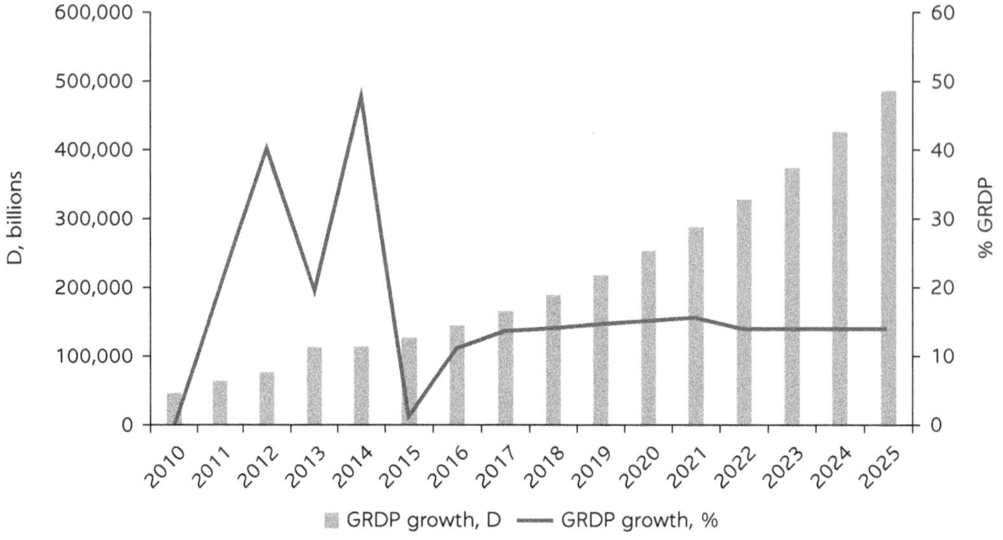

Source: Bac Ninh Province.

FIGURE 2.25
Actual and Projected Revenue to Gross Regional Domestic Product, Bac Ninh

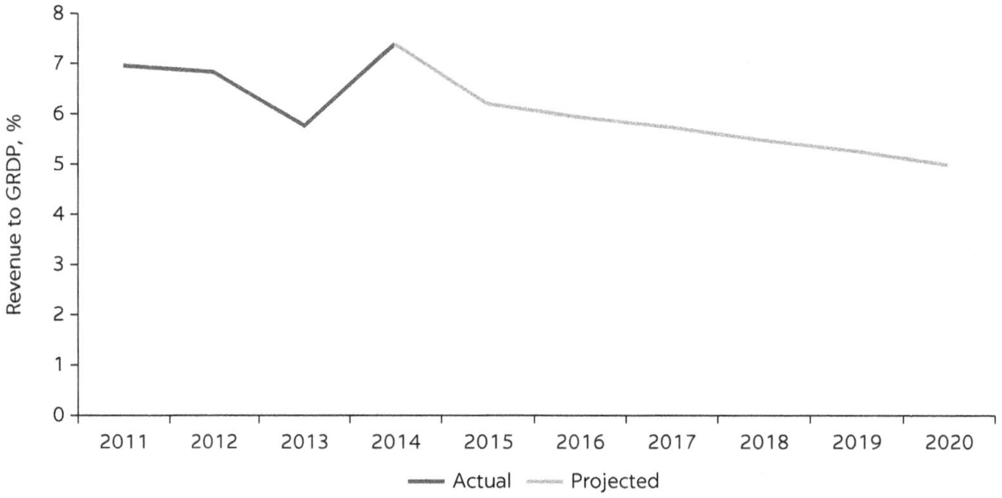

Source: Bac Ninh Province.

The delayed impact of Samsung's declining operations is also reflected in the revenue growth. Despite its past high growth, the province now is projecting an annual growth rate in revenue of around 10 percent on average, which can be viewed as reasonable and compares well with the predicted GRDP growth rate of around 12 percent (figure 2.26).

Recurrent expenditure

Recurrent expenditure is an important dimension because it determines the proportions of revenue that are committed (recurrent) and those that are

FIGURE 2.26
Actual and Projected Revenue, Bac Ninh

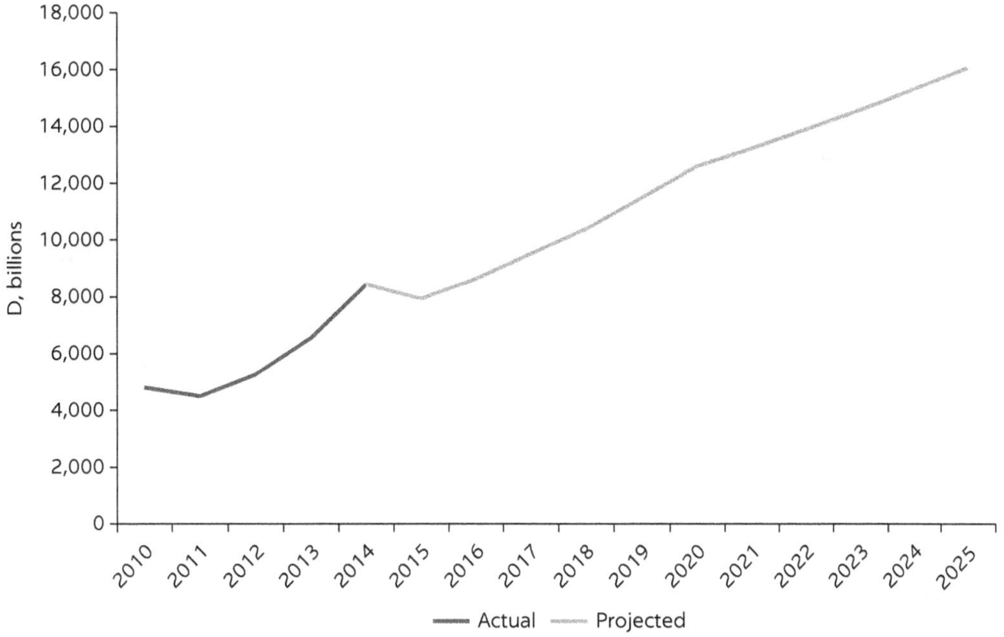

Source: Bac Ninh Province.

discretionary (figure 2.27). In the case of Bac Ninh the percentage used for recurrent expenditure is projected to be stable around 65 percent of revenue, allowing a substantial discretionary buffer, which will be viewed favorably in a credit rating if prudent debt levels are maintained. The drop in the percentage in 2012 was a result of recurrent expenditure growing more slowly than revenue.

Budgeted capital program

The province's investment program amounts to D 8.137 trillion (US$378 million) over 5 years, with the funding to come from the province's own resources (figure 2.28). Investment in transport dominates, which is understandable for a province that is undergoing rapid industrialization and that needs to use the quality of its transport routes to attract investors. Unfortunately, the provincial information gave no indication of longer-term planning that would incorporate all services or say what services were be delivered by the SOEs. The size of the projects in the budgeted capital program varies from small to substantial, as shown in figure 2.29.

Borrowing history

Bac Ninh has a loan of D 252 billion (US$11.7 million) with the VDB and a loan of D 100 billion (US$4.65 million) from the state treasury. The province has issued two municipal bonds of D 100 billion (US$4.65 million) and D 300 billion (US$13.95 million) at issue rates of 9.65 percent and 6.59 percent, respectively. The start and maturity dates are 2013–18 and 2014–19, respectively. Thus, Bac Ninh has experience in borrowing, and officials are confident about managing cash flows.

FIGURE 2.27

Ratio of Recurrent Expenditure to Revenue, Bac Ninh

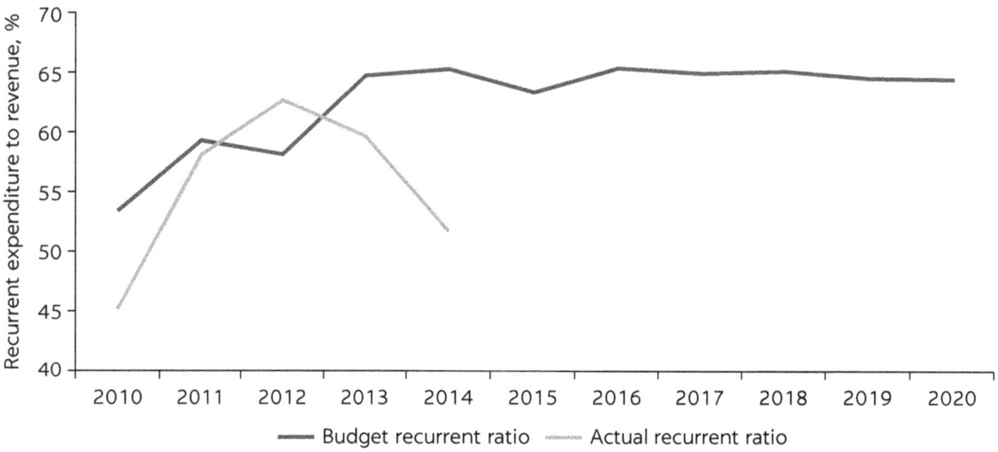

Source: Bac Ninh Province.

FIGURE 2.28

Actual and Budgeted Capital Expenditure, Bac Ninh

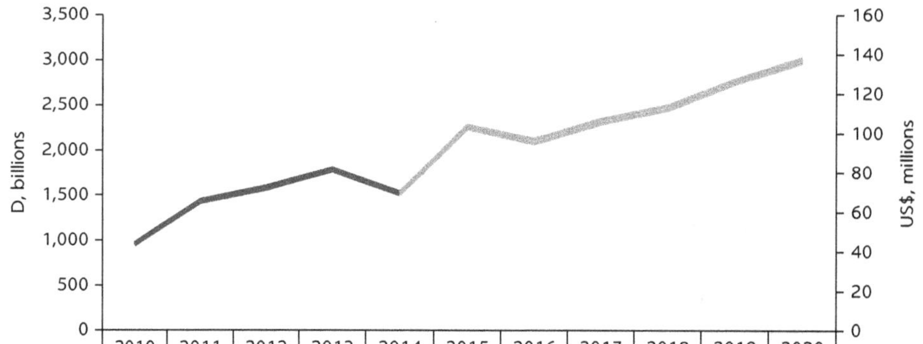

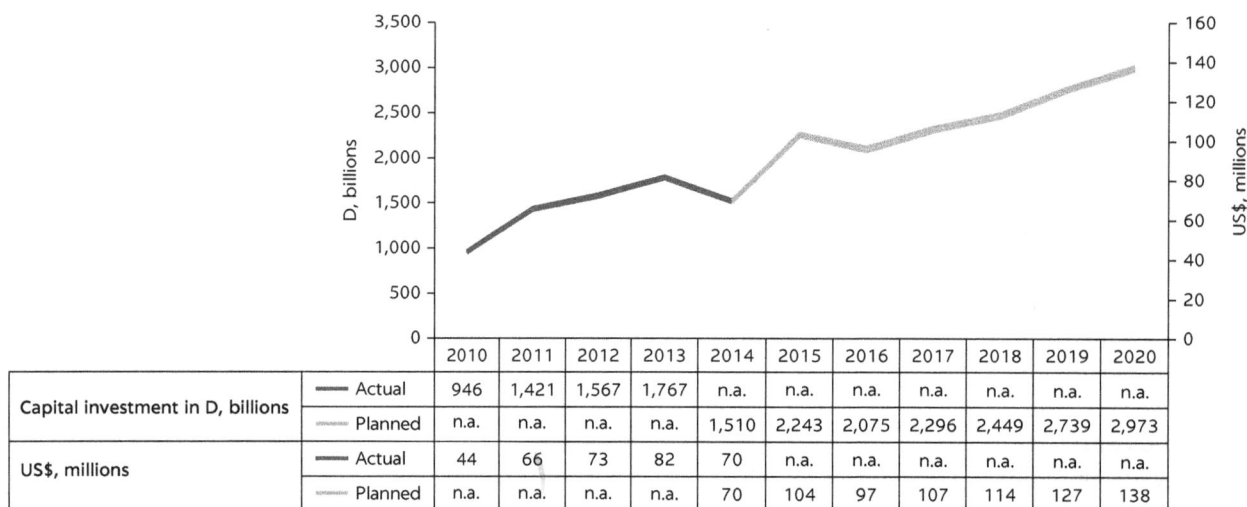

		2010	2011	2012	2013	2014	2015	2016	2017	2018	2019	2020
Capital investment in D, billions	Actual	946	1,421	1,567	1,767	n.a.	n.a.	n.a.	n.a.	n.a.	n.a.	n.a.
	Planned	n.a.	n.a.	n.a.	n.a.	1,510	2,243	2,075	2,296	2,449	2,739	2,973
US$, millions	Actual	44	66	73	82	70	n.a.	n.a.	n.a.	n.a.	n.a.	n.a.
	Planned	n.a.	n.a.	n.a.	n.a.	70	104	97	107	114	127	138

Source: Bac Ninh Province.
Note: n.a. = not applicable.

Projected debt capacity according to the free cash flow approach

Similar to the other two provinces studied, the constraining element for Bac Ninh is not the ability to service debt, but the 30 percent previous debt ceiling. This constraint indicates an allowable D 2.843 trillion (US$132 million) in 2016 and a maximum debt level of D 4.817 trillion (US$224 million in 2025). Cumulative capacity is D 37.642 trillion (US$1.751 billion) (figure 2.30).

Projected debt capacity using the debt sustainability analysis approach

In applying the DSA approach, the analysis assumes that the requirement of the balanced budget approach will still apply. When testing the fiscal space, no provision is made for borrowing for operational purposes to achieve a balanced budget (no budget deficits or surpluses). In practice, however, that approach is not always the case; instead, substantial carryovers or shortfalls are the norm.

Like the FCF methodology, the DSA approach aims to establish sustainable debt levels by developing a baseline scenario using the macroeconomic indicators and acceptable ratios. Similar to the FCF analysis, this approach has not taken into account short-term bridging loans from the treasury and ODA. It was assumed that cash flow management challenges would be bridged by short-term borrowing from the state treasury. Bac Ninh remains comfortably within all the financial ratios of the DSA approach (figures 2.31–2.33).

FIGURE 2.29

Composition of Planned Capital Program, Bac Ninh

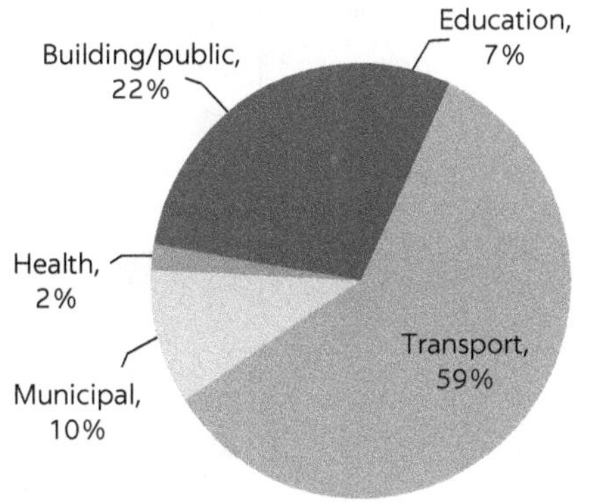

Source: Bac Ninh Province.

FIGURE 2.30

Debt Profile, Bac Ninh

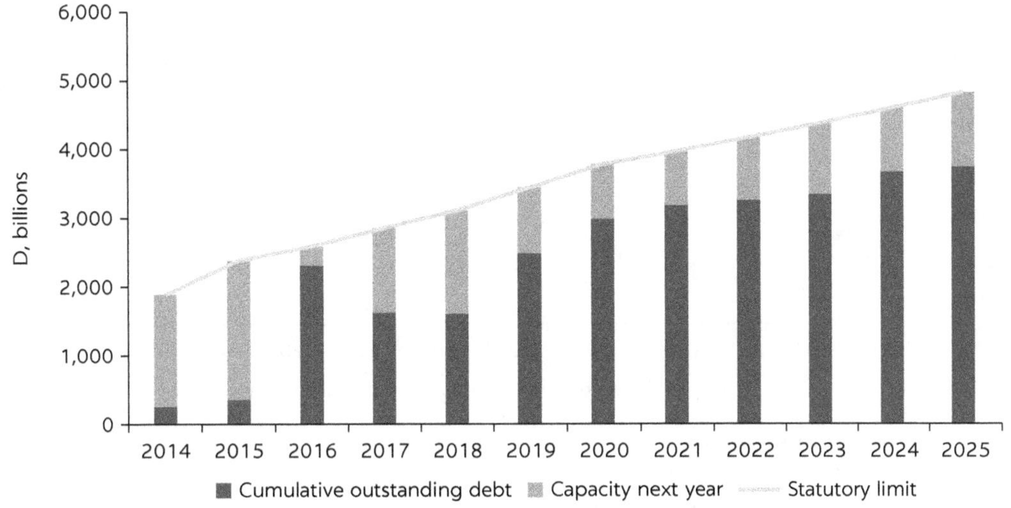

Source: World Bank calculations.

FIGURE 2.31

Debt Sustainability Analysis Indicators: Liquidity Ratio, Bac Ninh

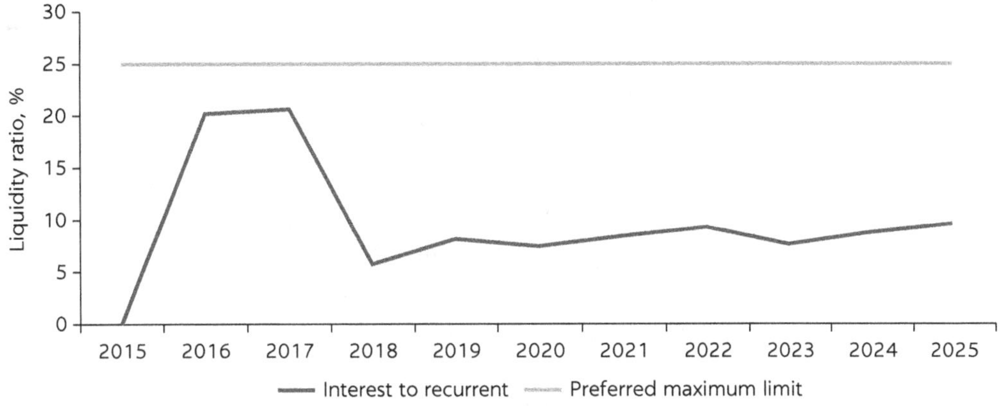

Source: World Bank calculations.

FIGURE 2.32

Debt Sustainability Analysis Indicators: Solvency Ratio, Bac Ninh

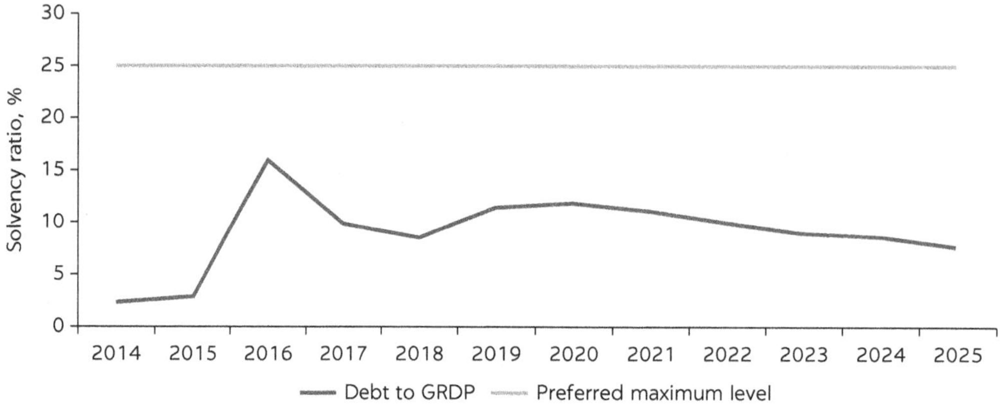

Source: World Bank calculations.

FIGURE 2.33

Debt Sustainability Analysis Indicators: Debt Service to Revenue, Bac Ninh

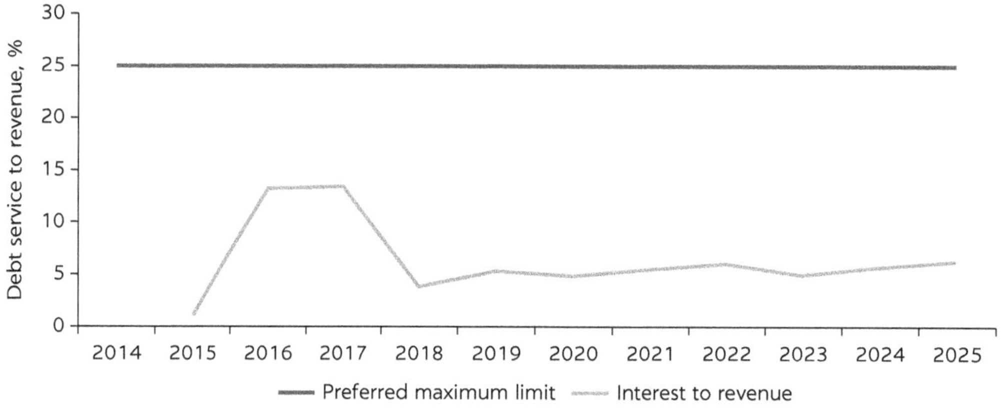

Source: World Bank calculations.

Potential capital program

Bac Ninh province has greater scope to accelerate the capital program by borrowing, mainly because of its lower recurrent expenditure. Figure 2.34 shows a smoothed potential capital program versus the budgeted capital program, which indicates that substantial acceleration is possible.

Constraints and summary

Bac Ninh is in a healthy financial position and, from a financial perspective, is able to borrow. As a rapidly developing province, it needs to develop its transport infrastructure to remain an attractive investment area. The province can sustainably borrow D 2.843 trillion (US$132 million) in 2016. This will escalate to D 4.817 trillion (US$224 million) in 2025, with total borrowing estimated at D 37.643 trillion (US$1.751 billion). Total borrowing will give the province substantial leverage on its capital because the province will be able to maintain a low ratio of recurrent expenditure to total revenue. The initial increase in the capital program is not substantial, and physical or planning constraints are not expected to have a significant delaying influence.

FIGURE 2.34

Capital Program with and without Borrowing, Bac Ninh

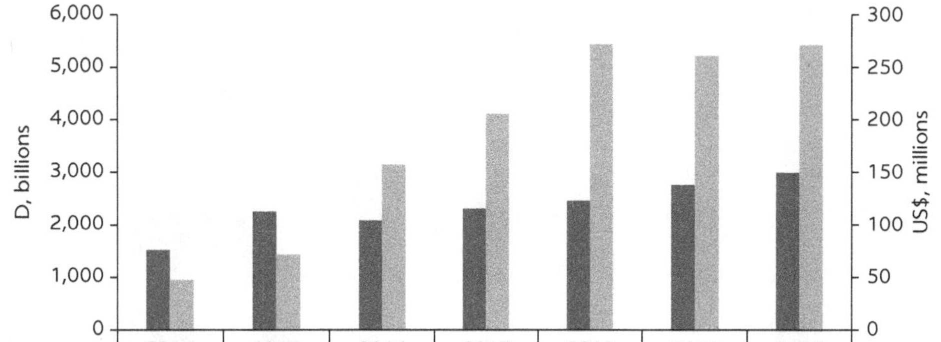

	2014	2015	2016	2017	2018	2019	2020
Budgeted capital program, D, billions	1,510	2,243	2,075	2,296	2,449	2,739	2,973
Capital program with borrowing, D, billions	946	1,421	3,129	4,090	5,414	5,193	5,398
Budgeted capital program, US$, millions	70	104	97	107	114	127	138
Capital program with borrowing, US$, millions	44	66	146	190	252	242	251

Source: World Bank calculations.

In summary, the province has the need, ability, and willingness to borrow, and the conversion of need into effective demand will be influenced more by the terms of access to borrowing than by interest rates and other terms. However, there is some concern about creditworthiness because of the province's dependence on a single contributor, Samsung, for nearly 50 percent of the its revenue. Bac Ninh was projected to have a demand for new debt up to D 2.843 trillion (US$132 million) in 2016.

All provinces contributing to central government revenues

This study considered eight more provinces that contribute to the central government budget. The sharing ratio, which is not the same across the provinces, varies from 40 percent to 91 percent. Economic growth and population growth also vary considerably, as does the relationship between capital investment programs and recurrent cost. The variation makes it quite difficult to extrapolate from that result with a reasonable degree of accuracy without doing an individual assessment. However, the data for individual assessments were not readily available. Thus, given the objective of this study—namely, to establish what effective market demand would be—the analytic approach aggregated the available data and collectively determined the effective demand of all 11 provinces.

A comparison of the provinces shown in figure 2.35 shows about equal populations and widely diverging total retained income profiles, but it shows substantially less divergence in discretionary income as a result of the transfers to and from the central government.

That result suggests that the demand for infrastructure funding would not be too divergent among provinces. However, substantial differences can be seen in economic growth (though calculation of GRDP was inconsistent across provinces, and therefore is unavailable), population growth, and capital investment needs. Another important step in assessing demand is to consider the current

FIGURE 2.35

Comparison of 11 Provinces Participating in Revenue Sharing, 2013

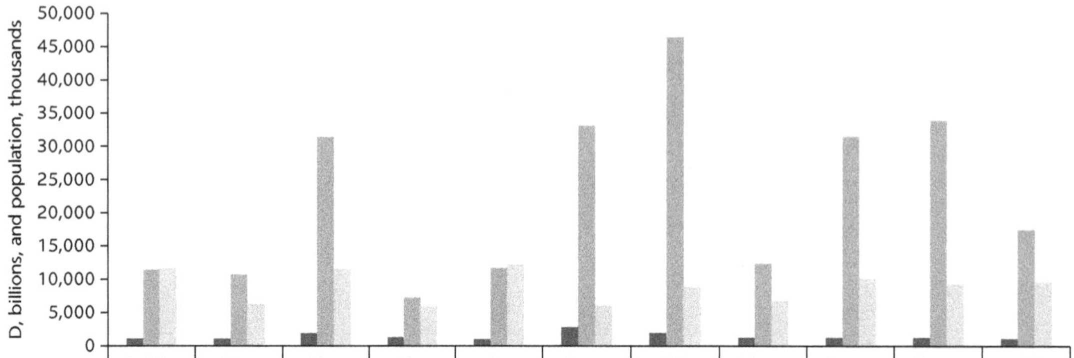

	Ba Ria-Vung Tau	Bac Ninh	Bing Duong	Can Tho	Da Nang	Nong Nai	Hai Phong	Khant Hoa	Quang Ninh	Quang Ngai	Vinh Phuc
Total population, in thousands	1,087	1,085	1,869	1,272	981	2,752	1,945	1,215	1,213	1,231	1,045
Total revenue in D, billions	11,417	10,718	31,400	7,235	11,678	33,070	46,448	12,367	31,450	33,840	17,498
Total retained income in D, billions	11,615	6,228	11,500	5,895	12,151	5,945	8,847	6,761	10,120	9,298	9,571

Source: Vietnam Statistical Office.
Note: There is a slight discrepancy between the figures provided by Dang Nai and by the Statistical Office, but not to the extent that it will materially influence the conclusion.

relationship between capital expenditure and recurrent expenditure, as this defines the discretionary income available for potential loan servicing. The relative recurrent expenditures of the provinces (figure 2.36) averages about 70 percent, indicating that all provinces have fiscal space that enables them to borrow under current conditions.

Aggregated provincial borrowing

Aggregated retained revenue for all 11 provinces contributing to central government revenues in 2013 is estimated as D 100 trillion (US$4.65 trillion), according to MOF estimates.

The analyses of the three pilot provinces indicate that, even with high recurrent costs, the total debt stock will most likely be determined by the cap of 30 percent of revenue and not by the affordability of loans or the ability to service loans from the discretionary portion. Given this likelihood, the aggregated initial ceiling on borrowing would be D 33 trillion (US$1.535 billion).

Assessment of provincial demand

The only way to assess the actual funding need for the 11 provinces is to make certain subjective assumptions and to use different approaches to estimate each province's potential capacity to absorb debt. The results of the different approaches must then be viewed with the understanding that the capacity will be used only if the other constraints are overcome. However, the conversion of capacity to effective demand will depend finally on how beneficial the provinces deem the terms.

FIGURE 2.36
Provincial Recurrent Costs, 2013

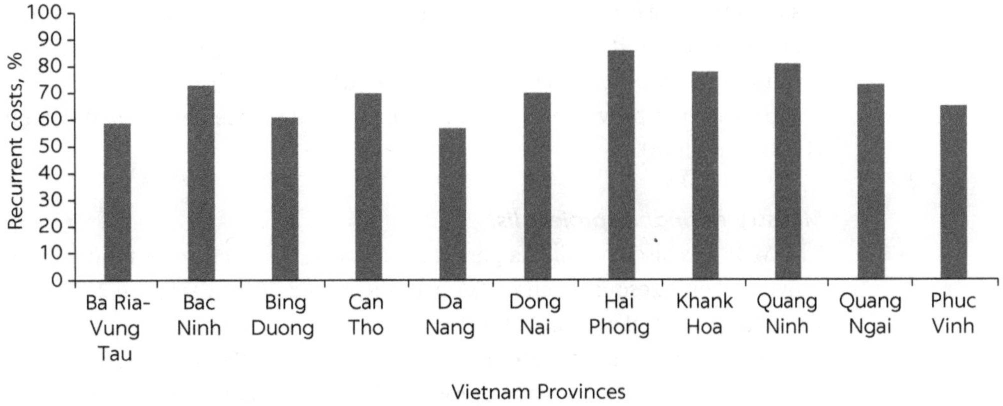

Source: Vietnam Statistical Office.

Aggregated revenue of provinces and debt ceiling

The analysis of 11 provinces assumed that the additional projects to be funded by debt would materialize over 5 years, given the lengthy process of being included in the budget, planning, and so on. Employing the total debt ceiling and a 70 percent ratio of recurrent debt to revenue and the aggregated revenue of all the provinces, the analysis put demand at between D 6.6 trillion (US$307 million) in 2016 and D 33 trillion (US$1.535 billion) in 2021.

Extrapolated demand

The total debt capacity of the three provinces was estimated to be D 10.19 trillion (US$474 million), given an average of D 3.397 trillion (US$158 million). Extrapolating to the 11 provinces would result in a total demand of D 37.363 trillion (US$1.738 billion). Although the three target provinces all have had exceptional GRDP growth and have clearly geared up their implementation capacity to support the rapid economic development, condition is unlikely to be true of all the provinces, especially the more rural ones. Not all provinces experience GRDP growth rates as high as the three selected provinces, as indicated by the national average of around 6 percent, and they probably do not experience the same demand for infrastructure spending. In addition, the more rural provinces, especially, have probably not built up the planning and implementation capacity required to rapidly accelerate the additional infrastructure spending to this level. To allow for the need to ramp up infrastructure projects across all provinces, the analysis assumes that potentially 20 percent of the total spending commitment could materialize. The demand would then be between D 7.473 trillion (US$348 million) and D 37.363 trillion (US$1.738 trillion).

Current capital expenditure and project size

Capital expenditure in 2013 in all provinces was estimated at D 33 trillion (US$1.535 billion), indicating that substantial implementing capacity was available. If the analysis assumes that this capacity could potentially increase by 20 percent, a borrowing demand of D 6.6 trillion (US$307 million) would not be unreasonable, with a 40 percent borrowing maximum. Thus, the demand could go up to D 13.2 trillion (US$614 million).

In the three target provinces, the average project size after eliminating the outliers would be on the order of D 200 billion (US$9.3 million). If the analysis assumes that the other eight provinces can increase their planning and implementation capacity to undertake two more projects, the additional funding need would be D 4.400 trillion (US$204 million). An additional two projects per province would increase the funding need by D 9.680 trillion (US$450 million).

Ministry of finance project list

The MOF has also compiled a partial list of capital projects to be funded from provinces' own resources and ODA over the period 2015–20 (figure 2.37). The list indicates a total need of D 17.610 trillion (US$819 million) for project implementation from domestic resources and a request for ODA of D 62.317 trillion (US$2.89 billion). The result is a provincial project implementation capacity of D 79.927 trillion (US$3.7 billion) over 5 years and a capacity of D 15.985 trillion (US$743 million) per year in addition to the current capital programs of D 33.000 trillion (US$1.535 billion). In summary, the provinces can be assumed to have the capacity to undertake a substantial number of additional projects.

The calculations indicate that despite the still-heavy dependence on and preference for ODA, Vietnam's changing status toward being a middle-income country could render its reliance on ODA unrealistic. In addition, there is a substantial need for project capital funding. Thus, if the ODA component is eliminated, the total from domestic resources could be D 17.610 trillion (US$819 million) for nine provinces, and D 1.956 trillion (US$91 million) per year over a 5-year period. However, should the ODA be substantially less than it is now, funding for higher-priority projects may be obtained from borrowing. If analysis assumes that this approach doubles the demand for borrowing, the total could be D 3.912 trillion (US$182 million).

Provinces' stage of readiness to borrow and the availability of a project pipeline will play a major role in determining the maximum effective demand for borrowing. However, provinces will need better budget and financial

FIGURE 2.37
Projects Identified by Provinces, 2015–20

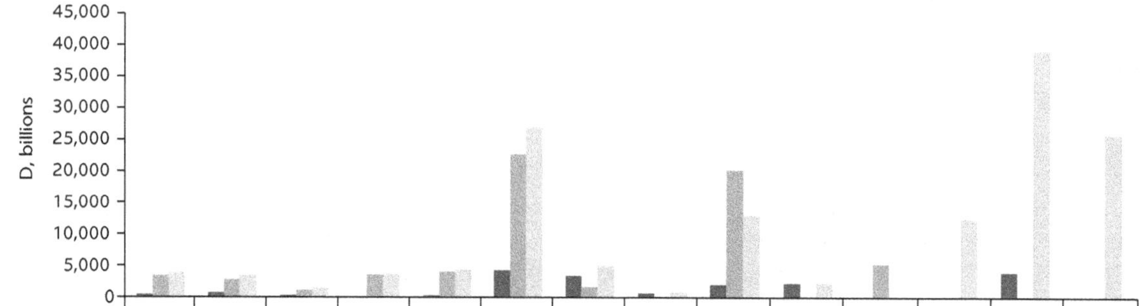

	Bac Ninh	Quang Nam	Thai Nguyen	Hai Durong	Hung Yen	Dong Nai	Thai Binh	Long An	Long Son	Binh Thuan	Quang Ninh	Hai Phong	Thanh Hoa	Da Nang
Domestic sources	368	674	266	98	275	4,155	3,271	612	1,924	2,150	n.a.	n.a.	3,817	n.a.
ODA requests	3,363	2,696	1,066	3,453	3,943	22,138	1,630	132	19,686	n.a.	5,110	n.a.	n.a.	n.a.
Total planned investments	3,731	3,370	1,332	3,551	4,218	26,294	4,901	745	12,629	2,150	n.a.	12,034	38,174	25,120

Source: Vietnam Ministry of Finance.
Note: n.a. = not available; ODA = official development assistance.

management practices before they can be considered creditworthy borrowers. Also, most projects need a preparation period, so analysts can assume that the provinces' borrowing ability will not be fully utilized. More research is needed to determine how much of the maximum allowable borrowing could effectively be used. Nevertheless, a summary based on the different approaches to determine provinces' readiness to borrow is shown in table 2.4. Using the FCF and DSA approaches discussed earlier, the study therefore estimates realistic maximum demand for the debt needed to take on other projects in addition to the existing capital program to be about D 6.700 trillion (US$311 million) in 2016.

Effective demand

Although the demand and capacity of D 6.700 trillion (US$311 million) is deemed to be within the absorption and additional implementation capacity of the 11 provinces, that demand will be influenced by the regulatory reform and the promptness of amendments as well as by the commercial banks' appetite for lending. It is also suggested (as discussed later in this chapter) that any

TABLE 2.4 **Debt Capacity Approaches**

ESTIMATION METHOD	2016 IN D, BILLIONS	MAXIMUM 2016 IN US$, MILLIONS	REALISTIC IN D, BILLIONS	REALISTIC IN US$, MILLIONS	UNDERLYING ASSUMPTIONS	NOTES
Total debt cap per Amended State Budget Law	33,000	1,535	6,600	307	Based on aggregate revenue of provinces in 2016; assuming that it will take up to 5 years to reach debt cap due to the need for smoothing capital expenditure on additional projects not budgeted	Will increase annually with increase in aggregate revenue Based on assumption that all debt would be used for additional projects
Extrapolated from three provinces	37,363	1,734	7,473	347	Discounted to 20% for capacity constraints Based on average (US$158 million) of 3 provinces extended to all 11	Based on assumption that all debt would be used for additional projects
Based on current capital expenditure	13,200	614	6,600	307	Ability to increase by 20%	Additional projects
Based on average project size	19,360	900	9,680	450	Average size of the projects planned in the three provinces, analyzed with 2–4 additional projects	Additional projects
Ministry of Finance project list	3,912	182	1,956	91	Also assuming a 5-year period	Assumed to reflect unfunded projects
The recommended potential demand as an average of the different approaches	22,533	5,240	6,695	311	Based on underlying assumption that all additional accelerated infrastructure funding will be by way of private-sector debt, though in reality, some of the additional projects could be funded from provinces' own resources	

Source: World Bank calculations.

borrowing initiative should be accompanied by capacity building in financial management, which will take time. The biggest factor in converting need or demand into effective demand will be the borrowing terms, especially considering the benefits of establishing interest-free access to the VDB.

One of the most important considerations in assessing effective demand will be the loan duration, or tenor, as illustrated by figures 2.38 and 2.39. Figure 2.38 indicates the repayment on a D 100 loan over a 10-year period and the impact it has on affordability. Figure 2.39 illustrates the changes in amounts that can be borrowed by a fixed installment of D 100 over a 10-year period. Both graphs

FIGURE 2.38
Projected Effect of Loan Period on Annual Installments

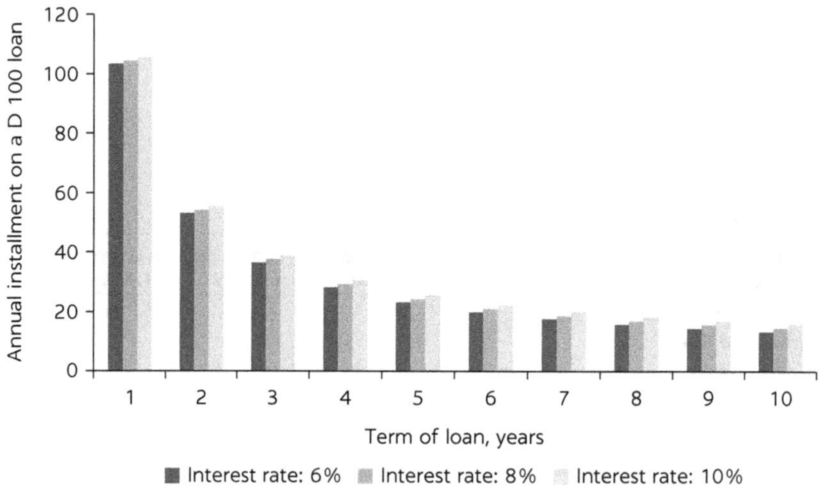

Source: World Bank calculations.

FIGURE 2.39
Effect of Loan Period on Amount Borrowed with Fixed Installments

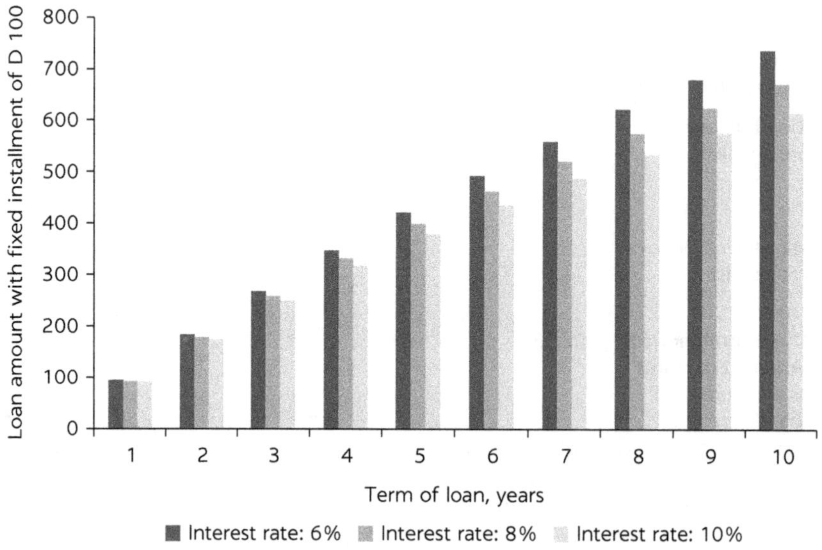

Source: World Bank calculations.

show that tenor has a greater effect on the potential amount of borrowing than interest rates do. Note that even if the amount borrowed reaches the prescribed debt ceiling, any reduction in the annual installments will leave a bigger portion of the discretionary, uncommitted revenue available for direct capital investment. Therefore, one can conclude that the most critical reforms for provincial borrowing would be to (a) amend the restriction on the duration of loans from commercial banks and (b) develop the capital markets to allow bonds of longer tenor to be issued.

Comparison and conclusion

In conclusion, all three provinces analyzed are financially healthy, and the ceiling on debt should be the 2015 SBL ceiling on provincial debt, which took effect in 2017. In the case of two provinces, sharp increases in the ratio of recurrent expenditure to revenue may become an issue in the future. Further, the increase in the implementation of additional projects would not constitute a barrier to changing demand into effective demand, given the substantial current capital programs already being managed by the provinces. In most instances, these carryovers reportedly are a result of accrual accounting with services or goods rendered but not yet paid for. It is unclear whether this could also be a sign that implementation capacity is insufficient.

The realization of effective demand will depend on capacity building, needed regulatory reform, the appetite of the banks, and the attractiveness of the terms of the financing facility. This analysis determined that the amount needed to launch a CIFF and have an impact and leverage to support the reform program is about D 6.6 trillion (US$307 million).

Provinces receiving grants from the central government

The fact that most of the provinces are still dependent on transfers from the central government does not rule those provinces out as potential, creditworthy borrowers. Intergovernmental transfers that occur on a dependable and predictable basis in many cases form an integral part of a province's overall planning and its capital investment planning. However, this observation is made with the condition that such transfers should not be subject to short-term arbitrary or interpretive decisions. Instead they should be formula driven and based on firm agreements derived from the overall intergovernmental fiscal framework. In assessing creditworthiness, such transfers are included as "other income," although one of the risk criteria would be grant dependency, which would create other thresholds to borrowing. In Vietnam, the SBL and the annual state budget, when taken together with the 5-year stability periods, have created this certainty and have made all provinces, in theory, potentially creditworthy and able to qualify for borrowing, depending on the individual financial analysis.

Although a high-level analysis of the needs and financial capacity of the provinces is necessary to generate a quantitative indication of the potential demand, it should be understood that any financing facility represents a potential borrowing demand. That demand is likely to increase as Vietnam's economy develops and more provinces become contributors rather than recipients of transfers. A facility may also be used to create market access for these provinces.

Water sector

Although the water utilities are officially independent, in practice they are subject to provincial authorities that set tariff levels and govern operational investments (Smetts 2014); thus, they should be regarded as potential direct or indirect borrowers. The financial investments needed by the rural and urban water and sanitation sector are extensive, about D 55.685 trillion (US$2.59 billion) a year, of which approximately D 13.975 trillion (US$650 million) will be provided by households and private resources. Approximately 87 percent of this need is in urban areas and represents about 2.5 percent of GDP. About 60 percent of the investment in the urban system is for replacing, rehabilitating, and refurbishing, so no new income will be generated. Therefore, incorporating this expenditure in revised higher tariffs to help the sector break even is difficult. The potential need of the water sector is excluded from the current analysis because a separate dedicated facility has been put in place by the Asian Development Bank, and drawdowns are currently limited.

Local development investment funds

The local development investment funds (LDIFs) in principle could be potential clients, and the need for their investments in revenue-generating projects is also substantial. However, substantial demand is not likely in the near future. The LDIFs are constrained by the requirement of an equity component, which only 17 LDIFs have achieved. Expansion of the existing LDIFs would have to be matched with further equity investments, which could limit the effective demand. The LDIFs therefore are not considered in this analysis, although some demand may manifest itself over time beyond that already being provided through ODA and their access to markets.

State-owned enterprises

SOEs play an important role in Vietnam because they have access to the capital markets. At the same time, they could represent substantial contingent liabilities to the national government. According to international standards, which are not yet adopted in Vietnam, those credit risks should be taken into account.

There may be advantages to regarding SOEs as potential direct clients of the provinces, especially in the smaller provinces. Doing so could remove the contingent liability aspects. Recent experience in China is an example of the issues that can arise when virtually off-balance-sheet lending by SOEs is not being coordinated in an integrated way (Lu and Sun 2013).[5] SOE participation would depend on whether the terms are more favorable than direct access to the markets would be. For the purposes of this study their potential demand, whether indirect or direct, is not taken into account as an immediate reality. This approach may be reconsidered, depending on future developments to boost the size of bond issues.

Constraints affecting access to debt financing

Provinces hoping to borrow funds and estimate effective demand face challenges, both in the provinces and in the overall intergovernmental system, that will affect their access to financing. How well provincial authorities meet those challenges could determine the banks' willingness to take on provincial credit risks and could slow borrowing. Banks need information if they are to make prudent and sound credit decisions. This section outlines the types of information that provinces must have and must make available to financing facilities.

Information should be readily accessible and accurate enough for banks to perform credit appraisals. First, because data are collected from multiple sources, the data often are inconsistent and may raise fundamental integrity concerns. Second, given long budget cycles and lack of final audited figures (which are not available often until 18–20 months after the fiscal year-end), actual figures are useless as a management tool or as a basis for assessing creditworthiness.

Financial statements often do not present a full picture for the following reasons: (a) ODA is regarded as off budget. (b) Debt is not reflected in financial statements. (c) The statements do not show the activities of SOEs and public sector enterprises that have various degrees of autonomy. (d) Carryovers are not formally reflected, with no limit or transparency on the carryovers. (e) On-bill financing can be as high as 5–20 percent of the budget (World Bank 2014a). (f) Contingent liabilities are not transparent.

Several factors indicate provinces' lack of financial management and insufficient management information systems. Provinces tend to underestimate revenue, to consistently overspend on capital, and to under- or overspend against budgets (figure 2.40 illustrates this for two provinces). Also, substantial year-to-year swings in projected data and a consequential loss of

FIGURE 2.40

Budget Deviations in Dong Nai and Quang Ninh Provinces

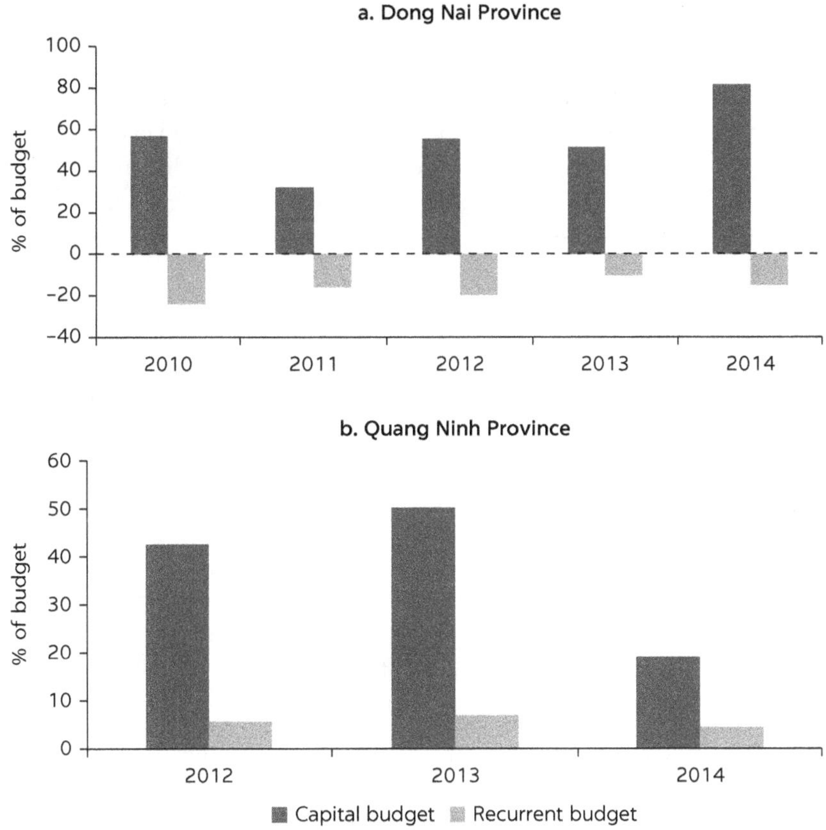

Sources: Dong Nai and Quang Ninh Provinces.

predictability make any degree of integrity in credit assessments impossible. Moreover, provinces have a tendency to disregard the development plan and regularly vary the allocations. For example, a policy of allocating excess revenue to salary reform and capital expenditure increases fixed recurrent costs in the long term and can threaten long-term sustainability. Both the provincial and central levels need to improve their budget, debt, and cash flow management capacity (World Bank 2014a). The preparation, planning, and coordination in project conception need improvement.

Reforming intergovernmental relations by allowing further fiscal decentralization would enable provincial credit risk to be perceived and legally differentiated from the central government debt repayment responsibility. This reform would be a crucial element in a structure that supports accountability and transparency.

The regulatory framework on lending needs to be clearly articulated to create certainty regarding the relationship between borrowers and lenders, especially as far as default and recourse measures are concerned.

Many of the constraints can be mitigated and the quantum of the potential sustainable debt can be substantially increased by an increase in revenue, that is, by faster increases in the tax rate, higher economic growth that increases the tax base, or decreased operational expenditure through reductions in recurrent costs, such as by reducing staff. For example, provinces collect only 60 percent of their potential revenue, on average, and they have no control over the structure of taxes and only limited authority over the quantum of taxes and tariffs.

Most of these issues are not new and have been highlighted in a World Bank report, "Assessment of PFM Arrangements at the Provincial Level" (World Bank 2011).

General creditworthiness considerations in provinces

In a unitary budget system, there is a perception that all credit risk at the local level effectively migrates to the central government and becomes part of the public debt. One objective of creating the CIFF is that of making a clear distinction between central and provincial debt. Provinces should start preparing for this separation of obligations by considering the following actions:

- Use sinking funds
- Quantify contingent liabilities
- Improve the management of recurrent expenditure (especially future commitments)
- Introducing cost recovery principles
- Concentrating on improved collections
- Making SOEs financially independent
- Developing stronger cash and debt management systems
- Developing default procedures with the central government to remove any ambiguity in how to deal with a local government default
- Improving data availability and reliability
- Building relationships with the commercial banks and capital market.

The World Bank has developed weeklong academies in a number of countries to strengthen the creditworthiness process at the local government level. These workshops help provinces become good credit risks and strengthen and develop good planning, management, and governance practices, which are preconditions for becoming creditworthy. The government of Vietnam should consider working with the World Bank to arrange this type of academy.

Risk for an entity like the potential city infrastructure financing facility

A province that is considering whether to work with an entity such as a CIFF or other instrument must conduct a high-level review of potential risks to such an entity. Provinces should note that credit risk depends on the structure of a CIFF as it concerns lending to the commercial banking sector, the provinces, or both. The CIFF should have a credit assessment system that allows prudent credit decisions, thus reducing the possibility of default.

Further, CIFFs must have clear rules on how to deal with defaults and the consequential likely workouts.[6] Other countries have made provisions granting substantial powers to an administrator appointed by the central government to oversee the financial rehabilitation of a defaulting local government if it cannot make an agreement for rescheduling payments with the creditors.

Other potential risks include (a) the lack of demand for the facility, (b) rejection of the terms or conditionality, (c) demand for the facility that is too high, (d) no accompanying reform program, (e) statutory limitation of debt, (f) total public sector debt exceeding safe limits, (g) lack of financial and credit management capacity in banks and provinces, (h) liquidity risk for CIFF due to delayed payments or nonpayments, (i) defaults and consequential loss, (j) inability to raise additional finance, and (k) fraud and mismanagement.

Provincial governments' willingness to participate in pilot city infrastructure financing facility

Consultations with the surveyed provinces on the need for future debt requirement and lending terms with key provincial government officials determined that the three provinces were willing to participate in a pilot CIFF. Key considerations for the establishment of CIFF include the following aspects:

- *Long-term financing.* The provinces are willing to borrow for infrastructure development, but currently long-term financing for infrastructure projects is not available. Provinces have shown preference and need for loans with a 10–15-year tenor, which would typically match the project life cycle period.
- *Preferential mechanism for CIFF.* As per SBL 2015, provincial governments are allowed to mobilize capital from all legal fund sources. However, for provinces, commercial banks may still be the last sources to tap for financing under the current market conditions. Without preferential mechanisms such as better interest rates or term conditions, provincial governments would not be interested to borrow from CIFF.
- *Interest rates.* Most provinces currently approach State Treasury or VDB for loans for infrastructure development. Provinces wish the interest rate applicable to commercial bank loans under the pilot CIFF program to be matched with that offered by the State Treasury and VDB.
- *Vietnamese dong-denominated loans.* The provinces have expressed their preference for Vietnamese dong-denominated loans rather than US dollar-denominated or any other foreign currency denominated loans, as they do not want the risk of foreign exchange to be passed onto them.
- *Moratorium period.* Against the current practice of fixed grace period, the provinces wish the loans to be of flexible grace period for each loan along with scope for pre-payments to be made by provincial governments.

Conclusions on effective demand

The financial analysis of the assessed provinces shows that all three are financially healthy. The debt ceiling that is imposed by the new SBL will determine the total debt exposure, not the ability to afford and service debt. However, the analyses show that the provinces have considerable room to improve management without substantial regulatory changes, which could increase the debt limits over time.

Some long-term trends that are of concern, such as the sharp rise in recurrent costs in some provinces, will need attention if the government is to achieve its goal of using substantial amounts of private sector debt sustainably. The short-term analysis shows an effective and realizable demand for long-term borrowing. Although the analysis could not derive definitive quantitative results, if the terms are attractive to the provinces in 2016, borrowing can realistically be expected to be D 3.3 trillion to D 6.6 trillion per year per province (US$153 million to US$307 million).

However, the limited availability of timely and accurate data may restrict the provinces' access to finance. Currently provinces have enough fiscal space to allow borrowing with only cursory credit assessments, but as recurrent costs increase with new debt, that opportunity will be diminished unless provinces streamline their access to data for submission to financing facilities. The central government and provinces therefore can consider the following interventions to improve the quality of financial management of the provinces to enhance creditworthiness.

In the short term:

- Prepare a sector-wise capital investment plan with clearly identified projects. The provinces should consider preparing medium- to long-term capital investments with clear sector-wise investments required, as well as taking into account the national and provincial priorities and bankability.
- Standardize budgeting, accounting, and financial reporting by provincial governments to bring transparency and uniformity into financial reporting. This can be built into the capacity building support in a pilot CIFF program.
- Identify training and capacity building requirements for officials on project identification, project preparation, procurement, and management, to help identify projects that are of national and provincial priority and at the same time are financially viable and bankable.
- Streamline the regulatory framework for provincial borrowing from commercial banks, allowing provinces to borrow from commercial banks as an eligible source of debt financing and defining payment security and a recourse mechanism.

In the long term:

- Implement reforms to improve the revenue income for provinces to meet the debt-service obligations. For instance, the provinces may undertake various tariff reforms and align taxes, user charges, and other levies to market or commercial levels, moving toward full cost recovery.
- Obtain credit ratings for provincial governments. To provide comfort to the commercial banks under a pilot program like a CIFF, the provinces may consider getting a domestic credit rating, international credit rating, or both.

Those conclusions, from the limited work conducted for this book, is reinforced by previous work by the World Bank—that governments hoping to receive any private sector financing at scale and for relatively long term need to upgrade their financial management systems. If countries expect the private sector to take on the full risk of infrastructure financing, as is the eventual objective, then the timeliness, availability, and accuracy of their data must meet the needs of the potential lender.

INTERNATIONAL CREDITWORTHINESS APPROACHES AT THE SUBSOVEREIGN LEVEL

National and central governments

Most governments adopt rules to manage and control subsovereign borrowing because of the need to prevent subsovereign debt defaults, which can damage the overall financial system and even jeopardize the central government's own rating. Thus governments face a delicate task in balancing autonomy and decentralization principles with the controls to be imposed. It is clear that there is no perfect set of rules.

Creditors often believe that a national or central government will not allow cities and provincial utilities to fail financially, creating a "moral hazard," in which one party takes more risks because another party bears the cost of those risks. In this view, the risk for governments is that proper credit assessments are not undertaken by creditors and excessive credit is granted, with subsovereign entities borrowing far beyond their means on the premise that risk will be transferred. The risk is exacerbated if creditors lack timely financial information, adequate controls, monitoring, and management of subsovereign debt.

However, decentralization policies also permit decision making at the interface with constituents, allowing local governments to use subsovereign borrowing to address backlogs and fund infrastructure for growth. Most governments embarking on decentralization have found it necessary to place some restrictions on subsovereign borrowing with the following goals.

First, restrictions prevent individual local governments from suffering financial distress as a result of borrowing and a potential consequential default on debt obligations. Defaults could lead to bailouts by central governments, which essentially defeats the goals of local autonomy and responsibility. There is also a real fear that one bailout, irrespective of how necessary it is, may undermine autonomy and financial discipline on a countrywide scale.

Second, aggregating overborrowing at the local government level can negatively affect the national macroeconomic environment. In extreme cases, it can even negatively influence a country's credit rating. An example is the overborrowing by local governments in China in the past few years, which necessitated sharp intervention by the Chinese government to curtail and manage the overborrowing by subsovereign entities. The government adopted measures to protect the solvency of local governments. However, such circumstances are changing as the central government moves to encourage deleveraging in the financial system, and protections on local debt may have been withdrawn (*Financial Times* 2017).

Restrictions on local government debt and borrowing

A number of controls and restrictions with respect to borrowing by local governments are used by both local and central governments:

- *Political restrictions* are enacted in some local governments, sometimes through a local referendum, so that no long-term borrowing can occur without the approval of the citizens.
- *Direct control* entails consideration and approval of borrowing on a case-by-case basis. Direct control—although good to manage and control debt and borrowing—has a severe downside in that the credit risks in the case of default are seen to migrate to the approving authority. The central government's approval of individual spending and borrowing initiatives of subsovereign governments introduces an implicit guarantee of local and regional public debt. Having granted permission, the central government may find it more difficult to refuse a bailout later on, should the local government run into trouble.
- *Administrative and numerical restrictions* comprise fiscal rules and regulations controlling the amount of new or overall debt levels.
- *Self-imposed restrictions* are approved by the central government.
- *Market-based control* provides clarity that the central government will not intervene and that local governments will be allowed to go bankrupt. The financial markets therefore must carry out diligent credit assessments similar to the credit assessments applied to private companies.

One rule that is virtually uniform is the prohibition on borrowing to cover operational costs, although short-term bridging loans are allowed. In addition, it is common practice to prohibit or require central government approval for borrowing in foreign currency. Most of those measures are self-explanatory, and the different approaches and the continuum are illustrated in figure 2.41, but the range of measures used in the administrative control environment of other countries are shown in table 2.5).

Administrative controls are seldom based on a thorough credit analysis to determine sustainable debt levels; in most cases they take the form of empirical formulas such as: x% of y.

The following are the most common empirical formulas used:

- A percentage of budgeted revenue or previous year revenue (Brazil, the Philippines, Poland)
- A percentage of budget or previous year's expenditure (Belgium, Germany)
- Debt service as a percentage of revenue (Brazil, Japan, the Republic of Korea, Spain)
- A percentage of the total property valuation (common in the United States)
- A fixed amount (the United Kingdom, £500,000 local)
- A percentage of capital program (Denmark, Vietnam)
- Total debt (Hungary)
- Overall budget deficit (Austria, Spain)
- New debt (Croatia, Lithuania).

Table 2.6 indicates some of the values adopted by different countries. In some countries, dual constraints have been adopted that restrict two components, such as overall debt level and annual debt service. The most common constraints involve restricting total debt and annual debt service; linking the restrictions expenditure or the capital program is less common. Administrative and numerical fiscal rules are attractive because they are clear, transparent, and relatively

FIGURE 2.41

Types of Controls over Local Government Borrowing

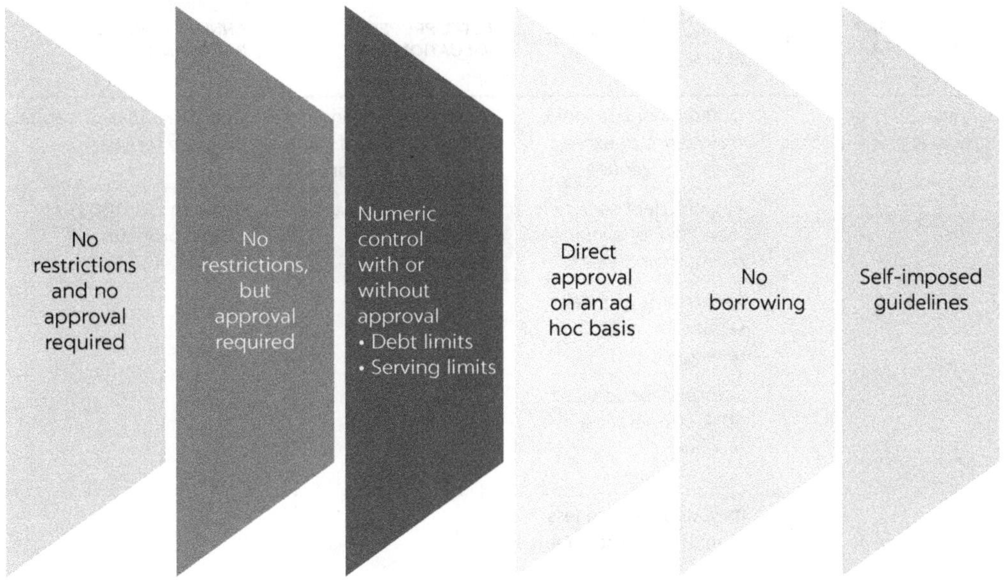

TABLE 2.5 **International Types of Control over Subsovereign Borrowing**

TYPE	COUNTRIES	COMMENT
Local autonomy, no restrictions/market-based	Finland, France, Japan, Netherlands, New Zealand, South Africa, Switzerland	Policy of no bailout is clearly articulated.
No restrictions, approval required	Argentina (province), Brazil (local), Peru (local), Turkey (local), United Kingdom (local)	Self-discipline is required.
Negotiated limits	Austria, Germany (regions), Spain (regions)	Debt ceilings are negotiated on the basis of fiscal targets.
Numeric control	Brazil (local), Croatia, Denmark, Estonia (local), Philippines, Poland, Spain, United States, Vietnam	Canada allows each province to set controls and uses virtually all types of restrictions.
Direct control	Bolivia, China, India (state), Thailand (local)	From unrestricted, China has now adopted a quota system.
Self-imposed	Argentina, Australia (state)	The subsovereign borrowers and their association have adopted guidelines.
Prohibition on borrowing	Cambodia (local), Indonesia, Latvia, Mexico (state), Nigeria (state external)	Latvia and Indonesia adopted central borrowing.

easy to manage and monitor. Appropriate rules also improve the credibility of fiscal policy. They have the drawback that they lack flexibility and do not normally distinguish between purposes or qualities, for example, income generation, project or general obligation borrowing, size of city, and other specific considerations such as investment in infrastructure to service a new economic activity such as a new mining development. One serious drawback to numerical rules, though, is that because they are not flexible, users can find loopholes and circumvent the purpose of the imposed controls. Local governments find it easy to create other vehicles to borrow and so bypass the controls, effectively negating the objectives. Therefore, even at the local government level, contingent liabilities should be tracked.

TABLE 2.6 **Sample of Numeric Control Measures Used Globally**

BORROWING AS PERCENTAGE OF TOTAL REVENUE: PREVIOUS OR CURRENT	PREVIOUS YEAR EXPENSES (%)	DEBT SERVICE PERCENTAGE OF CURRENT REVENUE	TOTAL PROPERTY VALUATION (%)	ANNUAL CAPITAL PROGRAM (%)
Philippines: 20% of regular income	Croatia: 30% of previous year expenses	Ontario, Canada: debt service not to exceed 25% of revenue	United States: various common 40% of property valuation	Denmark: 25% of capital program for year
Poland: 12–15% of recurrent revenue		Albania: debt service less than 20% of average revenue for 3 years	Prince Edward Island, Canada: 10% of property value	Vietnam: 30–100% of capital program
Nova Scotia, Canada: 30% of own source revenue		Czech Republic: debt service less than 30% of revenue		
Uganda: 10% of recurrent revenue without approval, 25% with approval		France: debt service 50% of operating revenue		
Albania: 77% of recurrent revenues		Italy: debt service less than 15% of total annual revenue		
Hungary: less than 50% of own revenue		Brazil: debt service less than 11.5% of current revenue		

South Africa and Spain have been at pains to announce that they will not financially bail out subsovereign entities that default; instead they would place offenders under administrative rules to "work out" the entity's debt and to restore it to sound financial standing. Nonetheless, despite a central government's efforts to prevent even psychological credit risk migration, in practice, bridging loans and other means are still sometimes considered.

Vietnam's current creditworthiness approach

Under the 2002 SBL, provincial borrowing was set annually at 30 percent of the annual capital budget, with exceptions made for Hanoi and Ho Chi Minh City, which were allowed up to 100 percent. Under the 2015 SBL, it has changed to a formula based on the previous year's revenue as in the following examples:

- Uses 60 percent of previous year's revenue for Hanoi and Ho Chi Minh City
- Uses 30 percent of previous year's revenue for the second tier of provinces that contribute to the central budget
- Uses 20 percent of previous year's revenue for provinces that generate at least 50 percent of their own budget

The adoption of this new formula would bring Vietnam more in line with global practice.

Additional clauses in the 2015 SBL also stipulate "[u]sing the state budget fund at a State Treasury beyond the budget estimate approved by a competent authority, except for the case of temporary funding or advance funding from next year's budget prescribed in Article 51 and Article 57 of this Law" (Article 18, Clause 11). Also, "Budget expenditures may only be realized after the budget estimate is approved by a competent authority; the standard, and expenditure limits imposed by competent authorities, must be complied with" (Article 8, Clause 4).

Where some defaults did occur in Vietnam in the past, they were handled not through the courts, as in many other countries. but administratively, essentially by employing the reserves at provincial level and using bridging support from the central government. The new approach under the 2015 SBL should facilitate borrowing within the affordability limitations and create more flexibility to deal with multiyear projects. However, it is also essential that the SOEs, which in principle pose a contingent liability to local government, be brought under the net.

Creditworthiness criteria of local government

No government uses the actual creditworthiness or debt absorption capacity of local governments when setting borrowing limits. However, commercial lenders that are taking a credit risk on provincial government have their own credit processes—most of them proprietary—that can vary from extremely rigorous to cursory, depending on their knowledge and risk perception of the sector. Globally a number of specialized intermediaries and local and regional development institutions specialize in subsovereign lending. All of them have over time developed their own credit assessment processes, which also vary from cursory to sophisticated. Some private intermediaries—such as Dexia in France (a privatized SOE, now a commercial bank), with 26,000 municipal clients—have developed an automated and very sophisticated credit assessment system to allow the setting of risk premiums. Similarly, INCA in South Africa has developed a sophisticated appraisal methodology allowing the determination of capital adequacy requirements and risk premiums as well as other conditions and loan caveats.

Most of these credit processes are confidential and proprietary, but in general they follow the broad methodology applied by the rating agencies, although on a more informal basis. Contractual savings institutions tend to rely more heavily on formal credit ratings, especially where exposure is through bond issue. They use the ratings to continually balance the portfolio to maintain the desired weighted credit quality. Monitoring the client, which is part of the formal rating procedure, is also more important to them than to the banking sector, which tends to undertake monitoring by regular client reports as one of the conditionalities. Contractual savings institutions often employ the caveats in the loan agreements, with punitive breach of contract conditions and default clauses to force regular reporting.

The sizes of the provinces in Vietnam and the potential volume of borrowing and bond issues indicate that it is probably time for credit rating agencies to start playing a more prominent role, and that formal credit ratings in due course may be considered as a precondition above a certain level of borrowing.

Basic approach to credit rating

The basic approach to rating of subsovereign entities is always based on the sovereign rating as a benchmark and ceiling, and it will follow a cascading approach in determining the risk and the eventual rating (figure 2.42).

Ratings have often been described as part science and part art, and they use the past to look into the future to predict the possibility of default and the likely

FIGURE 2.42
The Cascading Approach of Risk Evaluation

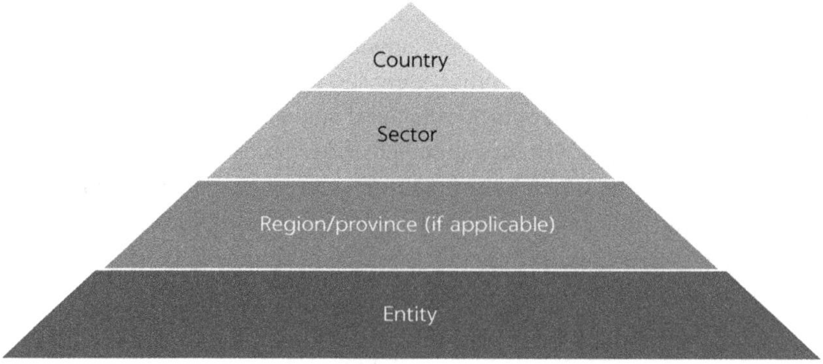

severity if a default occurs. The approaches of the three big rating agencies are fundamentally the same and follow this sequence[7]:

- Performing an in-depth study of documentation provided by the entity being rated (client)
- Performing in-depth and penetrating interviews
- Drafting the rating report
- Allowing the client to confirm the correctness of the information
- Submitting information to a rating committee for allocation of a rating
- Publishing the rating (if the client agrees)
- Regularly monitoring and issuing early warnings if required.

The actual aspects analyzed at the provincial level will differ from sector to sector but normally will focus on the long term and have both qualitative and quantitative focus. At the subsovereign level the approach will normally consist of an assessment and analysis of the following:

- *The economic base in its area of jurisdiction.* This step will cover aspects such as potential GRDP growth, unemployment rates, poverty indexes, concentration risk in a single client and industry, vulnerability to volatile inputs such as energy costs and other fixed costs.
- *Financial performance and stability.* This step will cover past performance and predicted future performance. Issues covered will be strength of the balance sheet, cash flow, and profitability as well as a number of semistandard financial ratios measuring solvency, liquidity, working ratio, debt-to-equity, or approximation in the case of a statutory entity, debt coverage, reserves, contingent liabilities, and operating revenues.
- *The experience and quality of management.* Although sometimes relatively subjective, this step will be based on an impression of whether management is a winning team or not. Specific items considered are succession planning, qualifications, experience, and training programs.
- *Operational performance.* This step looks at the efficiency and effectiveness of the entity with substantial reliance on peer comparisons.
- *Autonomy and transparency.* This step considers aspects such as the right to appoint management, the right to determine taxes and tariffs, the right to borrow, and so on. A slightly contradictory but substantial issue is also the

question of government support and, where subsidies are involved, the predictability and dependability of such transfers.

- *Risks.* The rating also includes a frank discussion of the external or internal risks faced by the entity. This step will cover aspects such as political and legislative changes, economic stress testing, and vulnerability to global events.

Ratings and shadow ratings

At the subsovereign level, where getting formal ratings is expensive, a preliminary step often is to conduct a private shadow rating process as a precursor to a formal rating. A shadow rating is a less in-depth assessment of an entity following the same basic methodology but usually carried out by a nonaccredited rating entity. This could be the institution itself, a bank, a consultant, or even a rating agency. A shadow rating has the advantage that it is cheaper, identifies the areas where improvement is needed before resorting to a formal rating, and can be easily adjusted to serve a specific purpose. For example, Afcapconsult in South Africa has developed Municat/Watercat,[8] a municipal water credit assessment tool that can be used as a model for municipalities and water utilities. Key outputs include shadow credit rating, benchmarking, trend analysis, and reform agendas. The Municat/Watercat tools are to be used by the following stakeholders:

- The municipality and utility, to identify performance improvement areas and to compare with their peers
- The donor community, to identify common areas in which technical assistance can have a substantial effect on a number of entities
- The regulator and government, to monitor performance
- The financial institution, to identify potential borrowing clients and to get comfortable in an unknown sector.

SUGGESTED CRITERIA FOR PROVINCES IN VIETNAM

General criteria

The study did not require the design of a detailed credit framework but instead involved the high-level identification of potential creditworthiness components. The list is not exhaustive but, as discussed in the assessment of the three provinces, it includes information that must be available and have a high level of integrity and dependability. Aspects that must be considered are presented in table 2.7.

If a borrowing support initiative is to be implemented, participation should be subject to meeting certain criteria. First, enough information must be compiled for banks to undertake a credit appraisal, and second, project preparation should be at an advanced stage ready for investment.

Initial credit risk assessment of provinces

The process of obtaining full creditworthiness at the provincial level will unfold over a number of years. However, that doesn't mean that development of a provincial debt market would be held in abeyance until full creditworthiness is achieved. Whereas full creditworthiness remains the long-term goal, provinces should be formally rated by accredited credit rating agencies to ascertain whether they

TABLE 2.7 **Criteria for Creditworthiness of Provinces**

<table>
<tr><th>ECONOMIC</th><th>LEGISLATIVE</th><th>POLITICAL STABILITY AND GOVERNANCE</th><th>OPERATIONAL EFFICIENCY</th></tr>
<tr><td>• Likelihood of support from the central government
• Ability to impose taxes and collect tariffs
• GRDP and growth projections
• Unemployment ratio
• Future challenges
• Dependency on grants
• Concentration on servicing a single industry client, or group of clients
• Future potential, such as in mining, export, or tourism</td><td>• Statutory limits imposed by the SBL and MOF
• Recourse mechanisms and default procedures
• Compliance with regulations
• Authority to borrow</td><td>• Autonomy
• Predictability and dependability of transfers
• Clarity of roles, responsibilities, and authority</td><td>• Collection efficiency (capability to collect billed accounts)
• Billing efficiency (capability to bill for services rendered)
• Staff costs per function
• Maintenance expenditure
• Quality of management information systems
• Use of private sector
• Customer complaint resolution norms</td></tr>
<tr><th colspan="2">FINANCIAL PERFORMANCE</th><th>HUMAN RESOURCES</th><th>RISKS</th></tr>
<tr><td colspan="2">• Collateral and reserves
• Operating surplus and deficit
• Percentage of cost recovery on trade services
• Solvency and liquidity ratios
• Debt service ratio (the proportion of annual revenue spent on servicing principal and interest obligations)
• Debt service coverage (the amount of cash available to meet principal and interest obligations)
• Working ratio (the ability to recover operating costs from operating revenues
• Cash reserves as a share of annual operating income (expressed as months of operating expense)
• Consumer bad debt provision (cash provision for bad and doubtful debt)
• Operating cost cover ratio
• Interest cover
• Debt maturity concentration
• Potential revenue not collected
• Ability to remain within budget
• Contingent liabilities
• Ring-fencing of revenue and expenditure for different functions and SOEs</td><td>• Management quality and experience
• Appropriateness of staff qualifications
• Quality of multiyear planning and budget
• Succession planning
• Training programs</td><td>• Changing legislation
• Economic volatility
• Interest rate volatility
• Political interference in day-to-day decisions
• Loss of financial control over SOEs</td></tr>
</table>

meet initial minimum conditions for access to CIFF support. The following are the suggested conditions for rating:

- Compliance with the criteria in the SBL as far as maximum debt limits are concerned
- Compliance with all legislative and regulatory requirements
- Operational and debt coverage ratio to be at least 1.3 (total unearmarked revenue divided by recurrent expenditure plus debt services)
- Actual deviations from budget to be within a specified norm (an initially acceptable 10 percent maximum deviation, gradually decreasing to 5 percent; partially as a proxy objective measurement of management capacity and skill)
- A satisfactory skills development plan to address project preparation and financial management that is to be developed and implemented
- Long-term recurrent expenditure projections not to exceed 90 percent of unearmarked revenue
- Liquidity cash reserves of at least 3 months to be maintained

- If financing is a bond issuance, an *external* sinking fund to be created
- At least a medium-term, climate-friendly development plan with the supporting capital investment plans to be developed and incorporated in the budgets.

These suggestions would apply in both retail and wholesale environments. In the wholesale environment, banks would also be free to apply their own credit criteria and would be expected to do so. For the commercial banks to participate and benefit in CIFF activities, they would be required, at minimum, to apply these conditions and credit principles.

Creditworthiness criteria of financial institutions

The assessment of banks to be used by the CIFF will be decided in consultation with the SBV. Basic high-level considerations in determining the creditworthiness of a bank are (a) earnings before interest, taxes, depreciation, and amortization; (b) liquidity; (c) capital adequacy; (d) solvency; (e) debt-equity ratio; (f) nonperforming loans; (g) asset quality; (h) portfolio diversification (sector, client, area); (i) fee to margin income; (j) management quality; (k) risk management systems; and (l) financial performance and ratios. A rating approach would also consider aspects such as the regulatory environment and economic prospects; however, because those factors will be common for all banks and other financial intermediaries to a large degree, it is not critical to take them into account.

CONCLUSIONS

The conclusion from this high-level assessment of the provinces' potential effective demand for access and support from a new financing facility is that demand is likely to be substantial but will take time to unfold. The three provinces assessed in this chapter are all financially healthy, and their debt will be capped by the new SBL prescription that total debt stock must be capped at 30 percent of the previous year's revenue rather than by the ability to service the debt. The detailed analysis of the three provinces indicates that the provinces must have considerable fiscal space for borrowing before the ceiling is reached or before the ability to service debt becomes an issue. The assessment raised some concerns that the recurrent expenditure trends in some provinces are rising to levels that can be regarded as curtailing fiscal flexibility; thus policy makers should initiate attempts to constrain the growth.

The chapter showed that the 11 second-tier provinces have the ability, capacity, and willingness to incur debt. Implementation capacity is not likely to present a challenge in most provinces, given the relatively small increase in capital investments. Therefore, the assessment concluded that provinces will have a substantial demand for access and support from a new financing facility to promote more borrowing and longer-term loans. Regulatory constraints and the financial attractiveness of the facility, however, will determine the effective demand. That demand will depend on the facility's conditions of such support and the degree to which reforms promote more autonomy, enhance revenue, and improve financial management capacity. If capacity building is efficient, if the regulatory environment is enabling, and if the conditions and terms are attractive, the effective demand by end-2016 is estimated to be between D 3.3 trillion

(US$153 million) and D 6.7 trillion (US$311 million) and to remain at around D 6.45 trillion (US$300 million) for the next 5 years.

Another conclusion noted that promoting sustainability and creditworthiness required that a credit evaluation system be introduced and that certain minimum parameters be articulated to allow access to support from the potential CIFF. Under the approach being considered—involving the private sector and structuring the support program for the private sector to take at least some real credit risk, even if partial—the commercial banks and capital markets will have limited appetite for the approach if timely and accurate information is not available. The lack of information from borrowers could prove to be more of a constraint than the availability of properly prepared projects, not in itself, but as a symptom of the inadequacy of provinces' financial management capabilities, management information systems, and budget skills. In light of these considerations, this chapter recommends that the CIFF initiative require, as a precondition, that participants in the borrowing support system and take part in a program to enhance financial management capacities at the provincial level.

NOTES

1. "The World Bank in Vietnam," World Bank country overview, http://www.worldbank.org/en/country/vietnam/overview.
2. Category 2 here means second-tier provinces that are net contributors to revenue of the government of Vietnam. Category 3, third-tier provinces, depend heavily on the central government's transfers and have very limited creditworthiness.
3. Ratios are generally accepted measurements used by commercial lenders to assess an entity's financial health and will typically include (a) debt service cover ratio, which is the ratio of cash flow available to service debt; (b) operating cost cover ratio, which indicates the operating costs as a ratio to total operating income; (c) liquidity ratio, which measures the short-term ability to meet obligations; and (d) loan life cover ratio, which measures the long-term ability to service a loan.
4. The MOF stated that this is not a provincial contingent liability but a charge on the national budget.
5. Since Beijing heavily restricted local governments' borrowing, local government financing vehicles were created to borrow on local governments' behalf. Such borrowing, which totaled over US$4 trillion in this IMF analysis, was responsible for one-quarter of the buildup in China's overall domestic debt since 2008.
6. A workout is the process whereby a debtor meets a loan commitment by satisfying altered repayment terms. This is often managed by an independent administrator and may consist of some radical interventions such as reducing staff.
7. The more detailed Moody's approach to credit rating can be obtained at https://www.moodys.com/researchdocumentcontentpage.aspx?docid=PBC_147779.
8. For more details of the assessment tool, please refer to "Presentation on Credit Assessment & Benchmarking Tools Developed (Watercat & Municat)," available at UN-HABITAT website: http://mirror.unhabitat.org/list.asp?typeid=54&catid=270.

REFERENCES

Albrecht, David, Hervé Hocquard, and Philippe Papin. 2010. *Urban Development in Vietnam: The Rise of Local Authorities: Resources, Limits and Evolution of Local Governance*. Paris: Agence Française de Développement.

Financial Times. 2017. "Rising Risk in Chinese Local Government Debt." FT Confidential Research. June 26.

Fitch Ratings. 2014. "Vietnam: Full Rating Report." *Fitchratings.com*, November 17, 2014.

Government of Vietnam. 2012. *State Budgets 2002 and 2013*. Unpublished documents. Hanoi: Government of Vietnam.

IMF (International Monetary Fund). 2014. *Vietnam: 2014 Article IV Consultation—Staff Report; Press Release; and Statement by the Executive Director for Vietnam*. Country Report 14/311. Washington, DC: International Monetary Fund.

Lu, Yinqiu, and Tao Sun. 2013. "Local Government Financing Platforms in China: A Fortune or Misfortune?" IMF Working Paper 13/243, International Monetary Fund, Washington, DC.

Smetts, Susanna. 2014. "Water Supply and Sanitation in Vietnam: Turning Finance into Services for the Future." UNDP Water and Sanitation Program. Washington, DC: World Bank.

UNDP (United Nations Development Programme). 2013. *2013 Human Development Report*. New York: United Nations Development Programme.

World Bank. 2011. *Vietnam: Assessment of PFM Arrangements at the Provincial Level*. Washington, DC: World Bank.

———. 2013. *Assessment of the Financing Framework for Municipal Infrastructure in Vietnam*. World Bank, Washington, DC.

———. 2014a. *Making the Whole Greater than the Sum of the Parts: A Review of Fiscal Decentralization in Vietnam*. Washington, DC: World Bank.

———. 2014b. *Subnational Debt Management Performance Assessment: Ho Chi Minh City, Vietnam*. Washington, DC: World Bank.

———. 2015. *Vietnam Socio-Economic Development Plan, 2010 to 2020*. Washington, DC: World Bank. http://www.worldbank.org/en/country/vietnam/overview.

3 A Supply-Side Analysis of the Vietnamese Banking Sector

The Vietnamese banking industry has shown impressive growth in the past decade along with the country's economy. Since the 1990s, the government of Vietnam has launched a series of restructuring and liberalization reforms to strengthen the banking sector as part of the country's shift to a more market-driven economy. These reforms also have paved the way for the diversification of commercial banks in the country (box 3.1). Overall, total assets of the commercial banks in Vietnam have been rapidly expanding, and forecast to increase from US$267 billion in 2015 to US$422 billion by 2019 (figure 3.1).

The Vietnamese banking industry is highly concentrated in the four state-owned commercial banks (SOCBs),[1] which control around 45 percent of total assets (Schmittmann et al. 2017). The remaining assets, held by 89 banks, are highly fragmented. Those banks are mainly composed of joint-stock commercial banks (JSCBs), joint-venture banks, and branches of foreign banks (figure 3.2). SOCBs dominate the market in terms of loans and deposits, although their share has been eroding since the 1990s, decreasing to 70 percent in the early 2000s and later to 45 percent in 2017. Traditionally, SOCBs have been the instrument of government policy lending, which often includes programs that focus on state-owned enterprises (SOEs). SOCBs continue to be the main funding source for SOEs. The majority of the income for SOCBs is from interest-based rather than fee-based products. More specialized segments, such as project financing and investment banking, have a limited presence in Vietnam.

The non-SOCBs, especially JSCBs and the wholly owned foreign banks, have increasingly imposed competitive pressure onto the traditional players in the banking sector (tables 3.1 and 3.2). Together, the non-SOCBs account for more than half of total assets in the sector. JSCBs have shown aggressive growth in recent years and have emerged as an important competitor for the SOCBs. They have more diversified shareholding structures, with both public and private shareholders. They focus on small and medium enterprises (SMEs) and on the retail segment. The foreign banks, which differentiate themselves with their global industry knowledge, expand rapidly into the retail market.

BOX 3.1

Vietnam Banking Reform Timeline

Over the past 65 years, various banking reforms in Vietnam have brought the sector to the point at which commercial loans could be used to finance local infrastructure projects.

FIGURE B3.1.1

Vietnam Banking Reform Snapshot

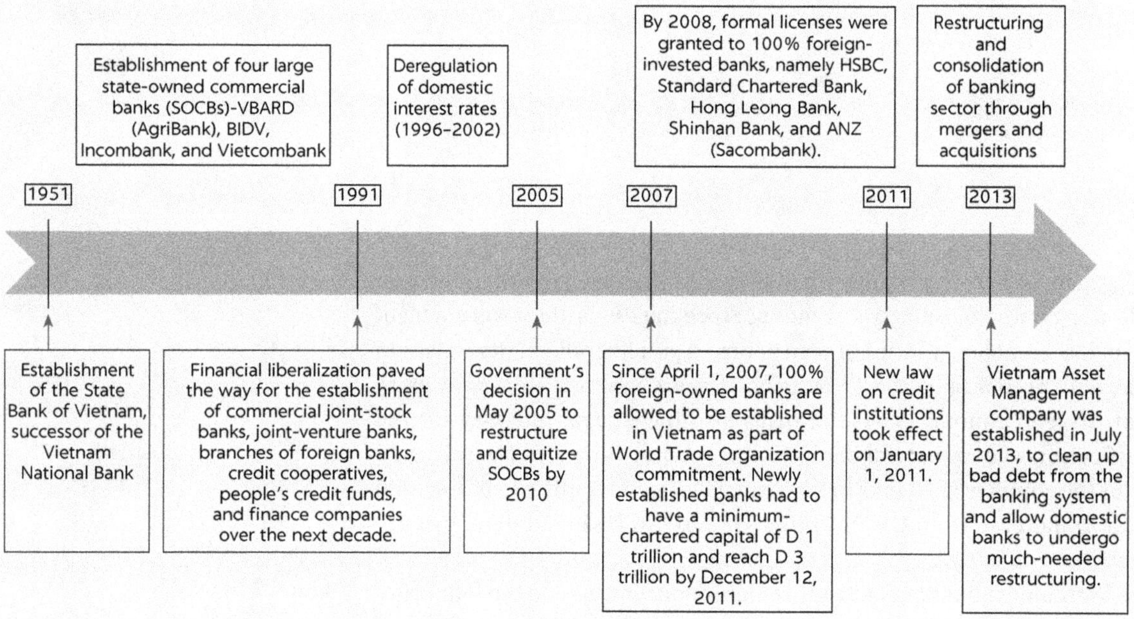
Establishment of four large state-owned commercial banks (SOCBs)-VBARD (AgriBank), BIDV, Incombank, and Vietcombank
Deregulation of domestic interest rates (1996–2002)
By 2008, formal licenses were granted to 100% foreign-invested banks, namely HSBC, Standard Chartered Bank, Hong Leong Bank, Shinhan Bank, and ANZ (Sacombank).
Restructuring and consolidation of banking sector through mergers and acquisitions
1951
1991
2005
2007
2011
2013
Establishment of the State Bank of Vietnam, successor of the Vietnam National Bank
Financial liberalization paved the way for the establishment of commercial joint-stock banks, joint-venture banks, branches of foreign banks, credit cooperatives, people's credit funds, and finance companies over the next decade.
Government's decision in May 2005 to restructure and equitize SOCBs by 2010
Since April 1, 2007, 100% foreign-owned banks are allowed to be established in Vietnam as part of World Trade Organization commitment. Newly established banks had to have a minimum-chartered capital of D 1 trillion and reach D 3 trillion by December 12, 2011.
New law on credit institutions took effect on January 1, 2011.
Vietnam Asset Management company was established in July 2013, to clean up bad debt from the banking system and allow domestic banks to undergo much-needed restructuring.

FIGURE 3.1

Total Assets of Vietnamese Commercial Banks

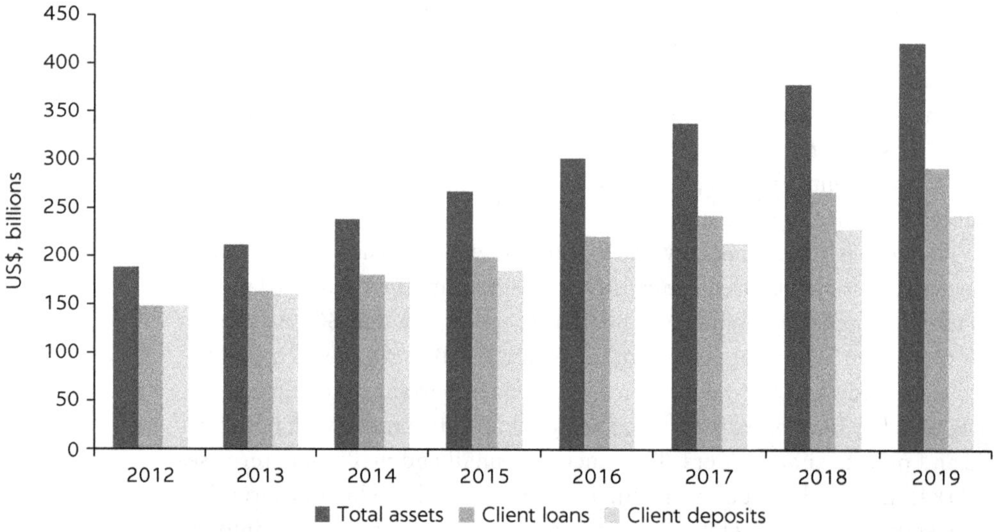

Source: "Vietnam Commercial Banking Report Q2/2015," BMI Research.
Note: Data for 2014 are estimated; 2015–19 data are forecast.

FIGURE 3.2
Chartered Capital and Number of Banks per Category

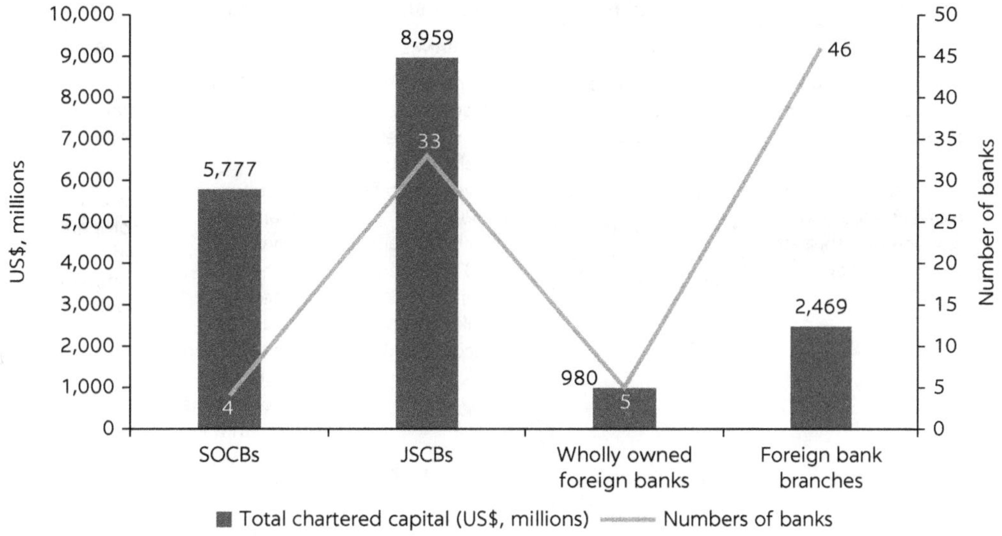

Source: State Bank of Vietnam.
Note: SOCB = state-owned commercial bank; JSCB = joint-stock commercial bank.

TABLE 3.1 **Key Groups of Banks by Market Focus and Strengths**

STATE-OWNED COMMERCIAL BANKS	JOINT-STOCK COMMERCIAL BANKS	FOREIGN BANK BRANCHES	WHOLLY OWNED FOREIGN BANKS	JOINT-VENTURE BANKS	POLICY BANK
4 BANKS	33 BANKS	46 BANKS	5 BANKS	4 BANKS	1 BANK
Characteristics					
• Dominate Vietnam's market in terms of assets, loans, deposits, and distribution network. • Traditionally focus on a certain segment. For example, Agribank focuses on the agricultural sector; Vietcombank specializes in trade finances, foreign exchange, and international payments. • Provide main source of funding for SOEs. • Have a good reputation with domestic depositors.	• Have a shorter history of operations than SOCBs. • Focus on SME and retail segment, with emphasis on banking products and services. • Had aggressive growth in recent years in terms of branch network and deposit mobilization. • Are strategic foreign investors. Most of the top JSCBs have large international strategic investors, such as HSBC (Techcombank), ANZ Bank (Sacombank), and ACB (Standard Chartered Bank)	• Are constrained by the regulation limiting the capacity to operate as local banks. • Historical focus on servicing multinational customers in Vietnam, but with increasing focus on larger Vietnamese companies. • Have key strengths in terms of capital, experience, and technological expertise.	• Differentiate themselves by offering innovative products that reflect their global industry knowledge. • Expand aggressively into retail market. • Have a limited branch network.	• Use joint-venture contracts for capital contributed by one or more Vietnamese banks and one or more foreign banks. • Are traditionally focused on relations with corporate customers, primarily export companies from the foreign joint-venture bank's country.	• Provides funds to carry out the policy-directed lending of the government.

continued

TABLE 3.1, *continued*

STATE-OWNED COMMERCIAL BANKS	JOINT-STOCK COMMERCIAL BANKS	FOREIGN BANK BRANCHES	WHOLLY OWNED FOREIGN BANKS	JOINT-VENTURE BANKS	POLICY BANK
4 BANKS	**33 BANKS**	**46 BANKS**	**5 BANKS**	**4 BANKS**	**1 BANK**
• Includes an extensive branch network with over 1,000 branches or transaction offices across Vietnam.	• Are under pressure to restructure. Many small JSCBs (such as Ocean Bank, GP Bank) with poor performance and high NPLs are under restructuring through mergers and acquisitions.	• Have a limited number of branches, each requiring a separate license. • Are geographically concentrated in urban areas.	• Announce their presence by buying stakes in local joint-stock players, such as HSBC (Techcombank), ACB (Standard Chartered Bank), and ANZ (Sacombank).	• Have a limited branch network. • Have difficulties expanding, given local partners' limited resources, thus requiring that joint-venture banks maintain their original capital structure between foreign and local partners.	• Has a limited branch network. • Does not have to compete with commercial banks.

Note: State-owned commercial banks include majority state-owned joint-stock bank (VietcomBank). Wholly owned foreign banks include ANZ (Sacombank), HSBC, ACB (Standard Chartered Bank), Hong Leong, and Shinhan Bank. JSCB = joint-stock commercial bank; NPLs = nonperforming loans; SME = small and medium enterprises; SOE = state-owned enterprise; HSBC = The Hongkong and Shanghai Banking Corporation; ANZ = Australia and New Zealand Banking Group.

TABLE 3.2 **Products of Key Groups of Banks in Vietnam**

STATE-OWNED COMMERCIAL BANKS	JOINT-STOCK COMMERCIAL BANKS	FOREIGN BANK BRANCHES	WHOLLY OWNED FOREIGN BANKS	JOINT-VENTURE BANKS	POLICY BANK
Major players					
• Agribank • Vietcombank • VietinBank • BIDV	• Techcombank • Sacombank • ACB (Standard Chartered Bank) • Military Bank • Maritime Bank • LienVietPostBank	• ABN Amro Bank • Bank of China • Citibank • Deutsche Bank AG Vietnam	• HSBC • Standard Chartered Bank • ANZ Bank • Hong Leong Bank • Shinhan Bank	• Indovina Bank • Vietnam-Russia Bank • VID Public Bank • Vina Siam	• Vietnam Bank for Social Policies
Product focus					
• Have an industry focus but are expanding into personal and SME products. Some still focus on serving the traditional industry customer groups (such as Agribank for rural and agricultural financial markets), while others are increasing their focus on catering to the needs of individual consumers and SMEs.	• Focus on individual consumers and SMEs if large. Large JSCBs also offer corporate banking, treasury, and capital market products, such as foreign exchange transactions, derivative trading, options, securities, leasing subsidiaries, and trade finance. • If smaller JSCBs, have limited product diversification with a focus on SMEs. • Are starting to offer more innovative deposit products to boost capital mobilization.	• Focus on sophisticated products for foreign-invested companies and large state-owned companies. • Have select products for foreign and high-income Vietnamese retail customers, including international payment services, foreign currency trading, and remittances.	• Focus on retail banking through automobile and housing loans, Internet banking services, as well as international credit card services. • Have introduced new products to the Vietnamese market, such as mortgage services and medium-term certificates of deposit.	• Focus on products for foreign-invested companies investing and doing business in Vietnam, such as export-import finance, overseas remittances, project finance, as well as export and import support services.	• Focus on lending to poor households, disadvantaged students, overseas workers, ethnic minority households, and other social development purposes, such as job creation and environmental protection.

Note: State-owned commercial banks include majority state-owned joint-stock banks (Vietcombank). Wholly owned foreign banks listed were granted licenses for 100 percent foreign-owned subsidiary banks in 2008. BIDV = Bank for Investment and Development of Vietnam; JSCB = joint-stock commercial bank; SME = small and medium enterprises; HSBC = The Hongkong and Shanghai Banking Corporation.

BANKING INDUSTRY ISSUES

Asset liability mismatch

A major constraint facing commercial banks' capability and appetite for lending to provincial governments is the mismatch between short-term capital and long-term loans. Because the primary sources of funding for commercial banks are the customers' deposits, which are short- to medium-term in nature, the banks' assets will always have shorter tenor compared with the long-term financing needs of infrastructure. Commercial banks are able to mobilize only a small amount of long-term capital: less than 4 percent of the total liabilities in four of the banks discussed here. However, a relatively significant portion of their loan portfolios (on average more than 20 percent) is allocated to long-term loans to clients (see later section, "Rapid Assessment of Performance of Selected Commercial Banks"). Thus commercial banks are exposed to the liquidity risk of using too much short-term capital for long-term lending (table 3.3 and figure 3.3). The ratio of long-term liabilities to long-term assets is generally lower than 16 percent, except for VietinBank, with 26 percent. In current conditions, further long-term loans to provincial governments could increase the gap between long-term assets and liabilities.

TABLE 3.3 **Characteristics of Selected Commercial Banks**

ASSETS AND LIABILITIES, D, MILLIONS	VIETCOMBANK	LIENVIETPOSTBANK	MARITIME BANK	VIETINBANK
Long-term assets	27,762,105	18,680,940	4,529,183	90,853,242
Long-term liabilities	2,017,282	2,872,705	182,515	23,366,272
Long-term liquidity gap	25,744,823	15,808,235	4,346,668	67,486,970
Long-term liabilities as share of long-term assets, %	7.27	15.38	4.03	25.72
Long-term liabilities as share of total liabilities, %	0.32	2.87	0.20	3.23

Source: Annual reports for 2015 of Vietcombank, LienVietPostBank, Maritime Bank, and VietinBank.

FIGURE 3.3
Liquidity Risks Facing Selected Commercial Banks

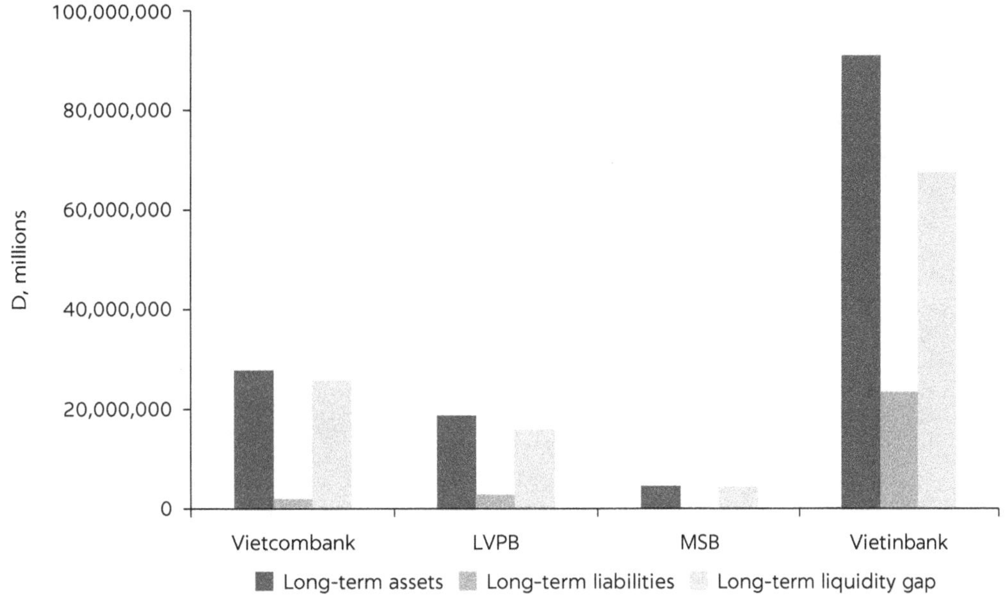

Source: Annual reports for 2015 of Vietcombank, LienVietPostBank (LVPB), Maritime Bank (MSB), and VietinBank.
Note: LVPB = LienVietPostBank; MSB = Maritime Bank.

Credit slowdown

Another constraint in the Vietnam banking industry is the slowdown of credit growth, which affects commercial banks' lending capability (figure 3.4). Vietnam's banking sector has shown impressive growth in both loans and deposits since 2000. In the period 2000–2012, total loans and deposits also grew at a compound annual growth rate of 28.3 percent and 28.9 percent, respectively. The fastest growth rate took place in the period 2002–07, when total loans and deposits grew at a compound annual growth rate of 35.8 percent and 37.5 percent, respectively. That growth peaked in 2007, when loans grew at 53.9 percent and deposits grew at 51.5 percent. Since 2013, both loan and deposit growth rates have been lower than they were earlier. The slowdown in loan growth has largely resulted from a large number of bad debts in Vietnam's banking sector, which have reduced the willingness of banks to lend. With room for policy easing, the State Bank of Vietnam (SBV) is expected to cut rates further to spur credit growth in the country in the short term.

Nonperforming loans

Dealing with high percentages of nonperforming loans (NPLs) is a top priority for banks in Vietnam. Banks must ensure that lending to provincial governments does not lead to a possible increase in NPLs. Reliable NPL data are difficult to obtain because of a big gap between Vietnamese bank practices and international standards on reporting NPLs (figure 3.5).

However, according to the SBV, reporting of NPLs across the banking sector has been increasing since 2009 and peaked at 4.1 percent in December 2012 (figure 3.6). Independent rating agencies as well as other economists believe the unreported number to be much higher. Many think that the 3.3 percent of

FIGURE 3.4

Growth of Loans and Deposits in the Banking Sector

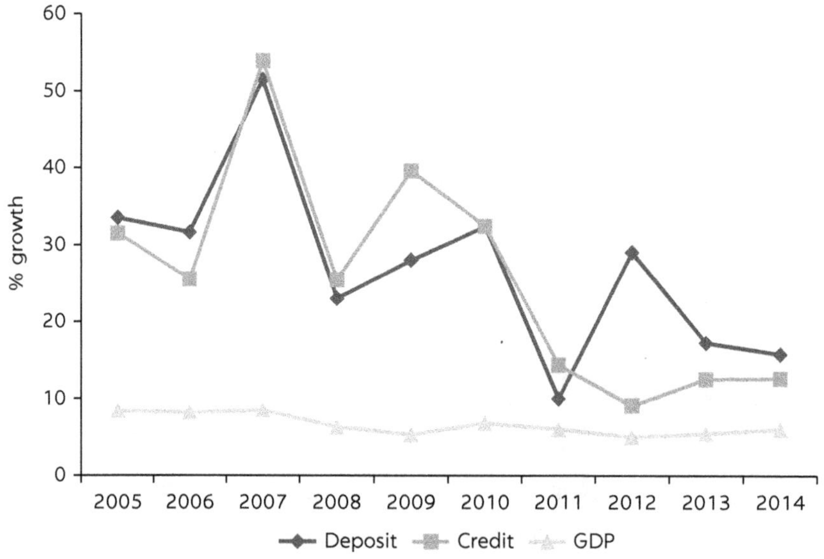

Source: State Bank of Vietnam.
Note: GDP = gross domestic product.

FIGURE 3.5
Estimates of Nonperforming Loans

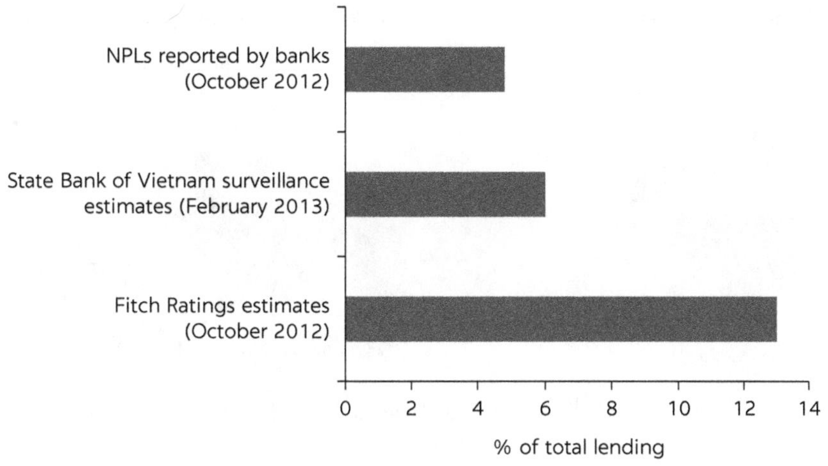

Source: State Bank of Vietnam and Fitch Ratings.
Note: NPL = nonperforming loan.

FIGURE 3.6
Changes in Nonperforming Loan Rate of Commercial Banks

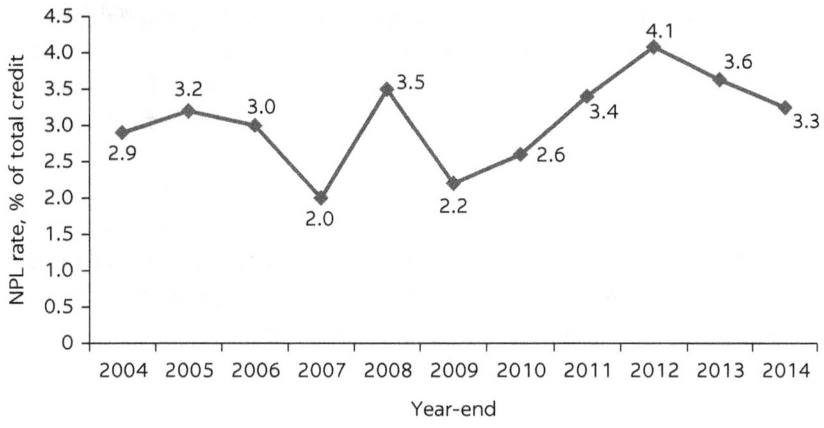

Source: State Bank of Vietnam.
Note: NPL = nonperforming loan.

NPLs in 2014 does not reflect the true troubled status of the Vietnamese banking industry or of the credit quality of bank lending. The SBV has issued many measures to control and manage NPLs at commercial banks, such as issuing Circular 02 on loan reclassification (effective June 2014) and establishing the Vietnam Asset Management Company in July 2013 to repurchase banks' NPLs. As a result, the NPL rate decreased from 3.6 percent in 2013 to 3.3 percent in 2014.

State-owned enterprises

SOEs currently account for more than half of the banking sector's NPLs (figure 3.7). Sour loans (in which interest is overdue and recovery of principal is uncertain) in the property sector are another main source of NPLs. Small banks have an overwhelming exposure to real estate loans and individual loans, resulting in highly skewed and risky loan portfolios.

FIGURE 3.7

Allocation of Credit and Nonperforming Loans

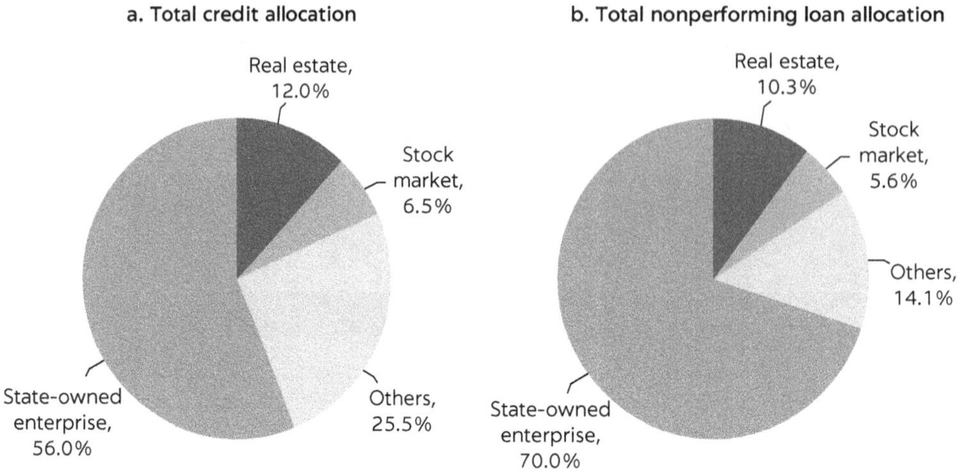

Source: Bank Reform Report 2011.

The relatively high proportion of NPLs in local commercial banks reduces the availability of domestic debt capital and, therefore, the potential for commercial banks to join syndicated loans for infrastructure projects. In addition, high bad debt levels in local commercial banks make it difficult for international investors (funds and banks) to on-lend through these local banks.

Under the current circumstances, commercial banks are hesitant to lend to provincial governments because such lending may lead to an increase in NPLs, which have limited or no recourse mechanism. Commercial banks need to learn how to properly manage credit risks specific to provincial government borrowing, knowledge that should be required both by commercial banks' policies and SBV regulations.

MACROECONOMIC INSTABILITY AFFECTS GOVERNMENT CREDITWORTHINESS

The track record of macroeconomic instability in recent years threatens the credibility of the government at both the central and provincial levels. That record could potentially affect the creditworthiness of provincial government borrowers. Moreover, the high level of government debt could trigger a fiscal crisis, undermining confidence in the ability of the banking sector to lend to provincial governments.

Falling inflation

Falling inflation provides room for further rate cuts, making borrowing from commercial banks more affordable for provincial government borrowers. Although economic growth has been sustained, headline inflation continues to fall, providing room for continued monetary easing. Consumer price inflation rose 4.1 percent on average in 2014, marking a significant decline from the

6.6 percent recorded in 2013. Easing price pressures in turn have led to a recent rise in the real policy rate. Real interest rates came in at 4.8 percent in 2014, suggesting that current monetary policy is not terribly loose.[2]

FIGURE 3.8

Proportion of Banking Industry's Short-, Medium-, and Long-Term Loans

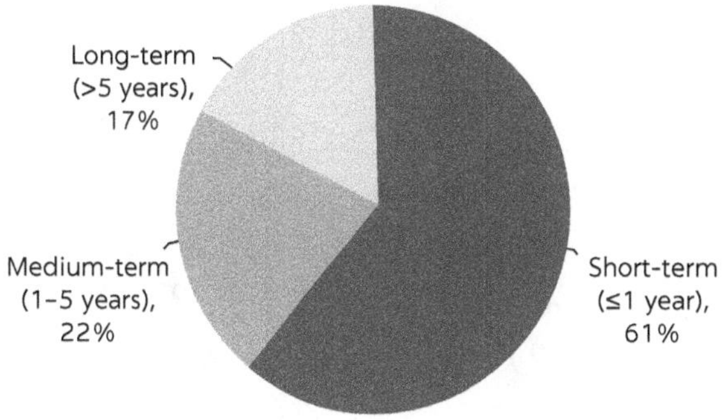

Source: Vietnam banking survey 2013, KPMG.

Domination of short-term loans

More than 60 percent of Vietnamese commercial banks' outstanding loans were short term, while the entire banking sector's total long-term loans (more than 5-year tenor) were estimated at US$31 billion by the end of 2012 (figure 3.8). In general, more than 85 percent of the Vietnamese commercial banks' total liabilities are due in less than 1 year; for some banks, that rate is up to 98 percent. Those percentages reflect a mismatch of financing tenor caused by provincial governments' long-tenor infrastructure projects and the short-term nature of commercial bank deposits.

The SBV set a limit, effective February 2015, allowing commercial banks to provide medium- and long-term loans up to 60 percent of their short-term funding mobilization.[3] The new regulation has increased the medium- and long-term lending capability of the commercial banks. However, many commercial banks believe that the credit market can neither function as nor replace the debt market; that is, they cannot provide the long-tenor loans to the allowable limit because of the tenor mismatching and the liquidity issue. The Vietnamese banking system does not want to repeat the recent painful experience with high NPLs and the liquidity crisis. In general, the new circular has some positive regulatory impact, but it has little effect on technically promoting long-term lending by commercial banks.

Less attractive government bonds

Within this macroeconomic context, yet another trend is that government bonds are becoming less attractive to the banking system. For many years, issuing a government bond was a traditional way that the Vietnamese government dealt with its fiscal deficit. However, the government has been very unsuccessful with its bond issuing plans recently, and in May 2015 issuing of government bonds reached a low point. Several factors explain this situation.

First, in 2015 the economy improved and credit grew higher than the previous year. As a result, the commercial banks can find better opportunities to lend, and they have shifted their portfolios to focus more on business sectors and less on government bonds. Second, the interest rates offered by government bonds with maturity in 5 and 10 years are 5.5 percent and 6.3 percent, respectively. Those interest rates are far below the market rate for commercial banks' medium- and long-term loans, which are 9.0–11.0 percent. Third, the SBV circular 36/2014/TT-NHNN set ceilings for government bond buying. JSCBs are not allowed to buy government bonds in excess of 35 percent of their short-term mobilization funds, and the ceiling for SOCBs is 15 percent. Some commercial banks have reached their ceiling and cannot buy more government bonds.

According to Resolution 78/2014 of the National Assembly, the government will not issue bonds with a maturity of less than 3 years. One reason is that the government is in the process of restructuring its debts and reducing capital costs; for example, bond proceeds are not yet disbursed to projects, but bond repayment is already due. Since April 2015, the government has issued only bonds with maturity of 5, 10, and 15 years, but bonds with the shortest maturity of 5 years account for 60 percent of total bonds issued. Since liquidity is still a big issue, buying long-maturity government bonds will be limited under the current banking business conditions.

EXPLORING NEW MARKET SEGMENTS

Ongoing restructuring in the banking sector and in SOEs may have improved commercial banks' strengths and credit assessment capability, giving the sector a fresh start in tapping into new market segments, such as lending to provincial governments. The Vietnamese government aims to speed up the process of privatizing SOCBs, which will help modernize the banking industry. SOCBs will play a smaller role in lending to provincial governments, and the risks associated with state-directed lending will decrease over time.

The government has already taken steps to address the high level of NPLs in the banking sector, which constituted 4.67 percent of total loans in 2013, according to the SBV. While it is expected that progress on this front will be gradual, the government's strengthening of the banking sector is a step in the right direction to secure the country's long-term growth prospects.

Ongoing banking reforms by the government are expected to help strengthen the sector and encourage bank lending, although it is notable that progress on this front will likely proceed at a gradual pace. The government established the Vietnam Asset Management Company in July 2013 to clean up bad debt from the banking system and to allow domestic banks to undergo much-needed restructuring and strengthening of their credit assessment mechanism. Meanwhile, the government also aims to speed up the reform of SOEs, which accounted for more than half of the bad debts in the banking sector, in a bid to improve operational efficiencies and reduce their need to borrow to finance their losses. In the government's latest efforts, the SBV will look to consolidate the banking sector through mergers and acquisitions and will seek to dissolve weak financial institutions that have little chance of recovery.

ASSESSMENT OF COMMERCIAL BANKS THAT LEND TO PROVINCIAL GOVERNMENTS

Some provincial governments have borrowed directly from commercial banks for their infrastructure projects. Commercial banks can lend directly to provincial governments with tenor up to 2 years if the source of repayment is the provincial budgets. A recent example is Dong Nai province. It is one of the 13 net contributors (including Hanoi and Ho Chi Minh City) to the state budget that signed two separate credit contracts with VietinBank in 2014 for loans of D 200 billion and D 1 trillion (US$ 46.5 million). The two contracts have 2-year tenor and the same annual interest rate of 7 percent. At the same time, Dong Nai province has also directly borrowed from the Bank for Investment and Development of Vietnam (BIDV); the loan for D 400 billion (US$ 18.6 million) has a 2-year tenor and annual interest rate of 6 percent. All of Dong Nai's infrastructure

TABLE 3.4 **Commercial Banks' Direct Lending to Provincial Governments**

LENDER BANKS	PROVINCIAL GOVERNMENT BORROWERS	PROJECTS AND LOCAL ENTITIES	LOAN AMOUNT (D, MILLIONS)	LOAN AMOUNT (US$, MILLIONS EQUIVALENT)	TENOR (YEARS)	INTEREST (%)
VietinBank	Ho Chi Minh City	Thu Thiem Tunnel Project Management Unit	8,000,000	372.0	2	—
VietinBank	Dong Nai province	Nonrevenue infrastructure projects	1,200,000	55.8	2	7
BIDV	Dong Nai province	Nonrevenue infrastructure projects	400,000	18.6	2	6
LVPB	Thai Nguyen province	Land development fund	80,000	3.7	2	7

Sources: Commercial banks VietinBank, BIDV, and LVPB.
Note: BIDV = Bank for Investment and Development of Vietnam; LVPB = LienVietPostBank; — = not available.

TABLE 3.5 **State-Owned Commercial Bank Lending Rates, by Recipient**

LENDING TERMS	CENTRAL GOVERNMENT (THROUGH GOVERNMENT BONDS)	LOCAL GOVERNMENTS	CORPORATIONS	INDIVIDUALS
Interest rate (%)	4.08 (5-year bond)	6.00–8.70	9.00–10.00 (short-term)	9.00–15.00
	6.19 (10-year bond)			
	7.05 (15-year bond)		10.5–12.0 (long-term)	
Collateral	No	No	Yes	Yes; creditworthiness
Tenor	3–15 years	2 years	1–10 years	1–5 years

Source: Selected state-owned commercial banks.

projects that are funded by such commercial borrowings are non-revenue generating. As reported by the lending banks, the provincial government borrowers have made their repayments as scheduled.

SBV documents that regulate lending to provincial governments by commercial banks are Decision 1627/2001/QD-NHNN of 2001 and Letter 576/NHNN-CSHT of 2005. In the SBV regulations, commercial banks are allowed to lend to provincial governments for infrastructure projects (tables 3.4 and 3.5). In general, all identified existing loans to provincial governments by commercial banks have more favorable lending terms—lower interest rates and no collateral required—than those of other corporate and individual clients.

However, the SBV set a limit on the amount of lending to each provincial government based on the capital gap between a provincial capital expenditure budget, with a 30 percent limit, and the total updated and planned commercial capital mobilization of provincial government during the year. The maximum tenor for provincial government lending is 2 years, and commercial banks take the full credit risk of lending to them. There is no implicit provision of a recourse mechanism and commercial banks are encouraged to work with provincial governments on their own loan repayment supervision.

Borrowing by provinces to issue municipal bonds

Provincial governments can borrow from the bond market by issuing municipal bonds. According to the Vietnam Bond Market Association, four provincial governments—Ho Chi Minh City, Hanoi, Dong Nai, and Da Nang—have successfully issued municipal bonds with total par value of about D 17 trillion (US$790 million), with maturity ranging from 1 to 15 years. Many of the bonds have expired on maturity and no case of default has been reported. Moreover, some smaller provinces have also issued municipal bonds to selected commercial banks in private arrangements.

The common tenor of provincial bonds is 3 to 5 years. However, in 2005 and 2006 Ho Chi Minh City was able to sell in Vietnam its 15-year bonds of about D 325 billion (US$15 million) and D 425 billion (US$20 million), respectively. The province's ability to sell 15-year bonds demonstrates that under certain conditions, commercial financing in Vietnam can match the long-term tenor needs of provincial infrastructure investment projects. Because Ho Chi Minh City is the richest province in Vietnam, and buyers believe that the city's bonds carry the implicit support of the Ministry of Finance, Ho Chi Minh City is considered "too big to be allowed to fail." Provinces that are not as well known to investors may have a harder time finding buyers than those relatively wealthy provinces that have already issued bonds. The assumption of some buyers that the Ministry of Finance will stand behind the bond issuers has not been tested.

The municipal bond buyers are dominated by SOCBs (Vietcombank, BIDV, VietinBank, Agribank); some JSCBs (VP Bank, Maritime Bank, Military Bank, Techcombank, Ocean Bank, LienVietPostBank); and insurance companies (AIA Vietnam). The commercial banks take the full credit risk in lending to provincial governments through bonds or loans within the current legal and market conditions, but they have little risk mitigation in such transactions. In fact, none of the existing loans to provincial governments by commercial banks have been provided with proper collateral or guarantee. The commercial banks have conducted some technical and risk assessment in lending to provincial governments, but even those assessments have taken shortcuts within their internal risk management procedure. And, in the absence of a recourse mechanism, the lender banks have been exposed to a great deal of credit risk, with very little risk mitigation in such lending to provincial governments.

Contingent liabilities of provincial governments

Many provincial governments have their own enterprises or hold the majority of shares. Those entities get loans from commercial banks, especially from SOCBs. Because the government is privatizing SOCBs, what the banks' risk strategy will actually be after such equitization is unclear, nor is it clear how the approach will affect their willingness to lend to provincially owned companies. Equitization may lead to more stringent lending criteria and somewhat reduce commercial funding access by provincial governments' infrastructure corporations. However, even after equitization, the central government is expected to retain a controlling interest in the large commercial banks. In such circumstances, the provincial governments may continue to retain some influence on directed lending to their own enterprises.

Current SBV regulations set a limit on the longest tenor of 2 years on the loans to provincial governments by commercial banks. As a consequence, long-term commercial bank lending is not available to provincial governments' infrastructure projects, which often require long-term capital.

Local capital markets and other financing sources

As in other countries, commercial financing to provincial governments in Vietnam can take many forms. It can come through projects that involve a degree of private management and private risk, such as public-private partnerships, joint-stock companies, build-operate-transfer (BOTs), and similar arrangements. Vietnam has had a number of BOTs and joint ventures in infrastructure (for example, the Phu My power plant, Thu Duc water treatment plant, and others). Such projects require both equity and debt.

However, under Vietnam's current conditions, debt is more difficult to arrange than equity. The equity markets in Vietnam are still in the early stages of development, but the debt markets are even more undeveloped. For infrastructure financing, debt is far more important than equity because debt is needed to make equity work, and commercial debt also is required for public sector projects when such projects are not commercially viable, particularly infrastructure that does not generate revenue. The sources of long-term financing available to provincial governments for infrastructure investment are very limited, mostly because debt capital markets in Vietnam are undeveloped.

Directed lending and government-guaranteed lending

Over the years, SOCBs have been lending, often directly, to provincial governments and SOEs to finance their investments. In addition, the commercial banks have three common forms of financing for infrastructure projects. First, some commercial banks have been appointed by the government as servicing banks for infrastructure projects that are considered official development assistance (ODA) projects. The banks are not responsible for project appraisal and, therefore, are not exposed to credit risks. In such cases, commercial banks simply collect fees for their bank services. Second, commercial banks can provide on-lending with original funding from ODA sources. And third, the banks can work with international financial institutions that make loans for long-term projects or to government entities that are secured with explicit government guarantees. In all cases, commercial banks in Vietnam are exposed to very little credit risk in dealing with provincial governments.

By comparison, provincial governments are currently not qualified to borrow from institutional investors and foreign banks. So far, no institutional investors and foreign banks have bought municipal bonds or provided loans to provincial governments. The simple reason is that provincial governments have no credit ratings, and neither their bond issuance nor commercial loans are backed by well-known financial institutions or the central government.

COMMERCIAL BANK CONSTRAINTS IN LENDING TO PROVINCIAL GOVERNMENTS

The current law is not completely silent on the possibility of provincial governments borrowing from commercial banks. However, as noted earlier, the longest allowed tenor of commercial bank loans to provincial governments is 2 years, making it impossible for the banks to provide long-term lending directly to provincial governments.

Another limitation is the SBV regulation that prevents any bank from lending more than 15 percent of its shareholders' equity to any single client, or more than 25 percent of its shareholders' equity to a client and its associate organizations and individuals.[4] Exemptions for such restrictions may be applied for on-lending from government and financial institutions. The regulation can be a constraint for large infrastructure projects, because the capital base of local banks is still relatively small; therefore, local syndication may be required, which limits the lending capability.

When calculating weighted risk of assets, banks consider the riskiest types of assets to be securities and real estate. How provincial governments' assets should be classified is unclear, both from a general regulatory standpoint and for internal risk procedure classifications within banks.

Tenor mismatching and liquidity risks

Because commercial bank deposits are short term, financing from commercial banks is not available at the long tenors needed for infrastructure projects. Generally, more than 85 percent of the total liabilities of Vietnam's commercial banks are due in less than 1 year; for some banks, the rate is as high as 98 percent.

The Vietnamese banking system suffered from an adverse liquidity crisis in 2011, when the interbank lending market was very active. As a result, Vietnamese commercial banks generally view liquidity risks as one of the key risks in their risk management system. In that regard, commercial banks will have some limitations, both in their lending capability and in their appetite for long-term lending to provincial governments, whether direct or indirect (for example, buying municipal bonds).

No recourse mechanism and high credit risks

The so-called self-budget balancing of provincial governments does not guarantee that provincial governments can repay their commercial borrowing. Some current loans to provincial governments are not fully market driven. In the absence of a clear recourse mechanism—leaving banks without any repayment guarantee from the government or international financing institutions—many Vietnamese commercial banks are unlikely to finance provincial governments because they view lending to them for infrastructure projects as too risky.

Historically, loans to government infrastructure projects at the central and provincial levels were covered with central government guarantees for repayment. Typically, those loans or lines of credit were neither tied to nor collateralized by any specific revenue source. More recently, a full credit risk guarantee is often required to reassure the lenders in the event government borrowers fail to make good on their debt service payments. As with any lending to provincial governments, banks have a difficult time understanding the financial condition of the borrowers (in this case, provincial governments) and the ability and willingness of the borrowers to make the required payments.

No credit ratings for provincial governments

The majority of commercial banks in Vietnam have their own credit rating system for local clients. However, this is not the case with provincial governments as clients. Market-driven lending to provincial governments is unprecedented for many of the banks. As a result, no credit rating system is available for provincial government borrowers. In addition, the quality of provincial governments' financial and budget information is very poor and unreliable because of the limited capacity at the local level and low accounting standards for preparing financial statements. Those conditions make it impossible for the commercial banks to assess the creditworthiness of provincial governments based on available information.

Poor project preparation and lack of accountability of provincial governments

Provincial government projects can be classified into two types: revenue generating and non–revenue generating. Commercial banks considering lending for projects of the first type will take a cautious approach to the project's credit appraisal by evaluating the provincial government on the basis of its cash flow. However, the poor quality and lack of transparency in the documents the provincial government submitted for appraisal may reduce the commercial banks' interest in evaluating such projects.

Regarding the second type, non-revenue-generating projects, some commercial banks view lending to provincial governments as grant funding from state or provincial budgets. Therefore, lending to this type of project will require some form of central government guarantee or tangible collateral. Although the repayment by provincial governments is not legally and financially mandated by commercial banks' policies, commercial banks likely will only act as agents to serve disbursements of government grant funding or on-lending if it is permitted. Commercial banks are not inclined to sue provincial governments that fail to meet their repayment obligations, however, because it would potentially damage their business operations in provincial governments' territories. Maintaining a good relationship with government at all levels is extremely important for commercial bank operations.

Reasons that banks are not inclined to buy municipal bonds

Buyers and potential buyers of municipal bonds, including commercial banks, have indicated that the interest rate (coupon) offered was not competitive; that is, alternative commercial fixed-term investments were available at more favorable rates. Central government bonds are preferred to municipal bonds because they are considered more trusted value assets. Another reason that banks avoid government projects is that provincial governments' disclosure and documentation before the sale of bonds were insufficient for municipal bonds and far below international standards and the banks' credit assessment requirements. When those conditions are not met within the commercial banks' internal credit analysis, the appetite for buying municipal bonds will be weaker.

Reasons that provincial governments are not inclined to borrow from commercial banks

Under current economic circumstances, many provincial governments are not motivated to seek commercial financing for their own investment projects. Provincial governments still compete with each other for the limited state budget, ODA, and favorable borrowings from the Vietnam Development Bank and the state treasury for their infrastructure investment projects. From the perspective of the provincial government, commercial rates are high compared with the favorable rates of the Vietnam Development Bank or state treasury. Thus, many provincial governments look at commercial borrowing only as an option of last resort to finance their infrastructure investment projects.

Another factor that hinders many provinces from issuing municipal bonds is that the procedures for issuing bonds are time consuming and cumbersome. They entail relatively high fixed costs, such as costs of documentation, advertising, and payment to securities companies, among others. Therefore, issuing municipal bonds is worthwhile only if a relatively large bond sale is being contemplated. Many provinces have borrowing needs below the economic cutoff point; thus, the high fixed cost of bond issuance means that this method will continue to be impractical for many provinces.

INCENTIVES FOR COMMERCIAL BANKS TO LEND TO PROVINCIAL GOVERNMENTS

Most commercial banks have expressed interest in entering a new market segment and lending to provincial governments, if they could know that market conditions would continue to improve. The following sections describe conditions that may act as incentives that would interest commercial banks in lending to provincial governments.

Entry into new market segments

Market-based lending to provincial governments is still new to the Vietnamese banking industry. However, commercial banks will be more willing to enter a new market segment if the government puts in place the balancing principle that addresses risk and return in lending to provincial governments. The commercial banks would prefer having the low-risk model in tandem with other financial mechanisms and instruments because, although their approach to such lending is cautious, they still need to diversify their bank portfolios. In addition, in 2013, the whole banking system had a large amount of unemployed capital—about D 200 trillion (US$9.3 billion). Although the unemployed capital was believed to be a short-term surplus, it indicated that the banking system was not short of capital during some periods. When the economy is stagnant and investment demand and individual consumption are decreasing, commercial banks often can more easily mobilize capital than they can lend or fund business activities. This has been the situation in recent years in Vietnam; thus, buying bonds is still the common practice of Vietnamese commercial banks to deal with the unemployed capital. However, in the long run, commercial banks are looking for new clients and funding opportunities to ensure their profitability. If market conditions improve, lending to provincial governments would be a new opportunity to use the unemployed capital of commercial banks.

Short-term lending to provincial governments

As a general principle, provincial governments should be free to borrow from the source that best matches their particular needs at a given time, which are not always for the long term. Provincial governments sometimes need to borrow short term for short-lived assets or short-term budget deficits. Also, they may have short-term cash management needs. Such short-term lending is an opportunity for commercial banks, which would be appropriate sources of funds needed on a short-term basis.

Other lending services needed by provincial governments

Many commercial banks believe they should be given an opportunity to earn additional profits by developing other business relationships with the provincial governments, including deposits, cash management, and wealth management. Changes in Vietnam's economic and market conditions that have raised it to a lower-middle-income country have made obtaining traditional ODA for funding infrastructure projects more difficult. Thus, such funding requires government at all levels to find ways to fill the financing gaps. The banking system and capital market will play a vital role in resolving this matter.

Many provincial governments have realized that overreliance on ODA and the state budget can lead to expensive and often inefficient infrastructure projects when contractors are appointed by ODA sponsors without international competitive bidding. In such cases, the positive effect of low interest rates can be superseded by significantly higher capital costs. In another scenario, waiting for funds from the central budget or ODA can lead to delays in infrastructure development and continued poor infrastructure services. With more autonomous power in provincial government budget planning, provincial governments that are not dependent on central budget support are expected to use their strong revenue streams to finance their investment needs. Some provincial governments have tried to improve simultaneously their business environment, to attract foreign direct investment, and their capability and accountability in infrastructure investment planning and budgeting. Those provinces will move ahead of other competing provinces and will be able to develop a sustainable business relationship with the banking sector.

New State Budget Law

The amended State Budget Law (SBL) of 2002 was approved in May 2015 and went into effect in January 2017. Accordingly, the debt ceiling of provincial governments has been set at a higher level. In the previous SBL, total outstanding borrowing could not exceed 30 percent of the provincial budget's total annual domestic capital investment. However, some important changes within the new SBL set the ceiling of outstanding borrowing as a percentage of the total provincial income. The changes affect the following:

- Special cities of Hanoi and Ho Chi Minh City, where the ceiling is 60 percent of city income
- Provinces whose actual income exceeded the budget in the previous year and that have repayment capability, which are allowed 30 percent of provincial income
- Remaining provinces that have an allowable 20 percent of provincial income.

The SBL also sets debt repayment as a priority in that it clearly requires provincial governments' annual budgets to include loan repayment.

Improved risk management and operations

Vietnamese commercial banks have improved their risk management capability tremendously over the past years, and many of them have adopted a rigorous and effective credit risk appraisal process. The overall operation of the banks has also been substantially improved. The greater accountability has made the commercial banks more confident in tapping a new segment of lending to provincial governments and project financing.

Provincial governments' preference for borrowing in local currency

Provincial governments that secure long-term debt through the central government find funding is more available in foreign currencies because these financial markets are more developed than those in Vietnam and interest rates are lower. But borrowing in foreign currencies increases the risk to the government, even with managed exchange rates, because it can increase the central government's vulnerability to external economic shocks and changes in the real exchange rate. One of the government's objectives in the medium term should be to increase the use of domestic savings to finance infrastructure improvements. Such an approach would lower the real cost of debt instruments available in Vietnamese dong. Provincial governments that fund investment projects from their own budgets also will require access to long-term private finance. To be sustainable, such funding should increasingly be denominated in Vietnamese rather than foreign currencies. Thus, commercial funding for provincial government projects would be better served by Vietnamese commercial banks.

SUMMARY OF KEY FINDINGS

The current status, key constraints, and incentives of commercial lending by Vietnamese commercial banks to provincial governments of Vietnam are summarized in table 3.6.

RAPID ASSESSMENT OF PERFORMANCE OF SELECTED COMMERCIAL BANKS

This section reports on this study's rapid assessment review of five banks that are potential candidates for the city infrastructure financing facility (CIFF) mechanism. The five banks, which are broadly assessed in a rapid assessment, include two SOCBs (the state-owned commercial banks Vietcombank and VietinBank); two JSCBs (the joint-stock commercial banks LienVietPostBank and Maritime Bank); and one foreign bank (HSBC Vietnam). The assessment is based on their performance, including balance sheets, NPLs, local government lending portfolios, corporate governance, and credit and risk management system. The analysis can help provide an initial idea of the size of the CIFF and qualification criteria during the CIFF design phase.

TABLE 3.6 **Key Findings on Lending to Provincial Governments by Commercial Banks**

	CURRENT STATUS	KEY CONSTRAINTS AND HINDRANCES	KEY INCENTIVES
1	Commercial banks can lend directly to provincial governments without guarantees or collateral. Repayment is based on the provincial governments' annual budgets. The longest tenor of lending to provincial governments is two years.	Prudent banking regulations.	Entry into new market segment.
2	Provincial governments' lending portfolios consist mainly of municipal bonds.	Tenor mismatching and liquidity risks.	Unemployed capital in banking system.
3	Commercial banks take full credit risk in lending to provincial governments under the current legal and market conditions, but they have unclear risk mitigation strategies.	No recourse mechanism and high credit risks.	Offer of other services to provincial governments through lending to provincial governments.
4	Provincially owned enterprises' borrowing raises the contingent liabilities of provincial governments.	No credit ratings for provincial governments and lack of reliable information to assess creditworthiness of provincial government borrowers.	Short-term lending to provincial governments.
5	Long-term commercial bank lending is not available to provincial governments.	Poor project preparation and accountability of provincial governments.	Changes in economic and market conditions.
6	Commercial financing to provincial governments is prevailing, but local capital markets are undeveloped.	Unattractiveness of municipal bonds for some commercial banks.	The State Budget Law and the possibility of introducing a recourse mechanism.
7	Directed lending and lending with government guarantees are common.	Insufficient motivation of many provincial governments to borrow from commercial banks.	Improvement of risk management capability and overall operations of commercial banks.
8	Provincial governments are currently not qualified as borrowers for institutional investors and foreign banks.		Preference of provincial governments to borrow in Vietnamese dong than in foreign currencies.

Although the banks consulted in the assessment have a limited appetite for lending to local governments now, they have expressed interest in such lending when the CIFF mechanism is in place. The local commercial banks generally view wholesale and credit enhancement options as low-risk and high-risk models, respectively, and the first option would be more favorable from the local banks' perspectives because the source of capital is secured by the CIFF. However, the foreign bank would be more interested in the credit enhancement option because it may reduce credit risks for the bank.

Vietcombank

Established in 1963 as a state-owned commercial bank, the Bank for Foreign Trade of Vietnam (Vietcombank) is the oldest commercial bank for external affairs in Vietnam. It was the first bank in the country to have a centralized capital management structure and the first commercial bank to deal in foreign currencies. After more than half a century in operation, the bank has more than 400 branches, transaction offices, representative offices, and affiliates, both in Vietnam and abroad. Its Vietnamese offices include a head office in Hanoi, one operation center, one training center, 89 branches, and over 350 transaction offices all over the country. The bank also has three subsidiaries in Vietnam, two subsidiaries in other countries, one representative office in Singapore, and six

TABLE 3.7 **Key Financial Information for Vietcombank**

	2014	2015
Indicators in D, billions		
Total assets	576,996	674,395
Loan portfolio	316,254	378,542
Deposits	422,204	500,528
Shareholder funds	43,473	45,172
Profit after tax/net income	4,585	5,332
Return on assets, %	0.88	0.85
Return on equity, %	10.76	12.03

Source: Vietcombank Annual Report 2015.

joint ventures. In addition, Vietcombank has developed an automatic banking system with 2,100 automated teller machines and 49,500 points of sale nationwide. The bank's operations are supported by a network of more than 1,800 correspondent banks in 155 countries and territories.

Vietcombank expanded from its original role as North Vietnam's foreign trade bank to become one of the country's largest universal banks. It is also an investor in a number of other financial institutions, including Vietnam Export Import Commercial Joint Stock Bank (CJSB), Saigon Industrial and Commercial CJSB, Gia Dinh CJSB, Military CJSB, International Commercial CJSB, Oriental CJSB, Chohungvina Bank, Petroleum Insurance Company, and Golden Insurance Company. In 2015, Vietcombank increased its charter capital from D 55 billion (US$2.6 million) to D 265 billion (US$12.3 million). The bank has been expanding its assets volume and it reached D 674 trillion (US$31.4 billion) in 2015 (table 3.7).

Balance sheet assessment

As figure 3.9 shows, the three main components of Vietcombank assets in 2013 were loans and advances to customers (56 percent), placement with and loans to other financial institutions (20 percent), and investment securities and other financial assets (16 percent). The majority of total outstanding loans are lending for SOEs, and 20 percent is for retail loans (figure 3.10).

In January 2015, the governor of the SBV said that Saigonbank would merge with Vietcombank as part of restructuring in the sector, resulting in the following shareholder structure: government (77.1 percent); Mizuho Corporate Bank Ltd., Japan (15.0 percent); and other shareholders (7.9 percent).

As shown in figure 3.11, Vietcombank's lending balance concentrates on manufacturing and processing (32 percent); trading (27 percent); and agriculture, forestry, aquaculture, and mining (8 percent). By far, the majority of its lending is for loans of less than a year (figure 3.12).

Exposure of lending to provincial governments

Vietcombank also lends to provincial governments as follows:

- **Municipal bonds.** Vietcombank has bought about D 1.839 trillion par value of Hanoi and Ho Chi Minh City's municipal bonds with 3- to 5-year tenors and coupon rates of 7.2–10.7 percent.
- **Direct lending to provincial governments.** So far, Vietcombank has not lent to any provincial governments, but it has lent to two major cities (table 3.8).

FIGURE 3.9
Vietcombank Asset Portfolio

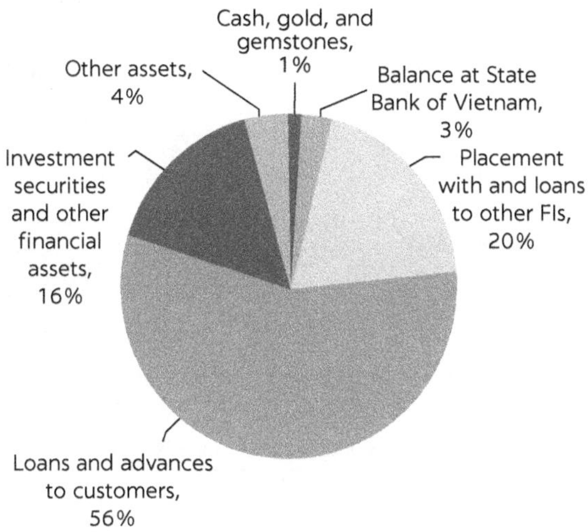

Source: Vietcombank Annual Report 2015.
Note: FI = financial institution.

FIGURE 3.10
Customer Shares of Vietcombank's Loan Portfolio

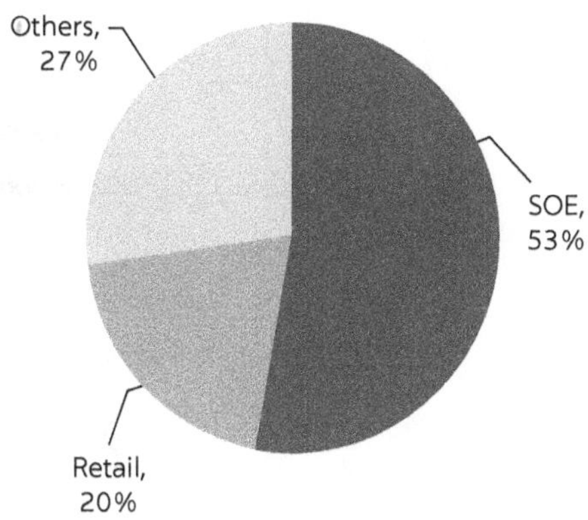

Source: Vietcombank Annual Report 2015.
Note: SOE = state-owned enterprise.

FIGURE 3.11
Vietcombank's Loan Portfolio, by Industry

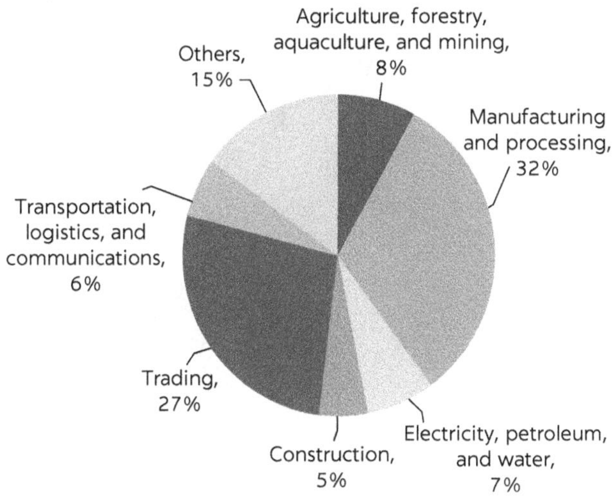

Source: Vietcombank Annual Report 2015.

FIGURE 3.12
Length of Terms in Loan Shares of Vietcombank's Loan Portfolio

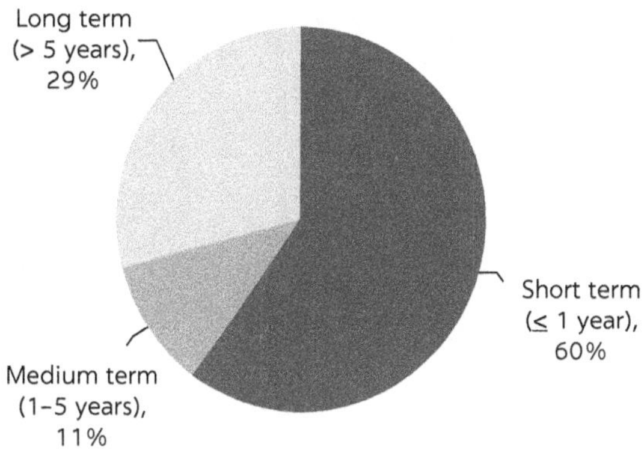

Source: Vietcombank Annual Report 2015.

- **Experience of lending to infrastructure projects (including provincial government projects).** Vietcombank has taken lending exposure to road and seaport projects undertaken by private companies and SOEs under the BOT route. The bank has also provided loans to subcontractors of the Ministry of Finance for big infrastructure projects. For such infrastructure projects, the tenor is 2–15 years, and interest rates are 10–10.5 percent.

Liquidity

Vietcombank has traditionally maintained a reasonable level of liquidity, and this has become even more important in view of economic instability and some

TABLE 3.8 **Vietcombank's Direct Loan Transactions with Vietnam's Two Biggest Cities: Hanoi and Ho Chi Minh City**

LOANS	D, MILLIONS
Provincial government bonds	**1,838,889**
Hanoi	688,889
Ho Chi Minh City	1,150,000
Direct loans to provincial governments	**None**
Total provincial government portfolio	**1,838,889**
Total loan portfolio	378,542,000
Total assets	674,395,000
Direct loans to provincial governments as a share of the total loan portfolio, %	**0**
Total provincial government portfolio as a share of total assets, %	**0.2**

Source: Vietcombank Annual Report 2013.

FIGURE 3.13
Vietcombank Liquidity Ratios

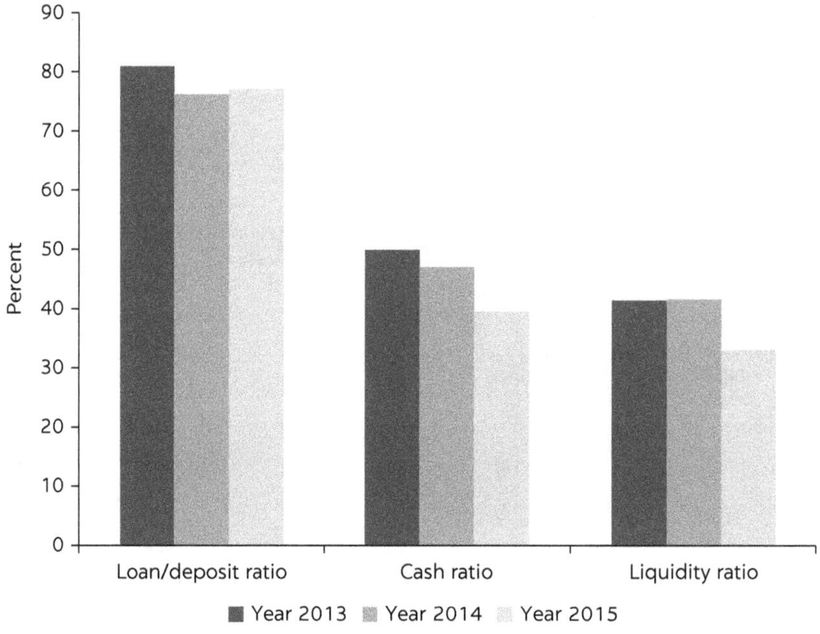

Source: Vietcombank Annual Report 2015.

tightening of liquidity in the local market. Though the bank's liquidity ratio declined from 41 to 33 percent from 2013 to 2015 (figure 3.13), it is still well above Vietnam's industry average liquidity ratio of 16 percent and the global industry average liquidity ratio of 15 percent, indicating a relatively solid liquidity position. The bank has been deploying customer deposits toward interest-earning assets, with a loans-to-deposits ratio above Vietnam's industry average (67 percent) and the global average (70 percent). Most of the liability is for less than a year (table 3.9 and figure 3.14), whereas around two-thirds of the loans are short to medium term in nature. The bank is focusing on developing new deposit products with a particular emphasis on lengthening the maturity profile of its

TABLE 3.9 **Vietcombank's Net Liquidity Gap (as of June 2016), D, millions**

	OVERDUE		NOT OVERDUE					TOTAL
	OVER 3 MONTHS	UP TO 3 MONTHS	UP TO 1 MONTH	1 TO 3 MONTHS	3 TO 12 MONTHS	1 TO 5 YEARS	OVER 5 YEARS	
Total assets	7,633,387	30,688,618	241,387,271	152,311,043	152,683,160	71,279,890	27,762,105	683,745,474
Total liabilities	n.a.	12,607,781	383,547,432	111,817,968	111,954,885	7,276,950	2,017,282	629,222,298
Net liquidity gap	7,633,387	18,080,837	(142,160,161)	40,493,075	40,728,275	64,002,940	25,744,823	54,523,176

Source: Vietcombank Annual Report 2015.
Note: n.a. = not applicable.

deposit portfolio, a strategy that is important in view of the current mismatch.

FIGURE 3.14
Length of Total Liability of Vietcombank

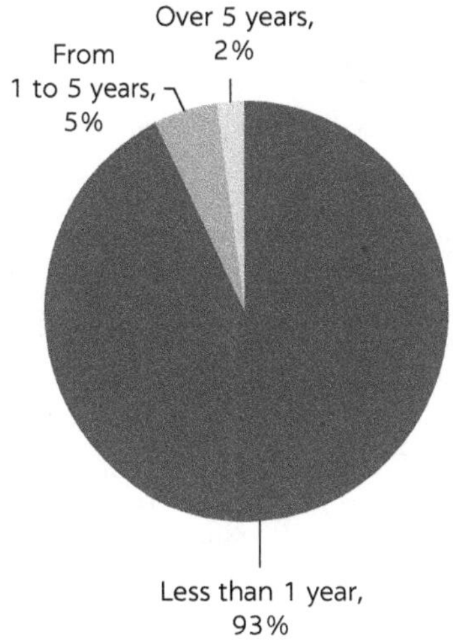

Source: Vietcombank Annual Report 2015.

Nonperforming loans

The level of NPLs at Vietcombank reached 2.7 percent in 2013 and decreased to 1.8 percent in 2015, well below the Vietnam industry and global industry NPLs average of 2.5 percent. An increase in the amount of bad debts in 2013 was entirely due to the higher proportion of lending to SOEs in the bank's loan portfolio.

Corporate governance

The system of bank governance and control in Vietnam is somewhat different from most other countries, which have a clear definition of roles and responsibilities and a clear separation of powers between board and management. They also have an internal audit function and a board audit committee that serve as a key mechanism in this overall governance and control structure. The board of directors of Vietcombank is a full-time board appointed by the government, which is a shareholder. In addition to the government-appointed members, the board has a representative from the Mizuho Corporate Bank Ltd., Japan. A supervisory board independent of the board of directors also reports to the general assembly of shareholders. The supervisory board is mainly responsible for operational control and internal audit of bank operations. However, the internal audit function differs from the standard international practice.

In Vietnam, an internal control function reports to the supervisory board and is actively involved in the control and compliance process. In addition, a State Audit Bureau carries out audit work on all SOEs, including the state banks. The supervisory board currently has four members, all of whom are full-time employees of the bank. The supervisory board meets monthly and reports to the bank's board of directors on a regular basis. The supervisory board also monitors the implementation of long-term strategies and goals at the bank, as well as ensures that the accounting systems at Vietcombank are in line with current regulations and principles.

Credit and risk management

The bank adopted a centralized management system for reducing credit risk that is structured procedurally into risk management, sales, and operations. The objective of separating the three types of functions is to minimize risks and take advantage of credit officers' expertise. The bank credit manual sets out procedures for credit policy, the credit management process, and credit assessment and control. The procedures are important because the bank has delegated authorities at the branch level for lending up to a certain amount. The board of directors, which has the highest responsibility for the bank's overall risk management, promulgates risk management policies and strategies for each period, establishes secured business limits, and directly approves high-value business transactions in accordance with both legal and internal requirements.

LienVietPostBank

In operation since 2008, Lien Viet Post Joint Stock Commercial Bank, or LienVietPostBank (LVPB), formerly known as LienVietBank, is a Vietnamese retail bank that provides banking products and services through its own transaction points across 42 cities and provinces and 1,031 postal transaction offices nationwide. By the end of 2015, LVPB had 4,023 employees.

The founder shareholders include Him Lam Joint Stock Company, Saigon Trading Group, and Southern Airports Service Company. In 2011 Vietnam Post Corporation became the LVPB's biggest shareholder by contributing capital to the bank equal to the value of the Vietnam Postal Savings Service Company, including cash. The merger was one of the most notable in Vietnam at that time and is a milestone in the development of the bank. The LVPB then changed its name to Lien Viet Post Joint Stock Commercial Bank and became the first postal bank in Vietnam. The bank focuses on developing banking products for households and SMEs and on expanding its activities to rural and remote areas using the post office network. The chartered capital by December 2015 was D 6,460 billion (US$300 million). In 2015, the total assets of LVPB reached D 107 trillion (US$ 5.1 billion), putting the bank among top 15 largest JSCBs in Vietnam (table 3.10).

Balance sheet assessment

As figure 3.15 shows, the three main components of LVPB assets in 2015 were loans and advances to customers (52 percent), investment securities and other financial assets (30 percent), and placement with and loans to other financial institutions (5 percent).

TABLE 3.10 **Key Financial Information for LienVietPostBank**

	2014	2015
Indicators in D, billions		
Total assets	100,801	107,587
Loan portfolio	40,815	55,470
Deposits	77,820	77,629
Shareholder funds	7,391	7,600
Profit after tax	466	350
Return on assets, %	0.46	0.33
Return on equity, %	6.31	4.60

Source: LienVietPostBank Annual Report 2015.

FIGURE 3.15

LienVietPostBank Asset Portfolio

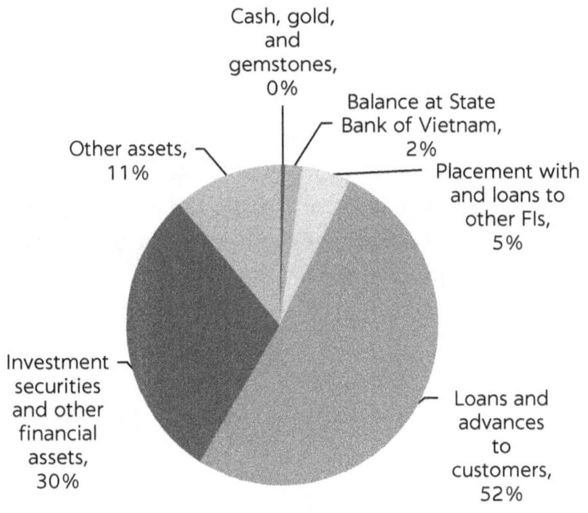

Source: LVPB Annual Report 2015.
Note: FI = financial institutions.

FIGURE 3.16

Customer Shares of LienVietPostBank Loan Portfolio

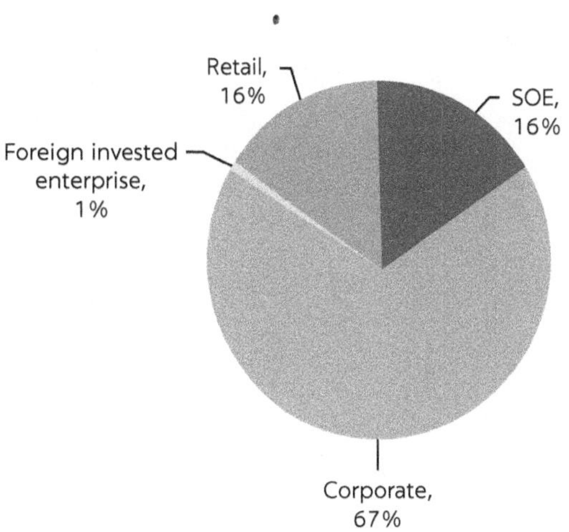

Source: LVPB Annual Report 2013. Annual report of 2015 has no available data on customer shares.
Note: SOE = state-owned enterprise.

FIGURE 3.17

LienVietPostBank Loan Portfolio, by Industry

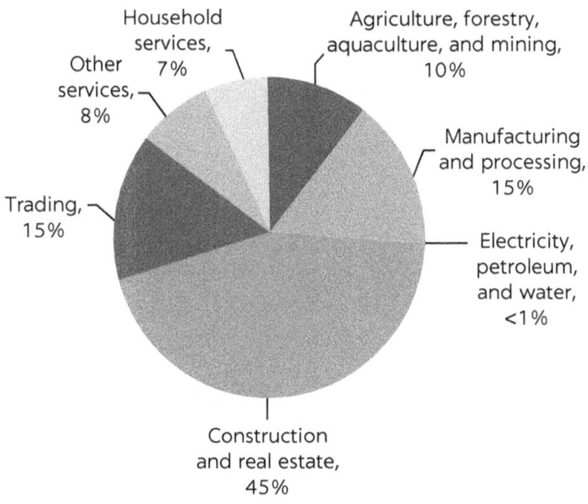

Source: LVPB Annual Report 2013. Annual report of 2015 has no available data on sector shares.

FIGURE 3.18

Length of Terms in Loan Shares of LienVietPostBank Loan Portfolio

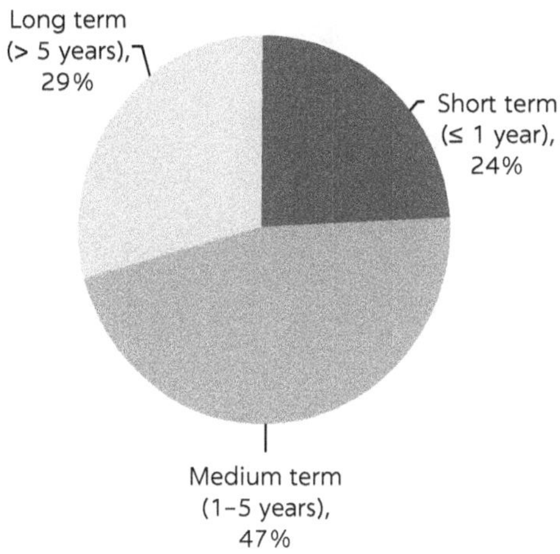

Source: LVPB Annual Report 2015.

Shareholder structure is Vietnam Post (13 percent); Him Lam (15 percent); individual and institutional shareholders (72 percent). LVPB's lending balance was concentrated in corporations (67 percent), retail (16 percent), and SOE (16 percent) (figure 3.16).

LVPB's lending balance concentrated on construction and real estate (45 percent), trading (15 percent), and manufacturing and processing (15 percent) (figure 3.17). Most of the loans are short to medium term in nature (figure 3.18).

Exposure of lending to provincial governments

As table 3.11 shows, LVPB also lends to provincial governments as follows:

- **Municipal bonds.** LVPB has bought D 780 billion par value of Hanoi and Ho Chi Minh City's municipal bonds with 3- to 5-year tenors and coupon rates of 6–7 percent.
- **Direct lending to provincial governments.** So far LVPB has only lent to Thai Nguyen province through the Thai Nguyen provincial land development fund with the loan amount of D 80 billion, tenor of 2 years, and interest rate of 9 percent. The repayment is a bullet repayment at the end of the project, and the source is assumed to be the provincial budget.
- **Experience in lending to infrastructure projects.** LVPB has experience in lending to roads and bridge projects (via the BOT route) through bilateral loans, syndicated loans, and subscription to government bonds. The bank also extends loans to subcontractors for the Ministry of Finance's large infrastructure projects.

Liquidity

The bank's liquidity ratio decreased from 31 percent in 2013 to 22 percent in 2015, and cash ratio decreased from 57 percent to 31 percent, mainly due to a greater allocation of customer deposits to fund customer loans and other interest earning assets (figure 3.19). While this may reflect that the solvency position of the bank has been deteriorating, the liquidity ratio for the bank is still well above the Vietnam industry average (16 percent) as well as the global industry average (15 percent). The vast majority of liability is less than 1 year (figure 3.20), however nearly half of the loans are medium term. The bank may consider paying more attention to addressing its potential asset liability mismatch problem.

Nonperforming loans

The level of reported NPLs declined from 2.5 percent in 2013 to less than 1 percent in 2015. That decline was completely due to the increase in the loan portfolio. The bank's NPLs were mainly from bad debts in construction

TABLE 3.11 **LienVietPostBank's Lending to Cities and Provinces**

LOANS	D, MILLIONS
Provincial government bonds	**780,000**
Hanoi	580,000
Ho Chi Minh City	200,000
Direct loans to provincial governments	**80,000**
Thai Nguyen province	80,000
Total provincial government portfolio	**860,000**
Total loan portfolio	55,470,000
Total assets	107,587,000
Direct loans to provincial governments as share of total loan portfolio, %	**0.01**
Total provincial government portfolio as share of total assets, %	**0.80**

Source: LVPB Annual Report 2015.

FIGURE 3.19
LienVietPostBank Liquidity Ratios

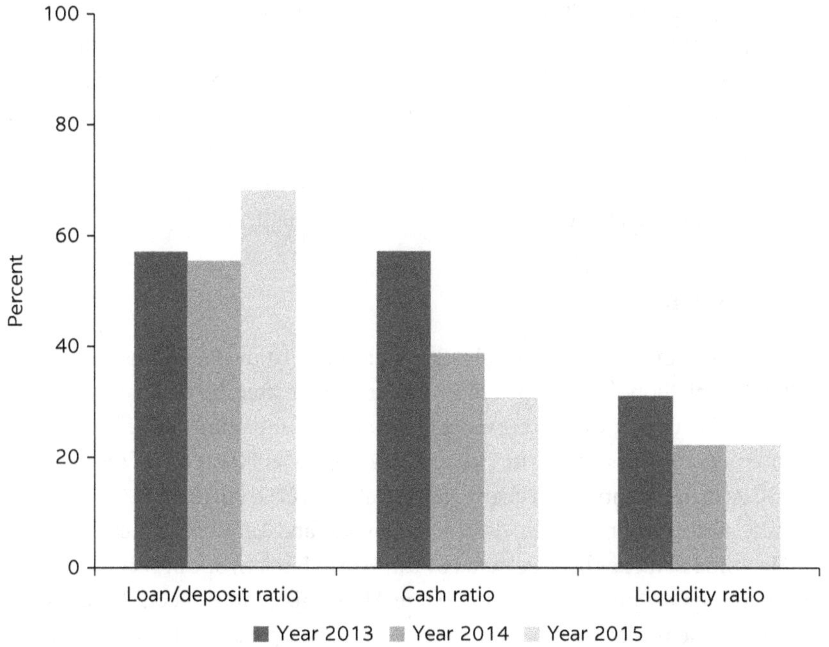

Source: LVPB Annual Report 2015.

FIGURE 3.20
Length of Total Liability of LienVietPostBank

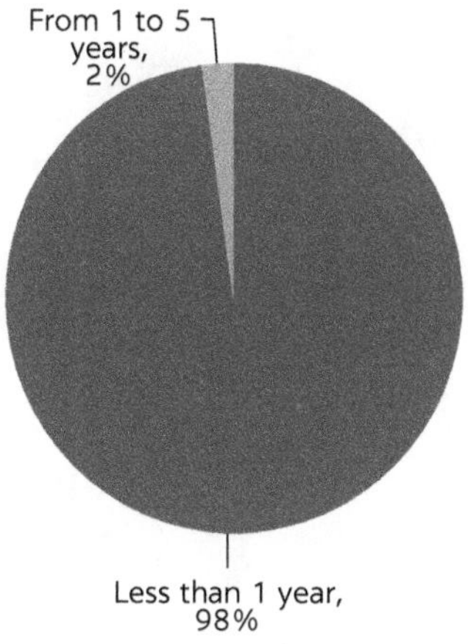

Source: LVPB Annual Report 2015.

TABLE 3.12 **LienVietPostBank's Net Liquidity Gap (as of June 2016), D, millions**

	OVERDUE		NOT OVERDUE					TOTAL
	OVER 3 MONTHS	UP TO 3 MONTHS	UP TO 1 MONTH	1 TO 3 MONTHS	3 TO 12 MONTHS	1 TO 5 YEARS	OVER 5 YEARS	
Total assets	404,743	139,812	24,736,775	8,991,710	15,205,108	40,479,159	18,680,940	108,638,247
Total liabilities	n.a.	n.a.	44,417,669	19,624,480	25,129,414	7,942,597	2,872,705	99,986,865
Net liquidity gap	404,743	139,812	(19,680,894)	(10,632,770)	(9,924,306)	32,536,562	15,808,235	8,651,382

Source: LVPB Annual Report 2015.
Note: n.a. = not applicable.

and real estate industries, which account for around 45 percent of LVPB's lending portfolio.

Corporate governance

LVPB has a good corporate governance structure in place with a clear separation of duties between the board of directors and management, although there are no members of management on the board. The board has three committees, each with a number of councils with different responsibilities. The three committees are the Strategy, Technology, Business, and International Relations Committee; the Human Resources, Credit, and Cost Management Committee; and the Asset-Liability, Risk Management, and Anti-Money Laundering Committee. The supervisory board includes an internal audit division and departments of backup, periodical audit, and regular supervision as well as a Postal Transaction Office audit. This board is independent of bank management. Overall, the bank has a strong organizational structure with a clear identification of the main functions and responsibilities.

Credit and risk management

The credit and risk management process of LVPB is not as straightforward as corporate governance. Credit and risk management seem to be both fragmented and duplicated among subcommittees and functional councils. Therefore, the bank implemented credit monitoring and centralized debt resolution at the head office in 2013, while enhancing credit granting monitoring at business units by promulgating internal regulations in compliance with the board's guidance and direction. In addition, in 2013 the bank also revised its organizational structure to enhance the effectiveness of credit risk management.

Maritime bank

Vietnam Maritime Commercial Joint Stock Bank (Maritime Bank) was established in 1991 in Hai Phong City. It opened for business right after the Ordinance on Joint Stock Banks, Credit Cooperatives, and Finance Companies took effect, and it became one of the first JSCBs in Vietnam. In 2015, the bank was one of the five largest JSCBs in the country, with chartered capital of D 11,750 billion (US$547 million), a branch network of nearly 300 offices nationwide, and 3,268 employees.

Maritime Bank has been selected by the World Bank as one of six commercial banks in the two-phased Banking System Modernization Project.[5] It has benefited from the project and built a modern banking operational system meeting international standards. The total assets of the bank maintained at around D 104 trillion (US$ 4.9 billion) in 2014 and 2015 (table 3.13).

Balance sheet assessment

As figure 3.21 shows, the three main components of Maritime Bank assets in 2015 were investment securities and other financial assets (47 percent), loans and advances to customers (26 percent), and placement with and loans to other financial institutions (11 percent).

Main shareholders were the Vietnam Post and Telecommunication Group (6.1 percent), the Phuc Tien Investment LLC (6.5 percent), and others (87.4 percent).

Maritime Bank's lending balance is highly concentrated in corporate sectors (79 percent), retail (12 percent), and SOE (9 percent) (figure 3.22). The loan portfolio is relatively balanced, both by industry and by length of loan (figures 3.23 and 3.24).

TABLE 3.13 **Key Financial Information for Maritime Bank**

	2014	2015
Indicators in D, billions		
Total assets	104,369	104,311
Loan portfolio	22,967	27,490
Deposits	63,219	62,616
Shareholder funds	9,446	13,616
Profit after tax	143	116
Return on assets, %	0.14	0.11
Return on equity, %	1.51	0.85

Source: Maritime Bank Annual Report 2015.

FIGURE 3.21

Maritime Bank Asset Portfolio

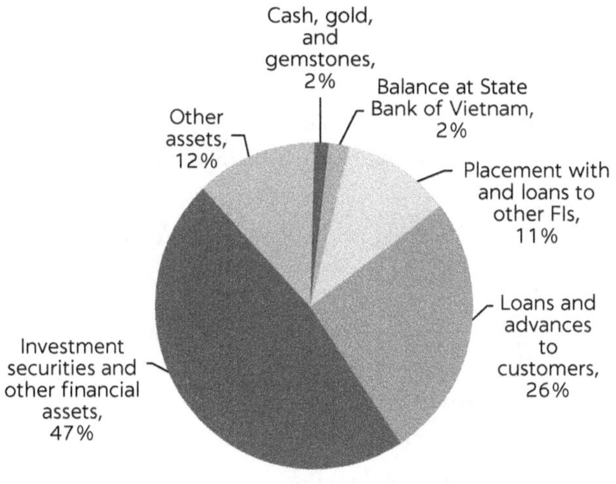

Source: Maritime Bank Annual Report 2015.

FIGURE 3.22

Customer Shares of Maritime Bank

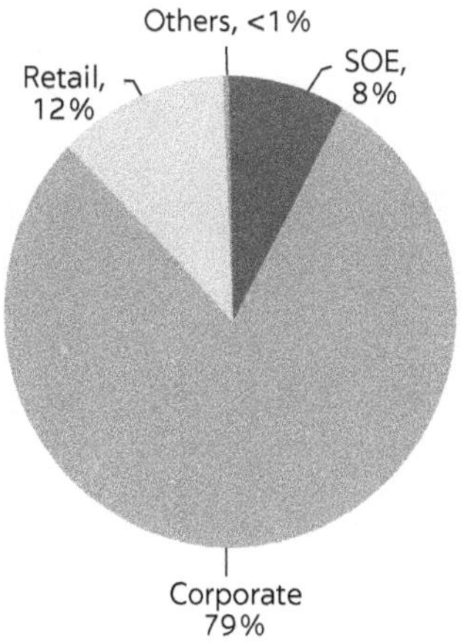

Source: Maritime Bank Annual Report 2015.
Note: SOE = state-owned enterprise.

FIGURE 3.23

Maritime Bank's Loan Portfolio, by Industry

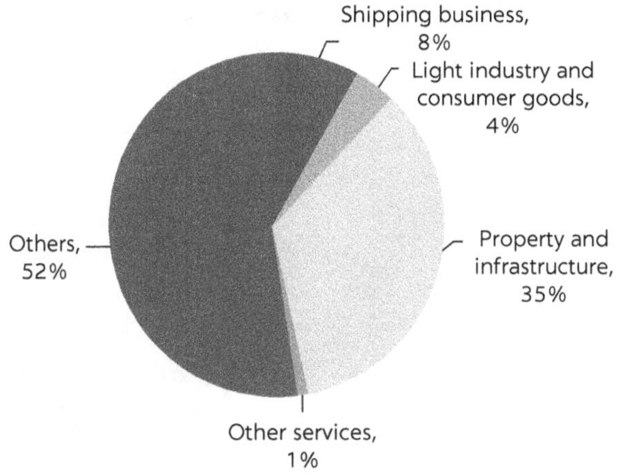

Source: Maritime Bank Annual Report 2015.

FIGURE 3.24

Length of Terms in Loan Shares of Maritime Bank's Loan Portfolio

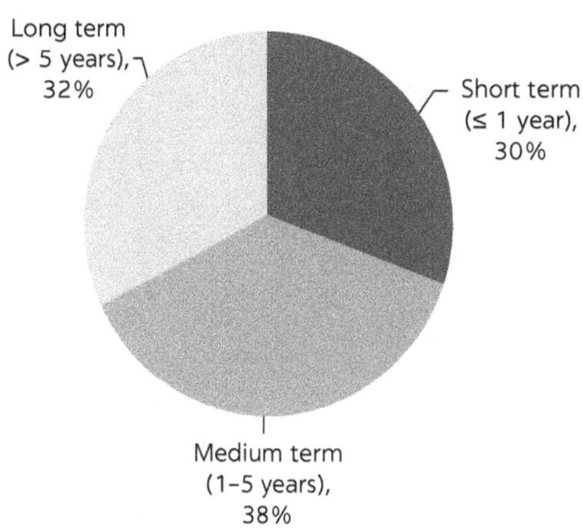

Source: Maritime Bank Annual Report 2015.

Exposure of lending to provincial governments

Maritime Bank has not been lending to provincial governments but has been buying some municipal bonds. The bank has not disclosed data about outstanding municipal bonds.

Liquidity

The bank may consider further improving its solvency position to manage fiscal risk. Its liquidity ratio and cash ratio are low compared with the Vietnam industry averages (figure 3.25), which are 16 and 21 percent respectively. The loans to deposits ratio is declining and well below the Vietnam's average of 67 percent and the global industry average of 70 percent, indicating that there is still liquidity margin for the bank to cover unforeseen funding requirements. Because the bank is deploying most of its deposits (short-term in nature) to provide short- to medium-term loans, the bank is less likely to face asset liability mismatch problems (figures 3.25 and 3.26, and table 3.14).

Nonperforming loans

The bank has been improving its asset quality. The level of NPLs at Maritime Bank declined from 2.7 percent in 2013 to 2.6 percent in 2015, around the industry average in Vietnam. The increasing amount of bad debts during 2012 to 2013 was mainly due to the high proportion of lending to the troubled shipping industry.

Corporate governance

Maritime Bank has a good corporate governance structure in place, with a clear separation of duties between the board and management. The bank's board of directors does not have any members of management on the board. The board has six committees: credit and investment board, board risk handling committee, board risk management committee, human resources committee, strategy committee, and audit committee. The supervisory board has an internal audit function in place that reports to the shareholders and is independent of the bank management.

FIGURE 3.25
Maritime Bank Liquidity Ratios

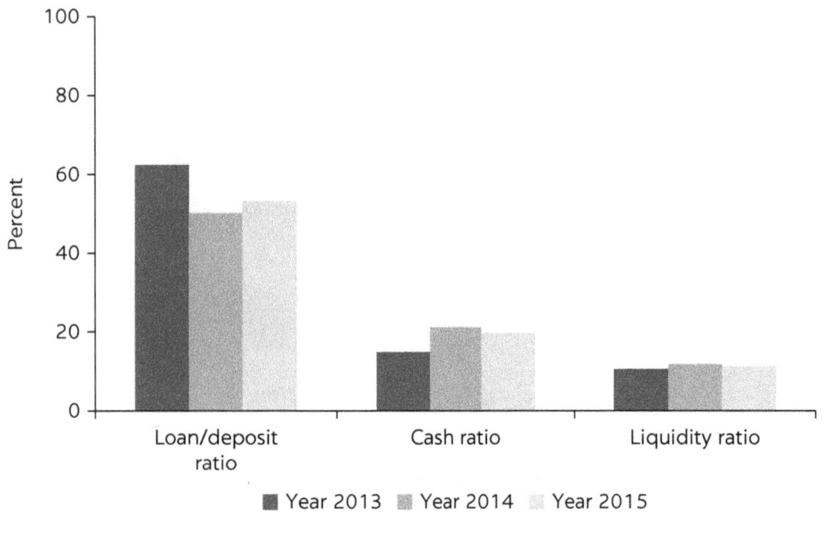

Source: Maritime Bank Annual Report 2015.

FIGURE 3.26
Length of Total Liability of Maritime Bank

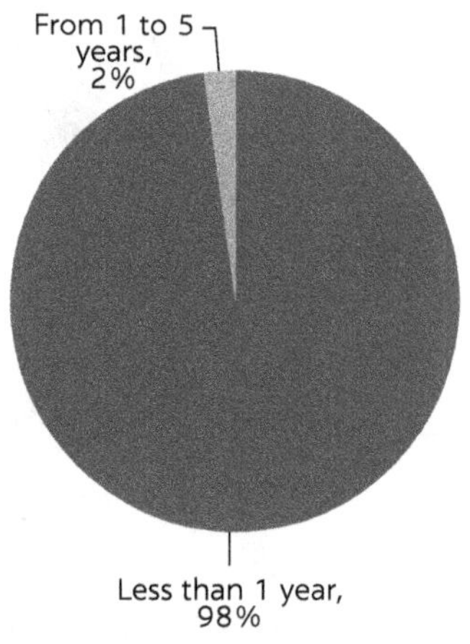

Source: Maritime Bank Annual Report 2015.

TABLE 3.14 **Maritime Bank's Net Liquidity Gap (as of June 2016), D, millions**

	OVERDUE	FREE OF INTEREST	UP TO 1 MONTH	1 TO 3 MONTHS	3 TO 12 MONTHS	1 TO 5 YEARS	OVER 5 YEARS	TOTAL
Total assets	4,287,125	16,981,986	39,366,852	5,472,341	15,043,764	20,161,719	4,529,183	105,842,970
Total liabilities	n.a.	2,767,891	33,827,211	22,102,512	25,323,225	3,136,680	182,515	90,844,456
Net liquidity gap	4,287,125	14,214,095	5,539,641	(16,630,171)	(10,279,461)	17,025,039	4,346,668	14,998,514

Source: Maritime Bank Annual Report 2015.
Note: n.a. = not applicable.

Credit and risk management

The bank has developed an internal rating system and credit policies that apply to specific customer segments: SMEs, large corporate and financial institutions, and retail and community.

VietinBank

The Vietnam Bank for Industry and Trade (VietinBank), formerly the Industrial and Commercial Bank of Vietnam, was established in 1988 when it was separated from the SBV. It became a state-owned corporation in 1993. As one of the four largest SOCBs in the country, VietinBank's total assets account for a significant part of the market share of the whole Vietnamese banking system. VietinBank's capital resources have continued to increase over the years and have risen substantially since 1996, with annual average growth of 20 percent. In December 2008 the bank carried out an initial purchase offer, and the shares were subsequently listed on the Ho Chi Minh Stock Exchange in July 2009. The shareholder structure is 64.5 percent SBV, 19.7 percent Bank of Tokyo-Mitsubishi, 8.0 percent International Finance Corporation (IFC), and 7.8 percent, others.

The bank has an extensive network of 150 branches and over 1,000 transaction offices throughout the country, employing 21,024 personnel. In 2015 the bank's charter capital was D37,234 billion (US$1.73 billion). The bank is particularly strong in certain sectors, such as the oil and gas industry, coal, and food processing and supply, and it has a strong relationship with many state-owned companies in these sectors. The asset size of VietinBank remained the largest in the local banking system, with a volume of D779 trillion (US$36.3 billion) in 2015 (table 3.15).

Balance sheet assessment

As seen in figure 3.27, the three main components of VietinBank's Assets in 2015 were loans and advances to customers (68 percent), investment securities and other financial assets (15 percent), and placement with and loans to other financial institutions (8 percent).

VietinBank's corporate lending accounted for nearly a half of total outstanding loans, and about 17 percent of outstanding loans were for SOEs (figure 3.28).

VietinBank's lending balance concentrates on manufacturing and processing (29 percent); trading (28 percent); and construction (11 percent) (figure 3.29). Its loan portfolio is more than half short-term loans (figure 3.30).

TABLE 3.15 **Key Financial Information for VietinBank**

	2014	2015
Indicators in D, billions		
Total assets	661,242	779,483
Loan portfolio	435,502	533,530
Deposits	424,181	492,960
Shareholder funds	55,259	56,109
Profit after tax	5,726	5,716
Return on assets, %	0.87	0.73
Return on equity, %	10.36	10.19

Source: VietinBank Annual Report 2015.

FIGURE 3.27
VietinBank Asset Portfolio

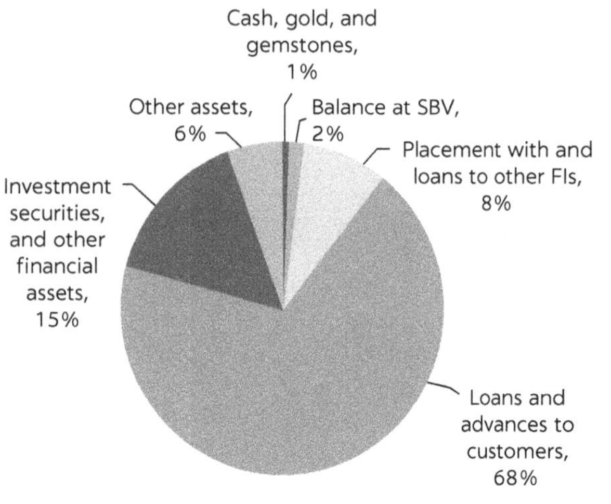

Source: VietinBank Annual Report 2015.
Notes: SBV = State Bank of Vietnam; FI = financial institution.

FIGURE 3.28
Customer Shares of VietinBank's Loan Portfolio

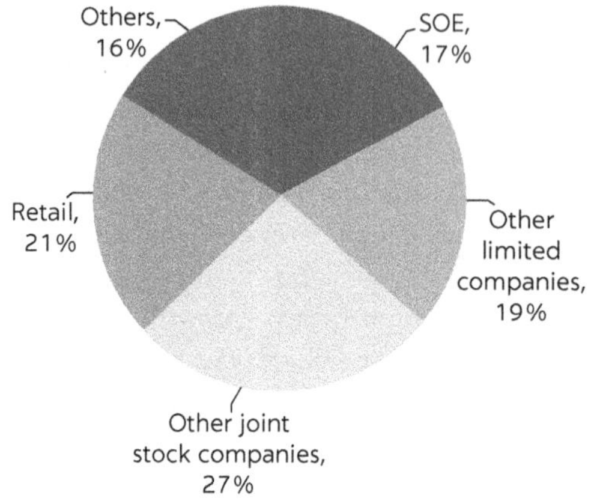

Source: VietinBank Annual Report 2015.
Note: SOE = state-owned enterprise.

FIGURE 3.29
VietinBank's Loan Portfolio, by Industry

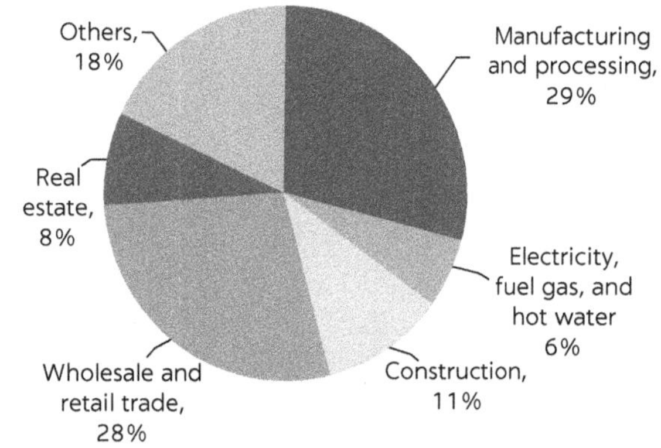

Source: VietinBank Annual Report 2015.

FIGURE 3.30
Length of Terms in Loan Shares of VietinBank's Loan Portfolio

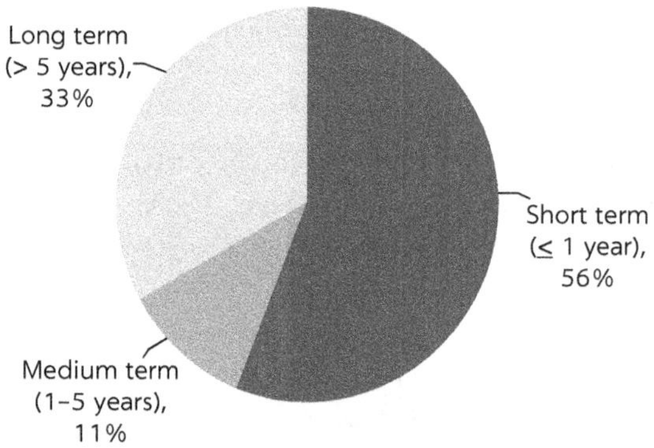

Source: VietinBank Annual Report 2015.

Exposure of lending to provincial governments

VietinBank also lends to provincial governments (table 3.16) as follows:

- **Municipal bonds.** VietinBank bought D 2.75 trillion par value of municipal bonds from four provinces: Hanoi, Ho Chi Minh City, Quang Ninh, and Bac Ninh, with the longest tenor of 10 years and coupon rates of 7.2–8.7 percent.
- **Direct lending to provincial governments.** VietinBank lent to two provincial governments. The first direct provincial government loan of D 8 trillion was granted to Ho Chi Minh City's Provincial People's Committee for its Thu Thiem Tunnel Project Management Unit. The second direct provincial government loan was to Dong Nai province for D 1.2 trillion, with a 2-year tenor and interest rate of 7 percent for non-revenue-generating infrastructure projects. The repayment source was assumed to be the provincial budget. The typical source of funding for these loans has been the short-term deposits of the bank.

TABLE 3.16 **VietinBank's Portfolio of Lending to Provincial Governments**

LOANS	D, MILLIONS
Provincial government bonds	**2,750,000**
Hanoi	1,000,000
Ho Chi Minh City	550,000
Quang Ninh province	800,000
Bac Ninh province	400,000
Direct loans to provincial governments	**9,200,000**
Ho Chi Minh City	8,000,000
Dong Nai province	1,200,000
Total provincial government portfolio	**11,950,000**
Total loan portfolio	533,530,000
Total assets	779,483,000
Direct loans to local governments/total loan portfolio	**1.7**
Percent total provincial government portfolio/total assets	**1.5**

Source: VietinBank Annual Report 2015.

Liquidity

The bank is operating on a liquidity ratio at par with the Vietnam industry average liquidity ratio (16 percent) and slightly above the global average level (15 percent). The bank needs to focus on maintaining a strong liquidity position, especially because the loan/deposit ratio of the bank stood at a very high level (nearly 100 percent). An ambitious credit growth plan will also put pressure on the liquidity of the bank. The bank may consider improving its solvency position by increasing the deployment of deposits toward liquid assets. Given that the majority of the bank's deposits are deployed to provide short- to medium-term loans, the bank is less likely to face asset mismatch problems (figures 3.31, 3.32 and table 3.17).

Nonperforming loans

The level of NPLs at VietinBank was 0.8 percent in 2013 further down to 0.7 percent, much lower than the overall market level. Part of the reason for the improvement was the strong growth in the portfolio during this period. The other cause was that VietinBank had sold its bad debts at their book value to the Vietnam Asset Management Company.

Corporate governance

The system of bank governance and control is somewhat different in Vietnam than in most other developed countries, which have a clear definition of roles and responsibilities and a clear separation of powers between board and management, as well as an internal audit function and board audit committee as a key mechanism in this overall governance and control structure. The board of directors of VietinBank is a full-time board appointed by the government as shareholder. In addition to the government-appointed members, representatives also come from the Bank of Tokyo-Mitsubishi and the IFC. There is also a supervisory board independent of the board of directors that reports to the general assembly of shareholders. One of the main functions of the supervisory board is to manage and control the internal audit function. However, this function differs

FIGURE 3.31
VietinBank Liquidity Ratios

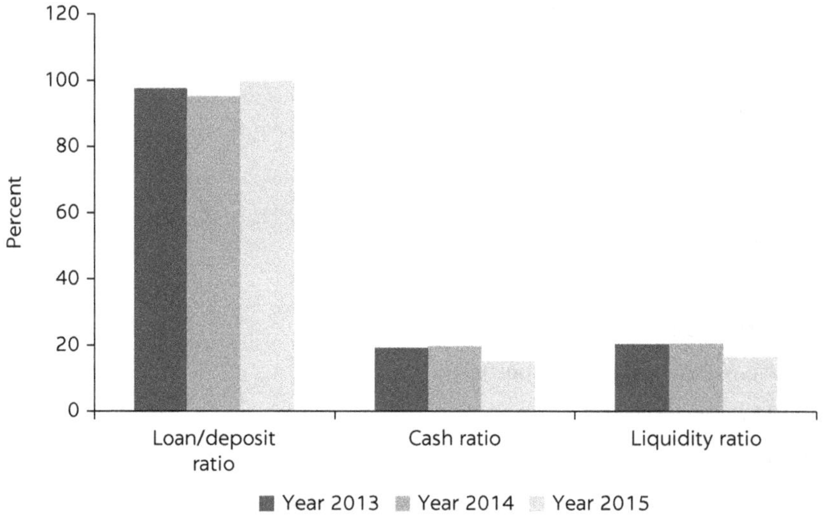

Source: VietinBank Annual Report 2015.

FIGURE 3.32
Length of Total Liability of VietinBank

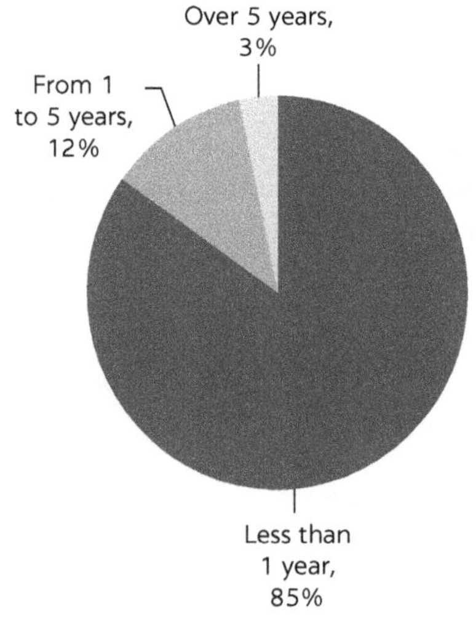

Source: VietinBank Annual Report 2015.

from the more standard international practice. In Vietnam an internal control function reports to the supervisory board, which is actively involved in the control and compliance process. In addition, a state audit bureau does auditing of all state-owned entities, including the state banks. The supervisory board has five members who are full-time employees of the bank. The supervisory board meets monthly and reports to the board of directors on a regular basis. The supervisory board also monitors the implementation of long-term strategy and goals at the bank, as well as ensures that the accounting systems at VietinBank are in line with current regulations and principles.

Credit and risk management

VietinBank has a well-developed credit and risk process that is defined in a detailed sequence of steps, from the application for a loan through the decision-making process. The bank has separated the customer relationship role from the risk management function by segregating those functions at branch level. It then established about nine centers for risk management to cover the whole country. At that step, the risk management committee is responsible for the credit assessment and appraisal of all larger business loans. The committee operates independent of the customer relationship staff, who have the primary responsibility for developing and expanding the business. That segregation is an important step in enhancing the credit and risk management capabilities at VietinBank.

The bank's risk management committee has overall responsibility for risk management, particularly with regard to credit, the major risk for VietinBank. The committee issued instructions that restrict and curtail the lending for sectors identified as higher risk in the current economic environment. The bank

TABLE 3.17 **VietinBank's Net Liquidity Gap (as of June 2016), D, millions**

	OVERDUE		NOT OVERDUE					TOTAL
	OVER 3 MONTHS	UP TO 3 MONTHS	UP TO 1 MONTH	1 TO 3 MONTHS	3 TO 12 MONTHS	1 TO 5 YEARS	OVER 5 YEARS	
Total assets	4,942,240	3,211,051	156,849,755	142,977,725	217,181,110	169,913,467	90,853,242	785,928,590
Total liabilities	n.a.	n.a.	211,577,410	169,112,861	232,792,667	86,508,512	23,366,272	723,254,165
Net liquidity gap	4,942,240	3,211,051	(54,727,655)	(26,135,136)	(15,611,557)	83,508,512	67,486,970	62,674,425

Source: VietinBank Annual Report 2015.
Note: n.a. = not applicable.

instituted a customer rating system based on qualitative and quantitative criteria developed by the bank over a number of years. All customers are rated by this system and must exceed a certain rating to be considered for a loan. The comprehensive risk management structure is designed to manage the bank's exposure to credit, market, and operational risks to the highest standards.

HSBC Vietnam

London-based Hongkong and Shanghai Banking Corporation (HSBC) opened its first office in Saigon (now Ho Chi Minh City) in 1870. In August 1995 the bank opened a full-service branch in Ho Chi Minh City and a second branch in Hanoi and established a representative office in Can Tho City in 2005. The chartered capital of the bank was D 7,530 billion (US$ 350 million) in 2015.

In 2009 HSBC became the first foreign bank to incorporate in Vietnam. The new entity, HSBC Bank (Vietnam) Ltd., is 100 percent owned by the Hong Kong SAR, China and Shanghai Banking Corporation Limited. HSBC Bank (Vietnam) Ltd. is also the first wholly foreign-owned bank to operate both branches and transaction offices in Vietnam. HSBC is currently one of the largest foreign banks in Vietnam to serve onshore and offshore clients.

The bank provides a comprehensive range of banking services, including retail banking and wealth management, commercial banking, global banking, global markets, global payments and cash management, global trade, and receivables finance and securities services.

Because detailed information on loan portfolio (by borrowers, tenor, and so on) was not available during the study, the analysis of HSBC focuses on the available financial information (table 3.18 and figures 3.33 and 3.34) and the governance structure of the bank.

Balance sheet assessment

As figure 3.33 shows, the three main components of HSBC Vietnam assets as of December 31, 2015, were loans and advances to customers (38 percent), placement with and loans to other financial institutions (32 percent), and investment securities and other financial assets (15 percent). Customer deposits account for a major portion of total liabilities, and the majority of the customer loans are short to medium term. The maximum tenor for U.S. dollar-dominated loans can be up to 10 years, while maximum tenor for Vietnamese dong-dominated loans ranges between 5 and 7 years. The funding sources for dong-dominated loans of HSBC are the local deposits of the bank, while long-term loans advanced by the bank are generally funded by long-term funds from the international markets.

TABLE 3.18 **Key Financial Information of HSBC Vietnam**

	2014	2015
Indicators in D, billions		
Total assets	84,293	72,215
Loan portfolio	32,790	27,085
Deposits	65,841	57,957
Shareholder funds	10,294	9,986
Profit after tax	814	935
Return on assets, %	0.97	1.29
Return on equity, %	7.91	9.36

Source: Financial statements of HSBC Vietnam 2015.

FIGURE 3.33

HSBC Vietnam Asset Portfolio

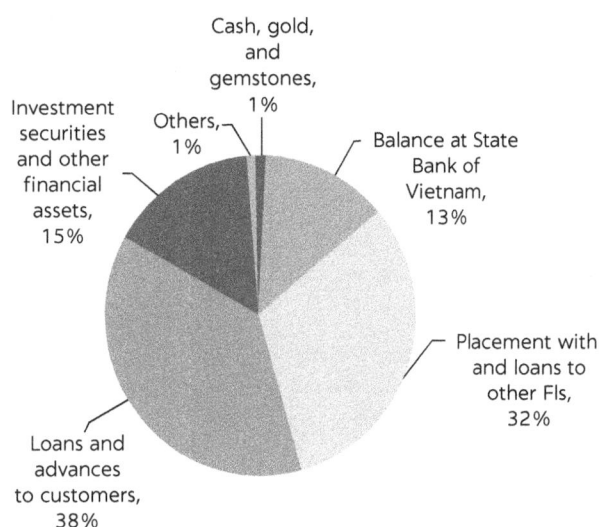

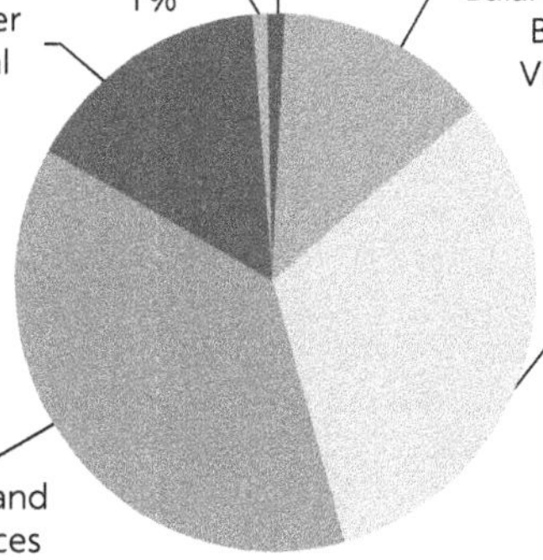

Source: Financial statements of HSBC Vietnam 2015.
Note: FI = financial institution.

Exposure of lending to provincial governments

HSBC Vietnam currently does not regard provincial governments as qualified borrowers. Therefore, the bank has no provincial government portfolio and has neither bought municipal bonds nor lent directly to any provincial governments. The bank is experienced in lending to infrastructure projects, mainly including loans to private sector and SOEs. The typical sources of finance for the Vietnamese dong loans are the local deposits. For U.S. dollar loans the funds are mostly from the international market, which has longer tenor.

Liquidity

HSBC Vietnam has been improving its solvency position by deploying more funds toward liquid assets. The bank's loan-to-deposits ratio decreased from 100 percent in 2014 to 48 percent in 2015, indicating that the bank has sufficient liquidity to cover unforeseen funding issues (figure 3.34). The cash ratio for the bank also reached 115 percent in 2015, implying that the bank has good liquidity to absorb credit losses. Because the bank is deploying short-term local deposits to fund short- and medium-term loans, while using international market to finance long-term loans, the bank is less likely to face asset liability mismatch problems.

Nonperforming loans

HSBC Vietnam's NPL rate reached 3.4 percent in 2013, due partly to the decreased outstanding loans in 2013. The rate decreased to 1.1 percent in 2015, well below the Vietnam industry average and the global industry average.

Corporate governance

As one of the world's largest banks, HSBC is committed to the high standards of corporate governance set by the code for the industry and its shareholders.

The Board of Directors of HSBC Holdings, led by a group chairman, is responsible for overseeing the management of HSBC globally. The authority of the

FIGURE 3.34
HSBC Vietnam Liquidity Ratios

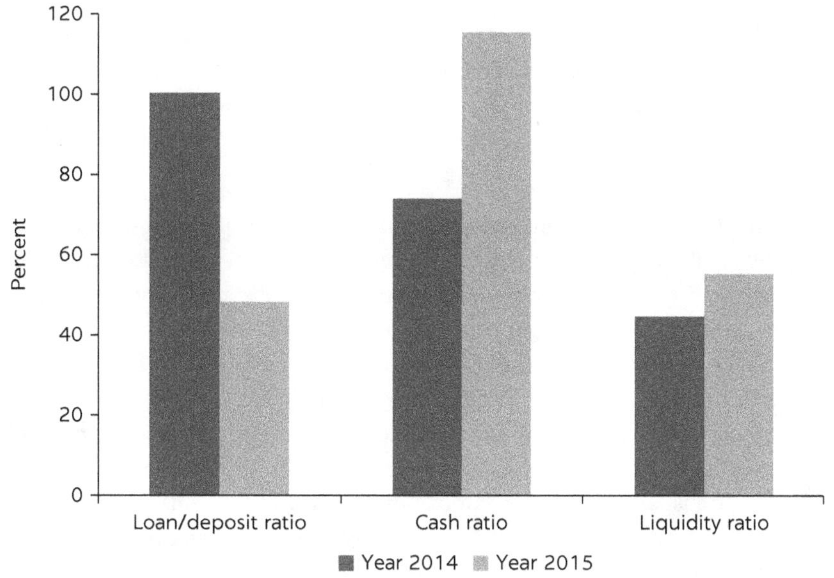

Source: Financial statements of HSBC Vietnam 2015.

board directors is exercised by collective action at the board meetings. The board sets the risk management strategy for the group and approves capital and operating plans presented by management. The board committees are the Group Risk Committee, Group Audit Committee, Group Remuneration Committee, Nomination Committee, Group Management Board (GMB), Financial System Vulnerabilities Committee, Code and Value Committee, and Chairman's Committee. Members of the board comprise a majority of independent nonexecutive directors to ensure that no individual or small group can dominate its decision making.

The board delegates the day-to-day management of HSBC Holdings to a GMB; heads of global business units or holding global functions and the chief executive officer of each region attend GMB meetings. The GMB is a key element of HSBC's management and reporting structure such that all line operations are accountable either to a member of GMB or directly to group chief executive officer, who in turn reports to the group chairman.

HSBC Vietnam's management team includes 12 members under the leadership of the first Vietnamese chief executive officer. More than half of the management team are foreigners who are the heads of the key business functions of the bank. There is no local board, but the management team of local business is under the delegation and supervision of the GMB and the global business and function. As a subsidiary of the global business group, the local business operations are aligned with the group strategy, principles, and objectives.

Credit and risk management

HSBC Vietnam has adopted a strong credit and risk management framework that meets the international standards and the HSBC Group's guidance and policies.

Key considerations by the five banks on participating in a city infrastructure financing facility

Consultation with the five banks assessed revealed that the banks are receptive to the concept of a CIFF and consider it as an opportunity for a new business segment of provincial lending. Having limited exposure to provinces and perceiving high provincial credit risks, the banks note that their key considerations on potential participation in a CIFF are the following:

- *Interest margin and terms.* The banks intend to earn an interest margin on provincial lending under a pilot CIFF program in line with the credit risk associated with the provincial governments that are under consideration. The banks are also willing to extend medium-term to long-term loans to provincial governments, depending on the tenor of available CIFF funding.
- *General obligation versus project finance.* The banks have been providing project-specific loans to provinces rather than general obligation loans, and they would prefer to provide project-specific loans to provinces because the lack of transparency and standardization in budgeting and financial reporting procedures makes it difficult for banks to assess the strength of provincial governments' balance sheets. For general obligation loans proposed under the CIFF program, the free cash flows available with the provincial governments from their overall operations may be escrowed for repayment to improve the debt security.
- *Capacity.* Commercial banks possess inadequate capacity for credit appraisal, risk management, and pricing of provincial loans. The banks have highlighted the need for support for building capacity in budgeting and financial management procedures followed by provincial governments, in analysis of provincial accounts and records, and for appraisal, pricing, risk management, and monitoring of provincial loans.
- *Currency denomination.* The banks prefer the provincial loans under a CIFF program to be denominated in Vietnamese dong, however they also indicated that they are open to receiving the CIFF funding in foreign currency. The banks would either pass on the risks to the provincial governments by including an appropriate foreign exchange risk premium, or they would hedge their exposure to the risks by using appropriate derivatives instruments.

CONCLUSION AND RECOMMENDATIONS

The banking sector in Vietnam has shown impressive growth with its ongoing restructuring and liberalization reforms. The sector is gradually recovering from the global financial crisis, and the commercial banks have just recently addressed the substantial NPL overhang. With substantial untapped capital sitting in the industry, the commercial banks are exploring new funding opportunities. Participating in the potential CIFF program may help commercial banks address issues such as asset liability mismatch, high provincial credit risks, and limited experience in undertaking credit assessment on the provinces, thus allowing provinces to use commercial banking resources in the short to medium term. More importantly, developing a CIFF program may also improve provincial governments' debt management and borrowing practice, thus ultimately building up a credit culture and enhancing their capacity to tap into the capital market for local infrastructure financing in the long term.

A rapid assessment of a sample of commercial banks in Vietnam was carried out to assess the potential of commercial banks to participate in the CIFF program. The SOCBs such as Vietcombank and VietinBank are among the largest commercial banks in Vietnam, with the greatest size of total assets, loans, and chartered capital, as well as a good business base across various sectors of the economy. These banks have made significant investments in infrastructure and have had considerable experience in lending directly and indirectly to provincial governments. Other smaller domestic commercial banks (LVPB, Maritime Bank) have built a provincial government portfolio but have some limitation in terms of lending capability. Finally, a foreign bank (HSBC Vietnam) is improving its solvency position and indicates sufficient bandwidth for provincial lending. Further assessment should be carried out thoroughly to identify a list of qualified commercial banks to participate in the CIFF program, once the program is launched.

The selected commercial banks have experience in providing loans at longer tenors. On average, four of the five selected banks used approximately 31 percent of their assets to make loans at tenors greater than 5 years (figure 3.35).

FIGURE 3.35

Average Loan Tenor of Four Vietnam Commercial Banks

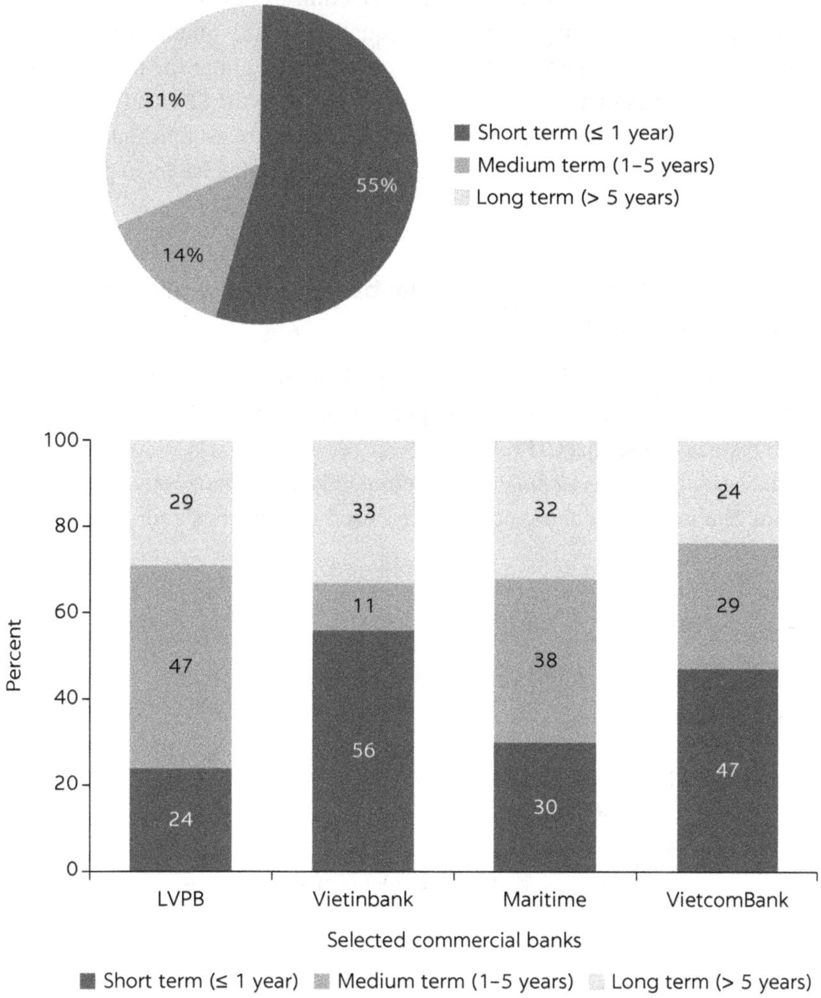

Sources: Bank for Foreign Trade of Vietnam (Vietcombank); Lien Viet Post Bank (LVPB); Maritime Bank; Vietnam Bank for Industry and Trade (VietinBank), as of December 31, 2015.

This suggests that the banks have the ability to lend at longer tenors and could possibly do so for provincial governments, if the appropriate regulations were put in place to authorize it. However, commercial banks would need to balance any expansion of long-term lending to provincial governments with the potential increase in liquidity risk, given existing conditions in which extensive mismatches already exist between long-term assets and long-term liabilities. Hence, the availability of a refinancing window through which the banks could obtain longer-term capital to fund long-term loans to provincial governments would potentially serve as a key market stimulant for commercial banks.

Overall, the banks still have limited exposure to provincial lending, given that banks still associate provincial lending with high risks and regulatory ambiguity. Bank officials have expressed their willingness to participate in a pilot program like the CIFF, provided that they are able to obtain sufficient information to assess the creditworthiness of the provinces. To do so would essentially require improved transparency of financial reporting by the provincial governments, as well as building the capacity of provincial governments to streamline financial reporting.

Proposed qualification criteria for selecting participating banks

Proposed qualification criteria for the selection of participating banks for the CIFF mechanism may include both qualitative and quantitative criteria (box 3.2). To propose appropriate qualification criteria under the local business environment, decision makers will have to consult with the SBV and Ministry of Finance in the later stage. Once qualification criteria are established, the study team can conduct a detailed bank assessment for selecting banks to participate in the CIFF program.

Recommendations for commercial banks under a pilot city infrastructure financing facility

Because commercial banks have limited experience in provincial lending in general, the following actions would be important for commercial banks planning to participate in a potential CIFF:

Business pipeline development. The commercial banks currently adopt a corporate relationship banking approach focused on private sector entities and

BOX 3.2

Qualifications for Banks to Participate in a City Infrastructure Financing Facility Program for Provincial Lending

At the preliminary stage, proposed qualification criteria could include the following:

- Risk and portfolio diversification
- Credit and risk management capability
- Financial performance
- Nonperforming loans
- Capital adequacy
- Liquidity
- Solvency
- Asset quality
- Size of bank in terms of assets, loans, and chartered capital
- Capability to assess project financing
- Bank strategy and risk appetite
- Management capability

SOEs for lending across various sectors. With their entry into provincial financing, the commercial banks would need to deal with a customer segment that will be more regionally dispersed and that will require cost-effective ways of business network expansion and of developing loan deals with provinces.

Appraisal procedures. Since commercial banks have very limited exposure to provinces currently, the credit appraisal procedure would need to be customized to adequately assess the provinces on various financial and institutional aspects. The appraisal procedure should consider and adequately price all the risks associated with the provincial governments.

Risk management function. Commercial banks would need to develop a rating tool, risk register, and risk control matrix for provincial government loans and integrate them into the wider organization risk management and decision-making process for better portfolio monitoring and management from the risk perspective.

Internal audit. More active internal audit processes and system automation, review of portfolio, and capacity building to adopt international best practices would be needed.

Capacity building. Banks would have to train staff and officials on various aspects related to the assessment of provincial loan proposals, including technical assessment, financial assessment, environmental and safeguards assessment, risk management aspects, and other related aspects.

Regulatory issues to be considered for the supply side

As the next chapter will discuss in detail, some fundamental weaknesses in the current legal and regulatory framework of provincial borrowing constrain provinces in efficiently and effectively using private capital to narrow the funding gap in public infrastructure investments. Here we highlight key regulatory considerations on the supply side.

First and foremost, the legal framework should clearly specify that commercial banks can lend to provincial governments and should provide guidelines for advancing and accounting of provincial government loans by commercial banks. The central government may also need to modify the SBV guidelines to allow commercial banks to lend to provinces for a longer tenor, compared with the existing maximum tenor allowed of 2 years. More important, the current legal framework lacks a clear recourse mechanism, making commercial banks and other creditors perceive that provincial lending is too risky. Thus, the legal framework should provide a clear recourse mechanism for the case of a provincial government's default or insolvency.

As the five selected banks highlighted, debt security related to provincial lending needs to be enhanced. The legal framework should allow provincial governments to service their debt through escrow accounts and collateralization agreements. The selected banks also highlighted the need for the legal framework to emphasize standardization of and transparency in the budgeting, accounting, and financial reporting procedures followed by provinces.

NOTES

1. The SOCBs are the partially privatized Bank for Foreign Trade of Vietnam (Vietcombank), Vietnam Bank for Industry and Trade (VietinBank), Bank for Investment and Development of Vietnam (BIDV), and Vietnam Bank for Agricultural and Rural Development (Agribank).

2. "Real Interest Rate," World Development Indicator, World Bank, https://data.worldbank.org/indicator/FR.INR.RINR?end=2016&start=2015.
3. Circular 36/2014/TT-NHNN issued by the State Bank of Vietnam, November 20.
4. Article 128 of the Credit Institution Law.
5. Phase I (P036042) of the project was to implement the international standard core banking solutions (CBS) and modules of banking operation systems to six participating commercial banks to improve their operational practice and capacity; phase II (P082627) of the project was a response to the urgent needs of expanding the core banking solutions to mitigate the risk of running both the new and legal systems in parallel.

REFERENCES

Vietcombank. 2016. *Vietcombank Annual Report 2015*. http://vietcombank.com.vn/upload/2016/06/09/20160613_AR_VCB_2015_EN.pdf?27.

LienVietPostBank. 2016. *LienVietPostBank Annual Report 2015*. https://www.lienvietpostbank.com.vn/sites/default/files/file_download/ANNUAL_REPORT_LPB_2015.pdf.

Maritime Bank. 2016. *Maritime Bank Annual Report 2015*. http://static2.vietstock.vn/data/OTC/2015/BCTN/VN/MSB_Baocaothuongnien_2015.pdf.

Vietinbank. 2016. *Vietinbank Annual Report 2015*. https://www.vietinbank.vn/web/export/sites/default/en/annual/annual-report-2015.pdf.

HSBC Bank Vietnam. 2016. *Summarized Financial Statements*. http://www.about.hsbc.com.vn/-/media/vietnam/en/hsbc-in-vietnam/financial-information/finance-report-2015-en.pdf.

Schmittmann, J., Corvino, D., and Katagiri, M., 2017. *Vietnam: Selected Issues*. IMF Country Report 17/191, International Monetary Fund. https://www.imf.org/~/media/Files/Publications/CR/2017/cr17191.ashx.

4 An Assessment of the Legal Framework for a City Infrastructure Financing Facility in Vietnam

Provincial governments in Vietnam have their respective rights, duties, and responsibilities established in laws, including those related to the local budget and capital mobilization. Budgets of provincial governments are prepared and submitted to the central government through a bottom-up process in which local legislatures review and appropriate the local budgets before submitting them to the upper tiers of government. The National Assembly ultimately adopts a budget for the entire country, which is a consolidation of the central and local budgets. Provincial budgets are an integral part of this unitary budget, but with a high level of spending decentralization.

As discussed in previous chapters, for provinces to effectively leverage their budget surpluses to obtain private sector capital to finance public infrastructure investments, a comprehensive legal and regulatory framework is needed to address constraints on both the demand and the supply side. This chapter provides a detailed review of the legal and regulatory framework for provincial financing in Vietnam to help identify the key legal and regulatory constraints to the establishment of the city infrastructure financing facility (CIFF) and the adjustments needed to launch the potential program.

VIETNAMESE JURIDICAL FRAMEWORK FOR CAPITAL MOBILIZATION BY PROVINCIAL GOVERNMENTS

This section presents an assessment of Vietnam's juridical framework for capital mobilization by the provincial governments. It analyzes the legal framework governing the capital mobilization capability of the provincial governments, including the provincial governments' borrowing from commercial banks, the Vietnam Development Bank's (VDBs) lending, and provincial governments' bond issuance. The findings from that assessment helped the report team in making final recommendations for this chapter.

Capital mobilization capability of provincial governments

Under Vietnamese law provincial governments comprise the provincial People's Council (PPCo) and the provincial People's Committee (PPC), which are organized in administrative units at the provincial, district, and commune levels.[1] The provincial governments have their respective rights, duties, and responsibilities as provided by law, including those related to the local budget and capital mobilization. The current capital mobilization capability of the provincial governments is mostly governed by the State Budget Law and the public debt management laws, the former related to management of the provincial government's budget and the latter to the debt management of the provincial governments.

State budget laws

The principal legislation or backbone of the legal framework governing the state budget is the Law on State Budget (or State Budget Law, SBL),[2] which constitutes the overall legal framework for the budgeting and financing of national and provincial infrastructure. The law not only stipulates the budget formulation process and the definition of revenues and expenditures, but also sets forth the framework for the provincial governments' capital mobilization. The provincial committees and councils (the PPCs and PPCos) constitute the main level of local government and have responsibility for defining the provincial budget—the estimated revenues and expenditures for the district and commune levels that fall under their jurisdiction.

Although the SBL empowers provincial governments with certain budgetary autonomy, all of the budgets must be integrated into a unitary state budget. The budget process starts with the lowest level of provincial government and progresses through the different administrative stages until it reaches the National Assembly for final approval. At the provincial levels, all the budgets of communes and districts under provincial administration are compiled into a single budget, which, once approved by the PPCo, is submitted to the Ministry of Finance (MOF) at the national level. The National Assembly approves the integrated state budget and distributes the results to the provincial governments and to treasury offices around the country, which are responsible for recording the revenues and expenditures of the local governments under their jurisdiction.

According to the SBL, revenues available for provincial budgets include tax revenues that are fully assigned to local governments, tax revenues that provinces have to share with the central government, other revenues assigned to local governments by the central government, and domestic borrowing.[3]

The SBL also provides a "list of spending tasks" associated with provincial budgets, with broad definitions for capital and recurrent expenditures. Such capital expenditures include investments in the construction of socioeconomic infrastructure projects and investments in state enterprises, economic organizations, and financial institutions. The provincial governments also are allowed to mobilize domestic capital, so although the former law, SBL 2002, indicates that, in principle, provincial budgets should be balanced,[4] it also contemplates domestic borrowing for investment in infrastructure projects that are included in provincial budgets and are part of the 5-year plan of the PPCos.

The former law, SBL 2002, limited the amount of capital mobilized, which must not exceed 30 percent of the annual investment capital for capital construction included in the provincial budget (with an exception allowing

100 percent for Hanoi and 150 percent for Ho Chi Minh City).[5] In that regard, the former law, SBL 2002, is further guided by Decree 60/2003 and Circular 59/2003,[6] which state that when demand exists for mobilization of investment capital for the construction of infrastructural works (covered by the provincial budget), the PPC must prepare the investment capital mobilization plan and submit it to the PPCo for approval. After PPCo approval, the plan must then be reported to the Ministry of Planning and Investment (MPI) and the MOF for supervisory purposes.

The new budget law, SBL 2015, raises the borrowing limit to 30 percent of provincial revenues for provinces that are net contributors to the national budget.[7] Provincial governments are allowed to borrow to offset their local budget deficit and to repay the principal of debts. The borrowing can be in the form of bond issuance, on-lending of a provincial government's foreign loan, or loans from other sources in accordance with the laws. Generally, the annual budgeting process of local government considers the balancing capacity of the local budget, the borrowing balance limit, and the demand for development investment capital. The PPC bases the estimate on local deficit, borrowing, and repayment of debt, then submits it to the PPCo for approval. Once approved, it is submitted to the central government for approval. The government of Vietnam is required by the SBL to prescribe in detail cases in which the local budget deficit is permitted so as to ensure the debt repayment capacity of localities and suit the total deficit of the state budget.[8]

This assessment noted that the SBL and its guiding legislation are silent on a recourse mechanism, including in its detailed procedures. Such a mechanism would ensure that, in the case of local government default, the lenders or financiers could recover the funds from the provincial budget. The recourse mechanism would play an important role in credit enhancement for local governments by providing financiers with the necessary security currently absent in the market in Vietnam. The study found that the absence of the recourse mechanism in the SBL is one of the legal barriers that discourages the credit institutions from lending money to the provincial governments. For example, a 2-year limitation on lending by commercial banks to provincial governments was established by the State Bank of Vietnam (SBV) Official Letter 576/NHNN-CSTT, and the inability of commercial banks to access the government's foreign loans for subsequent on-lending or lending to provincial governments was due to a restriction in Decree 78/2010.

Public debt management laws

The purposes of provincial government borrowing are defined in Article 37 of the Law on Public Debt Management.[9] Those purposes include (a) non-revenue-generating projects for socioeconomic development *within the provincial budget spending task* under the SBL and (b) revenue-generating projects capable of recovering capital. Articles 37 and 38 of the Law on Public Debt Management defines the forms of domestic borrowing and introduces the possibility of indirect international financing through the central government. Local borrowing potentially could be in the form of bonds or loans from other legitimate sources. However, the law does not specifically define the other legitimate sources—it just generally states that those other legitimate sources must be in accordance with the laws. One could therefore interpret that capital mobilization by provincial governments from credit institutions (as further assessed in the next section) is not contrary to the Law on Public Debt Management.

Conditions for domestic borrowing by provincial governments (under public debt management laws)

Regarding borrowing by the provincial governments for investment in non-revenue-generating projects, Article 39.1 of the Law on Public Debt Management states that the following conditions must be satisfied. First, the project must have completed investment procedures under the investment law and other relevant laws and must be on the investment list under the 5-year plan already decided by PPCos. Second, bond issuance schemes and plans for use of loans and debt payment must have been adopted by the PPCo and approved in writing by the MOF. Third, the value of the domestic borrowings must be within the provincial budget's borrowing limits under the SBL. And fourth, for on-lending of the government's foreign loans, the conditions specified in Articles 24.3 and 25.5 of the Law on Public Debt Management must be satisfied.

With regard to borrowing by the provincial governments *for investment in revenue-generating projects,* the Law on Public Debt Management[10] states that the following conditions must be satisfied: First, the projects must have completed investment procedures under the investment law and relevant laws and must have been determined by competent agencies as capable of recovering capital, and second, schemes on issuance of bonds for project investment must have been evaluated and approved in writing by the MOF.

Borrowing limits by provincial governments (under public debt management laws)

According to the Law on Public Debt Management and its guiding legislation, based on the state budget laws, the PPCs must set borrowing limits for provincial budgets that they report to PPCos and submit to the prime minister for approval.[11] Consequently, borrowings of, and bonds issued by, provincial governments must be made within the approved borrowing limits. However, the legislation makes it possible for a provincial government's limits to exceed the approved limit, provided that the PPC submits a specific plan to the MOF for its appraisal and for reporting to the prime minister for a decision. In that regard, it is noted that, according to Resolution 10/2011 of the National Assembly and Decision 958/2012 of the prime minister, the public debts (including the government debts, the debts guaranteed by the government, and the provincial governments' debts) may not exceed 65 percent of gross domestic product (GDP) by 2020 and 60 percent of GDP by 2030.[12]

According to Article 19 of Decree 79/2010, in accordance with the borrowing limits under the SBL, the capacity to balance provincial budgets for debt payment, the projects' implementation schedule, and the projects' needs for funds of loaned projects, the PPC must elaborate *the annual detailed plan on borrowing* and *the annual detailed plan on debt payment* and must submit them to the PPCo for approval. The first plan, the borrowing plan, must elaborate borrowing sources (bond issue, other lawful financial sources, and borrowing from foreign on-lending of a government loan), and it must show the funding being used for the declared purposes. The second plan must elaborate debt repayments from the provincial budget and from capital recovery of projects. The plan on debt repayment is to be made and approved by the PPC only on a year-by-year basis, even for revenue-generating projects.

Thus, the assessment determined that for medium- and long-term financing of infrastructure development projects, the SBL may cause credit institutions providing such financing to be concerned and uncomfortable.

This requirement also seems to be one of legal barriers discouraging credit institutions from lending to the provincial governments, because it means that provincial governments have a higher risk of not meeting repayment terms for their medium- and long-term financing.

Implementation of provincial government debt payment (under public debt management laws)

The Law on Public Debt Management (Article 42) provides a debt payment principle that states that the provincial governments' sources for repaying debt are provincial budgets and funds recovered from the investment projects of the locality. Guiding this law, Decree 79/2010 (Article 21) establishes principles for the repayment of provincial government debts; that is, where loans are included in the budget, repayment must come from provincial budget funds, and when loans are used for programs and projects, repayment must first come from revenues generated by the projects. When such revenues are insufficient for debt repayment, provincial budget funds must be allocated to repay the outstanding debts.

Management of provincial government debts (under public debt management laws)

According to Decree 79/2010 (Article 21.1), the PPC must borrow money and pay provincial governments debts according to approved borrowing limits and plans. The MOF is assigned to supervise provincial governments for both borrowing and debt payment.

For the purposes of administration and supervision, under Decree 79/2010 (Article 21.3) the PPC must direct provincial departments and functional sectors to closely monitor the use of funds from loans for programs and projects and must report on its borrowing and debt payment in accordance with the laws. The owners of programs and projects are responsible for reporting quarterly to the PPC on the implementation, fund withdrawal, disbursement, and debt payment of programs and projects.

On-lending of the government's foreign loans

According to Article 23 of the Law on Public Debt Management, the MOF must directly provide or authorize a financial or credit institution to provide on-lending. The on-lending beneficiaries include the following: (a) financial and credit institutions borrowing for further lending to users under credit programs or credit components of programs and projects using foreign loans; (b) enterprises borrowing for investment in programs and projects capable of recovering part or all of the loans; and (c) provincial governments borrowing for investment in socioeconomic development within the provincial budget spending task. According to Article 18 of Decree 78/2010, (a) the MOF must directly provide on-lending for provincial governments and for financial and credit institutions for implementation of credit limits or programs that are not subject to specific conditions and (b) the MOF must authorize financial and credit institutions to act as on-lending agencies in certain cases. The first case is on-lending to enterprises for execution of specific investment programs or projects, and second is implementation of credit limits or programs subject to conditions on borrowers, areas, sectors, on-lending interest rates, and other relevant conditions.

Further, in case of on-lending of the government foreign loan to the provincial governments, the decree states: (a) the MOF must evaluate the debt repayment capacity of the provincial governments (Article 19.5 of Decree 78/2010), (b) the on-lending interest rate must be the same as the foreign loan interest (Article 7.3 of Decree 78/2010), and (c) the on-lending currency must be the original foreign currency in which the foreign loan has been borrowed (Article 4.3 of Decree 78/2010). The research team therefore offers an interpretation that, for on-lending of the government foreign loan to the provincial governments, the on-lending agency is always only the MOF itself.

Thus, the study highlights the need to clarify those stipulations or to make an appropriate amendment to Decree 78/2010 to clarify that point. Without that clarification or amendment, a model of a CIFF with wholesale function (that is, having two tiers of lending as described later in this chapter), which proposes to use the government's foreign loan, may not work. The recommendations in the final section of this chapter reflect this interpretation, though the MOF would have to agree with it.

Further, for provincial governments to be eligible to benefit from central government on-lending, they must fulfill the following conditions: (a) be permitted by competent authorities to borrow the government's foreign loans, (b) have socioeconomic development investment projects within the local budget spending task that have completed investment procedures under the investment law and other relevant laws, and (c) have a provincial budget with sufficient capacity to repay the debt.[13]

The MOF's Department of Debt Management and External Finance (DDMEF) must sign the on-lending contracts on behalf of the MOF.[14] That means that the DDMEF may play a similar retail-like role within the CIFF, as discussed later in this chapter. In addition, according to Decree 78/2010, the following conditions must be met. First, before approving the loan, the MOF must evaluate the provincial budget plan for the year in which the foreign loan agreement is signed and the loan use and payment plan are approved by the PPC.[15] Second, provincial governments have certain advantages relative to other eligible subborrowers; for example, (a) they are not charged an on-lending charge fee by the government or the MOF (Article 10), (b) the on-lending interest rate is the same as the foreign loan interest rate (Article 7), and (c) no security is required or applicable (Article 12).

With regard to on-lending interest rates that are applicable to official development assistance (ODA) loans provided to organizations other than provincial governments, Article 7 of Decree 78/2010 stipulates the following: First, in the case of "on-lending in the original foreign currency," the on-lending interest rate is equal to two-thirds of the commercial interest reference rate corresponding to the on-lending conditions. If two-thirds of the commercial interest reference rate is lower than the foreign lending interest rate, then the on-lending interest rate is equal to the foreign lending interest rate. In case of on-lending in foreign currency without a commercial interest reference rate, then the on-lending interest rate is equal to the foreign lending interest rate.

Second, in the case of "on-lending in Vietnam dong," the on-lending interest rate is determined as equal to the foreign currency lending interest rate previously specified, plus the exchange rate risk ratio between the relevant foreign currency and the Vietnam dong. The MOF (in coordination with the SBV) shall be calculating and announcing the exchange rate risk ratio between the Vietnam dong and three major foreign currencies, namely US dollars, euros, and Japanese yen. In the case of major fluctuations on the foreign exchange market, the MOF may announce another exchange rate risk ratio during the applicable period. If the original foreign currency in the loan agreement is different from the three foreign currencies, the exchange rate risk ratio is the one applicable to US dollars.

Third, a number of trades and sectors are eligible for the preferential interest rate, which is equal to 30 percent of the corresponding foreign currency or Vietnam dong on-lending interest rate; however, the preferential interest rate must not be lower than the foreign lending interest rate. Given those conditions, the study determined that such provision on the on-lending rates in Vietnamese dong should be taken into account for proposing a CIFF with a wholesale function.

Further, according to Article 4.3 of Decree 78/2010, in the case of on-lending to a PPC, the on-lending currency is the original foreign currency in which the foreign loan has been borrowed. That implies that any on-lending of a government foreign loan to the provincial governments under a CIFF model should be made only in foreign currency (that is, not in Vietnamese dong) to comply with the decree. The recommendations at the end of this chapter will reflect that implication.

Capital mobilization by provincial governments from commercial banks

Organizational forms and permissible operation of commercial banks

According to Article 6 of the Law on Credit Institutions, credit institutions include, but are not limited to, (a) domestic commercial banks, established and organized in the form of a joint-stock company; (b) state commercial banks, established and organized in the form of a single member limited liability company (LLC) that is wholly owned by the state; and (c) joint-venture credit institutions and the wholly foreign-owned credit institutions established and organized in the form of a LLC that comprises a single member LLC and a multimember LLC.

The permissible operation of commercial banks, which includes receiving deposits, extending credits, and providing payment services through the account, must be specified by the SBV in the license issued to each commercial bank. Extension of credit seems to be the current major source of revenue of commercial banks, which could be made in the form of (a) loans, (b) discounts and rediscounts of negotiable instruments and other valuable papers, (c) bank guarantees, (d) issuance of credit cards, (e) domestic factoring, or (f) international factoring applicable to banks authorized to conduct international payment services.

Credit assessment and risk mitigation

For its purposes of assessment and approval to extend credit, the commercial bank must, on principle, require its client to provide data proving that the client has (a) a feasible plan on the use of its capital and financial capability, (b) a lawful capital use purpose, and (c) measures to secure the loan before the credit institution makes a decision on extension of credit.[16] Further, in extending the credit, the commercial banks are required to comply with the relevant provisions of the Vietnamese laws to ensure the security of the credit institutions' operations regarding the limits on extension of credit,[17] the prudential ratios,[18] and the reserves for risks occurring during their operation.[19]

With respect to credit assessment and risk mitigation, the SBV issued Circular 36/2014, which stipulates minimum safety limits and ratios for transactions performed by credit institutions and branches of foreign banks that must be constantly maintained to ensure security during their operation. Those limits include (a) minimum capital adequacy ratio, (b) credit limit, (c) solvency ratio, (d) maximum ratio of short-term capital sources used as the medium- and long-term loans, (e) limit on capital contribution and stock purchase, and (f) loan-to-deposit ratio.

Specifically with regard to the use of short-term capital sources, credit institutions (including commercial banks) are entitled to use short-term capital sources for providing medium- and long-term loans in Vietnamese dong (including foreign currencies converted into Vietnamese dong) at a certain permissible percentage (60 percent).[20] Credit institutions also are entitled to purchase and invest in government bonds at the maximum rate of 15 percent (state-owned commercial banks) or 35 percent (joint-stock commercial banks, joint-venture banks, and wholly foreign-owned banks). Investment in government bonds may include entrusted credits granted to other organizations to purchase and invest in government bonds, but it excludes credits used to purchase and invest in government bonds by means of entrusted capital derived from other organizations.

Further, the SBV has also issued Circular 02/2013 (as amended by Circular 09/2014) on classified assets, levels and methods of setting up of risk provisions, and use of provisions against credit risks in the banking activity of credit institutions and foreign bank branches. The circular classifies the debts into five groups: group 1, standard debts; group 2, debts that need attention; group 3, substandard debts; group 4, doubtful debts; and group 5, potentially irrecoverable debts. The debts are classified following quantitative and qualitative methods, and they are generally based on the capability of the borrowers to pay obligations and the performance of the borrowings in paying their debt obligations. Of the debt groups, groups 3, 4, and 5 are nonperforming loans. Accordingly, credit institutions (including commercial banks) are required to set up provisions, including specific provisions for each customer and general provisions, in accordance with the laws.

Thus, regarding the use of the CIFF model with a wholesale function, this study determined that the SBV must promulgate specific guidance or regulations on the assessment of credit risks relating to the loans to be provided by commercial banks to provincial governments. Taking into account the lack of detailed regulation on the matter and the lack of experiences of commercial banks in assessing the loans to provincial governments, such promulgation would support the credit assessment process used by the commercial banks when they are assessing whether to provide loans to provincial governments.

Borrowing from commercial banks

Generally, according to the Law on Credit Institutions, credit institutions (including commercial banks) will have autonomy in the conduct of their business operation and will be liable for the results of their business operation. On one hand, no organization or individual will be permitted to illegally intervene in the business operation of credit institutions.

On the other hand, credit institutions will have the right to refuse any request for extension of credit or for provision of other services if they consider that conditions are neither fully satisfied nor inconsistent with the laws.

Regulations on lending by credit institutions (including commercial banks) to clients that are not credit institutions[21] apply the following rules:

Borrowers or client.[22] The client could be Vietnamese or foreign organizations or individuals that are capable of repayment and that have demand for funds to perform investment projects; have a plan of production, business, and service activity or investment projects; and have a plan of domestic and overseas living standard improvement.

Borrowing principles.[23] The client must (a) use the loan capital for the correct purpose agreed to in the credit contract and (b) repay the loan principal and interest on time as agreed to in the credit contract.

Borrowing conditions.[24] The client will be required to satisfy all of the prescribed conditions, which include the following. (a) It has the civil legal capacity and capacity for civil acts and bears civil responsibility as stipulated by the applicable laws. (b) It must have a lawful purpose for using the loan capital. (c) It must have the financial capacity to ensure repayment of the loan within the time limit undertaken. (d) It must have an investment project or plan for production, business, and services that is feasible and effective, or it must have an investment project or a feasible plan to service living conditions that complies with the laws. (e) It must comply with the regulations of the government and the guidelines of the SBV on security for loans.

Loan types and term.[25] The loan could be (a) a short-term loan (with a duration up to 12 months), (b) a medium-term loan (with a duration over 12 months up to 60 months), or (c) a long-term loan (with a duration over 60 months).

Loan interest rates.[26] The loan interest rate shall be agreed in the loan contract in accordance with the regulations of the SBV.

Lending method.[27] It is permissible to use lending to provide loans to an investment project for development of production, business, and services or an investment project for servicing living conditions.

Although Decision 1627/2001 and its subsequent amendments do not have a specific clause on credit institutions' lending to provincial governments, the study team could see from the description of types of clients (as noted earlier) that commercial banks are allowed to extend credit to provincial governments provided that provincial governments are "capable of repayment and have demand for funds to perform investment projects."

Further, according to Decision 1627/2001, in the case of lending in foreign currency, (a) credit institutions must be licensed for foreign exchange activities, and (b) the credit institutions and the client must strictly comply with the government regulations and the SBV guidelines on foreign exchange control. SBV Circular 43/2014 stipulates that on foreign currency loans provided by credit institutions and branches of foreign banks for clients who are residents, commercial banks may only provide the foreign currency loans to meet borrowers' specific capital demands that are permissible, which include the following:

- Short-term, mid-term, and long-term loans used as outward remittance for payments on imported goods or services, if the borrowers' foreign currency derived from their operating revenues is sufficient to repay such loans
- Short-term loans granted to key petroleum importers who are given quotas on petroleum imports in 2015 by the Ministry of Industry and Trade to repay foreign debts incurred from such importing, if the borrowers lack operating revenues in foreign currency required to repay such loans
- Short-term loans used to meet the domestic enterprise's demands for capital needed to implement its plans to manufacture and trade goods exported through Vietnam's border gates and that the borrower's foreign currency derived from the export turnover is sufficient to repay
- Loans used as direct outward investments regarding important national projects that are subject to investment decisions made by the National Assembly, the government, or the prime minister, and the offshore investment certificate granted by the MPI.

In addition to the specified capital demands of the borrowers mentioned earlier, subject to the prior approval of the SBV, commercial banks are permitted to consider lending decisions on foreign currency loans if the demands for capital are regarded as a priority and fulfill policy incentives to develop production and business as prescribed in resolutions, decrees, decisions, directives, and other documents of the government and the prime minister. Under the CIFF wholesale model, lending by the commercial banks to the provincial governments may need the prior approval of the SBV, in case the loan is in foreign currency.

In compliance with Decision 1627/2001, in 2002 the SBV issued an official letter guiding lending to support provincial budgets for infrastructure development. In 2005, at the request of the MOF, the SBV sent its official letter to the commercial banks,[28] which guides commercial banks' lending to provincial governments, with the following main specifications:

- *Purpose for borrowing.* Loans are used for the construction of infrastructure works that are in the provinces' investment portfolio, included in the 5-year investment plan, and within the scope of the provincial budget that ensures the payment (as approved by the PPCo).
- *Loan amount and limits.* The maximum lending limit (of commercial banks) to a provincial budget (as of the signing date of the loan agreement) is equivalent to the difference between 30 percent of total annual domestic capital investment of the provincial budget and the total mobilized capital of the provincial budgets, including (a) the actual mobilized capital (at the date of signing the loan contract) and (b) the amount of capital expected to be mobilized in accordance with the plan (as approved by the PPCo). (*Actual mobilized capital* includes borrowings from commercial banks and investment bonds issued in compliance with the provisions of the government and borrowings from other legitimate funding sources.)
- *Loan term.* The maximum loan term is 24 months.

- *Loan contracts.* The loan contracts are entered into between commercial banks and the relevant PPC (or the provincial departments of finance and pricing, if so authorized by the PPC).
- *Loan disbursement.* The whole amount will be disbursed into the accounts of the provincial budgets at state treasury.
- *Loan use supervision* Commercial banks will agree with the PPC on the application of measures for checking and supervising the loans in compliance with the Vietnamese laws on lending and the state budget.

According to the Law on Promulgation of Legislation, any official letters of state agencies in general, and the SBV Official Letter 576/NHNN-CSTT in particular, are not regarded as a type of legislation. Though from a legal perspective this type of letter has only guiding power, not binding power, practically all the commercial banks seem to strictly follow the SBV guidance in the official letter to avoid any subsequent consequences. That explains why the commercial banks have not provided medium- and long-term loans to finance the infrastructure development projects of the provincial governments. Thus the study team determined that a new SBV circular needs to be drafted that would facilitate the commercial banks' medium- and long-term lending to provincial governments and would invalidate the application of Official Letter 576/NHNN/CSTT.

Both SBL 2015 and public debt management law have given regulation on the authority of the local governments incur debt, but the regulation has not yet clearly specified the form of bank loan as one eligible source, which could lead to interpretation that provincial borrowing from commercial banks is not fully legally supported. This perception is further sustained given the existence of the prime minister's Instruction 25 issued in 2014, which forbids provinces from borrowing from commercial banks to cover the expenditure of local budgets. In order to create an enabling subnational borrowing environment, it would be important to clarify the effectiveness of prime minister's Instruction 25 and specify that commercial bank loans are a legal lending source to provincial/local governments.

Capital mobilization by provincial governments from the Vietnam development bank

The VDB was established by Decision 108/2006 of the prime minister as part of reorganizing the Development Assistance Fund (DAF) (established under Decree 50/1999) to implement the state's policies on development investment credit and export credit, regulated in Decree 75/2011. The VDB, which will be assessed later, offers loans with favorable terms to provincial governments, including longer tenor, but only under national target programs approved by the government.

For instance, one of the national target programs was the program for solidifying and rebuilding the canals to develop rural transport roads, infrastructure for aquaculture, and infrastructure for craft villages in rural areas, during the period 2009–15.[29] According to the decision, the VDB is responsible for providing loans to provincial governments, and the provincial governments are responsible for repaying the debts to the VDB when due. For the repayment of the debts, the provincial governments must use the domestic development investment capital sources (including investment capital sources from the collection of land use fees) that are allocated in the annual budget balance of the locality to repay the debts. The canal rebuilding program was further guided by Circular 156/2009, which stipulates that the loans are made through the VDB once approved by the MOF, and the loan agreements are signed between the VDB branch in the locality and the provincial Department of Finance and Pricing.

Capital mobilization by provincial governments from local government bonds

As noted earlier, the Law on Public Debt Management authorizes provincial governments to issue bonds to finance local investment projects that meet certain conditions. Guiding the Law on Public Debt Management on this legal matter is Decree 01/2011, which consolidated the regulations for the issuance of both domestic and international government bonds, and Circular 81/2012.[30]

Decree 01/2011 defines local government bonds as debt securities that are issued by the PPC to raise funds for local investment works and projects. The local government bonds can be issued to fund investment in (a) socioeconomic development projects that are included in the provincial budgets, both under the spending task, according to the SBL, and under the investment portfolio defined in the 5-year plan decided by the PPCo; or (b) "local repayable projects" identified by the PPCo.[31] The PPCs are responsible for arranging for the payment of interest and principal on the bonds when due. The PPCs are required to ensure repayment of debt obligations coming from the provincial budget and from local revenue-generating projects.

Local government bonds are issued under bond issuance plans prepared by the PPCs, accepted by the PPCo, and approved by the MOF. Article 25.1 of Decree 01/2011 stipulates that bond issuance plans must include (a) the bond issuance objective and information on the projects to be funded; (b) capital sources of project and capital demand on bond issuance; (c) projected volume, term, interest rates, and method of bond issuance; and (d) a repayment plan and the projected amount, maturity, and interest rate on the bond. Local government bonds have to be registered and deposited at the Vietnam Securities Depository and listed and traded on a stock exchange following the guidelines established by the MOF. Local government bonds are issued through tendering, underwriting, or bond issuing agents and must be issued with maturities of 1 year or more.

For the issuance of local government bonds, the following conditions are required under Article 24 of Decree 01/2011:

- The local government bonds must be for investment in (a) projects of social and economic development, which are under the duties of the provincial budget in accordance with the SBL and the portfolio of the 5-year plan decided by the PPCos; or (b) projects determined by the PPCos as being able to meet capital recovery requirements. Such projects must complete the investment procedures prescribed by the investment laws and the relevant provisions of the Vietnamese laws.
- They must have a bond issuance scheme, with the required contents,[32] approved in writing by the PPCos and appraised and approved in writing by the MOF.[33]

- The maximum total capital raised by issuing bonds must be within the debt limit from funds mobilized annually from the provincial budget in accordance with the SBL and guiding legislation.
- Regarding projects that are able to meet capital recovery requirements, the total value of the loan, including the issuance of bonds to invest in such a project, must not exceed 80 percent of the total investment of that project.

Also, according to Article 7 of Decree 01/2011, the bond buyers (including buyers of local government bonds) generally could be Vietnamese organizations and individuals and foreign organizations and individuals. However, Vietnamese organizations are not permitted to use funds allocated by the state budget to buy bonds, including local government bonds. This means that under the current legal framework, commercial banks, including the state-owned commercial banks, are allowed to use their mobilized capital (for example, saving deposits) to buy local government bonds.

The local government bondholders have such rights and obligations as provided by Article 8 of Decree 01/2011. In particular, the local government bondholders, on one hand, are guaranteed full payment in due time when the principal and interest of bonds come to maturity, or the local government bondholders can use the bonds for transfer, donation, inheritance, and mortgage discount in civil and credit relations in accordance with the current regulations or laws. On the other hand, local government bondholders are obliged to pay tax (that is, institutions pay corporate income tax and individuals pay personal income tax) for interest income arising from local government bonds and income arising from transfer of the local government bonds (as a kind of income arising from securities transfer) in case of transfer of such bonds, in accordance with the tax laws.

OVERVIEW OF PAST AND CURRENT CREDIT AND FINANCIAL INSTITUTIONS

This section is an overview of the past and current credit and financial institutions (including VDB, formerly the DAF) that have functions, with certain limitations, of wholesale, retail, and credit enhancement similar to what will be set up in the CIFF. Those credit institutions share characteristics in areas such as establishment, capital mobilization sources, managerial organization tasks, and borrower eligibility, among others. The characteristics were used as a reference by the study team to assess optional legal structures and to make recommendations at the end of this section.

Development assistance fund

The DAF, now reorganized as the VDB, was established under Decree 50/1999/ND-CP, dated July 8, 1999. Its purposes were to mobilize medium- and long-term capital, and to receive and manage the state's capital sources used for development investment credit to implement the state's development investment support policy. The DAF was structured as a state financial organization that operates as a nonprofit. It had status as a legal person; it had charter capital, a financial balance, and its own seal; and it was entitled to open its accounts at the state treasury and banks in Vietnam and overseas.

Charter capital and capital mobilization sources

The DAF's charter capital was D 3 trillion (equivalent to US$136 million) derived from the existing charter capital of the National Investment Support Fund[34] and annual supplementary state budget allocations. Any change of the charter capital of the DAF was subject to the approval of the prime minister.

Decision 231/1999 of the prime minister stated that the DAF could mobilize capital from the following sources: (a) state budget, (b) loans from other funds (for example, post savings, social insurance fund, and so on), (c) government bonds, (d) foreign loans used for on-lending, (e) trust capital, and (f) other sources.[35]

Managerial organization of the development assistance fund

The DAF was composed of the Management Council, the Board of Supervision, the general director, the deputy general directors, and the professional bureaus and sections. The appointment, dismissal, commendation, and discipline of Management Council members, the head of the Board of Supervision, the general director, and the deputy general directors of the DAF were as decided by the prime minister at the proposal of the head of the Government Commission for Organization and Personnel.

The Management Council of the DAF comprised five members (two full-time members, the chairman and vice chairman-cum-general director; and three part-time members representing the MOF, MPI, and SBV). The council had the following tasks and powers:

- Submit to the prime minister for approval any supplements or amendments of the DAF charter, as well as matters concerning the development investment credits that were beyond its jurisdiction.
- Adopt the operation orientations, financial plans, and final settlement reports of the DAF.
- Perform tasks and exercise powers as stipulated in the DAF charter.
- Supervise and inspect DAF operations according to the DAF charter and decisions of the Management Council.
- Scrutinize reports of the Board of Supervision, settle complaints, and report cases beyond its jurisdiction to the prime minister for consideration and settlement.

The Board of Supervision of the DAF was responsible to the DAF Management Council for supervision of all operations of the DAF. The board had the following tasks and powers:

- Inspect and supervise the observance of the guidelines, policies, and professional regimes and rules in DAF operations to raise their efficiency and ensure the safety of the state's property and the DAF's assets.
- Report to the DAF Management Council on the inspection and supervision results and propose the measures to resolve any issues.
- Carry out its work independently according to the program already adopted by the DAF Management Council.
- Present its reports or recommendations on the inspection and supervision results and/or report on financial settlement evaluation at meetings of the Management Council (but not entitled to vote.

- Consider and submit to the competent authorities for settlement all complaints about DAF operations that were lodged by capital lending organizations, investors, credit institutions undertaking the entrusted loan provision, and other organizations and individuals.

The general director was the DAF's legal representative who took responsibility before the prime minister, to the DAF Management Council, and before the law for the entire operations of the DAF. The general director's tasks and powers complied with the provisions of the DAF's charter. The general director was assisted by the deputy general directors and an assisting apparatus. The general director was responsible for setting up and dissolving professional bureaus and sections, branches, and transaction offices, as well as appointing and dismissing heads and deputy heads of bureaus and sections. Directors and deputy directors of branches and transaction offices were decided by the general director after obtaining consent of the Management Council.

Eligible borrowers

Decree 43/1999, on development investment credit, stipulates that eligible borrowers will be development investment projects of different economic sectors that are capable of capital recovery in a number of areas, including the transport and water sector and some socialization projects in education, health, culture, and sports.[36] However, the decree does not make clear whether revenue-generating projects carried out by provincial governments, such as by a project management unit (PMU) or a sectoral department, are eligible borrowers or not. As for non-revenue-generating or insufficient-revenue-generating projects, provincial governments could not get financing from the DAF, except for programs and projects approved by the prime minister.

Development assistance fund tasks

According to Article 5 of Decree 50/1999, the DAF had the following tasks:

- Mobilize medium- and long-term capital and receive the state's capital sources (including domestic and overseas capital) for implementation of the state's development investment support policy.
- Use its capital sources efficiently and for the right purposes.
- Provide investment loans and recover debts.
- Provide postinvestment interest rate support.
- Provide guaranty for investors to borrow investment capital to reguarantee, and to undertake the reguarantee for investment funds.
- Entrust or take the entrusted provision of investment loans.
- Perform other tasks assigned by the prime minister.
- Strictly abide by the state's laws and other regulations concerning its operation.
- Observe the regime of periodical reports to the prime minister and the concerned ministries and branches as prescribed.

Note that (a) the DAF had no function to provide on-lending loans to commercial banks for lending to provincial governments, and (b) the DAF could provide eligible investors with guarantee services (that is, a type of credit enhancement). However, it is uncertain whether those investors could be provincial governments (via a PMU or sectoral department).

Taxation regime

Article 2 of Decree 50/1999/ND-CP states that the DAF is exempted from taxes and state budget remittances in order to reduce its lending interest rate and guaranty fee. The DAF was assigned the centralized economic cost-accounting and financial regime decided by the prime minister at the proposal of the MOF.

Vietnam Development Bank

The VDB was established pursuant to Decision 108/2006/QD-TTg of the prime minister, dated May 19, 2006, to reorganize the DAF and to implement the state's policies on development investment credit and export credit.

The VDB has legal person status, charter capital, and a seal. It is allowed to open accounts at the SBV, the state treasury, and domestic and foreign commercial banks and to join the system of payment with banks and provide payment services according to the provisions of laws. The VDB took over all the rights and responsibilities of the DAF.

The VDB operates on a not-for-profit basis. Its compulsory reserve ratio is 0 percent. The VDB is not required to buy deposit insurance. The VDB's payment capacity is guaranteed by the government.

Charter capital and capital mobilization sources

VDB's charter capital is D 5 trillion (US$227 million), which comes from the previous charter capital of the DAF. Adjustments to the charter capital of the VDB depend on its specific requirements and tasks, ensure the capital adequacy ratio, and are considered and decided by the prime minister.

According to Decision 108/2006 (Article 3) and Decision 110/2006 (Article 21), the capital sources of the VDB are as follows:

- State budget sources, including (a) the charter capital of the VDB, (b) state budget capital allocated to projects according to annual plans, and (c) ODA capital assigned by the government)
- Mobilized capital, including (a) issuing of bonds and deposit certificates according to the provisions of laws; (b) loans from the Postal Savings, the Social Insurance Fund, and domestic and overseas credit and financial institutions)
- Receipt of entrusted deposits of domestic and overseas institutions
- Nonrefundable capital voluntarily contributed by individuals; economic, financial, and credit institutions; sociopolitical organizations; and domestic and overseas associations, societies, and organizations
- Receipt of entrusted capital from local governments; economic organizations; sociopolitical organizations; and domestic and overseas associations, societies, and organizations for granting and lending
- Other capital sources as provided by law.

Further, pursuant to Decisions 108/2006 and 110/2006, the prime minister issued Decision 44/2007, dated March 30, 2007, promulgating the Regulations on Financial Management of the VDB, according to which, for its operation capital, the VDB could mobilize capital from the following sources:

- Issuing of the government bonds, bonds guaranteed by the government, bonds of the VDB, bills (of exchange) of the VDB, deposit certificates

- Borrowing from Vietnam Social Insurance, the domestic financial credit institution
- Borrowing from foreign financial and credit organizations
- State budget provisions for postinvestment assistance
- ODA funds as authorized by the MOF to provide on-lending loans
- Receipt of entrusted deposits from domestic and foreign organizations
- Mandated capital (for releasing to projects and collecting debts from clients) of domestic and foreign organizations through the mandate contract between the VDB and mandate organizations
- Volunteered and nonrefunded capital from individuals; economic, financial, and credit organizations; as well as sociopolitical organizations, associations, and domestic and foreign nongovernmental organizations
- Capital provided by the state budget to fulfill the mission on investment and credit, export credit, and objectives and programs of the government.

Managerial organization of the Vietnam Development Bank

The managerial organization of the VDB is stipulated in Decision 110/2006, according to which the VDB must be composed of the Board of Management, the Board of Supervision, and the executive apparatus. The appointment or dismissal of members of the Board of Management and the general director of the VDB are to be decided by the prime minister (at the proposal of the minister of home affairs after consulting the MOF and relevant agencies). The appointment or dismissal of deputy general directors, the head of the Board of Supervision, and the chief accountant shall be decided by the Board of Management. The appointment or dismissal of other managerial tittles of the VDB shall be decided by the general director.

The Board of Management of the VDB has five members, including full-time members and part-time members, of which, the chairman of the Board of Management and general director are full-time members, and the leaders of the MOF, MPI, and SBV are part-time members. The Board of Management of the VDB has the following powers:

- Manage the VDB in compliance with stipulations of Decision 108/2006, its charter, and other related regulations.
- Decide on the development plan and operational direction of the VDB.
- Approve the VDB's yearly business plan based on the proposal of the general director.
- Ratify the establishment, division, separation, mergence, and dissolution of operations centers, branches, and representative offices in domestic and foreign locations based on the proposal of the general director.
- Decide appointment or dismissal for the VDB's management titles, including deputy general director, controller-general of the Board of Supervision, and chief accountant based on the proposal of the general director.
- Ratify the appointment scheme and the general director's appointment or dismissal of the director of a department at the head office, and directors of branches, operations centers, and representative offices domestic and abroad.
- Issue documents on such matters as (a) general regulations on the operation of the Board of Management and Board of Supervision, (b) general regulations on the professional operations of the VDB, and (c) guidance documents to implement the state regulations.

- Examine and supervise the executive apparatus in implementing the government's regulations on the development of investment credit, export credit of the state, the VDB charter, and related decisions of the Board of Management.
- Approve the Board of Supervision activity plan and consider its supervision result report and financial liquidation appraising report.
- Approve the annual performance report, financial statement, and cleared-balance sheet of the VDB.
- Report to the minister of internal affairs for submission to the prime minister to appoint or dismiss the chairperson of the Board of Management, its general director, and members.
- Write a proposal to the MOF for submission to the prime minister to do the following: (a) amend or supplement policies on the development of investment credit and export credit, (b) amend or supplement the charter on the operation and organization of the VDB, and (c) amend or supplement the general regulation of financial management of the VDB.
- Fulfill the other rights and missions of the VDB in accordance with the laws.
- Be responsible before the prime minister for the Board of Management's decisions.

The Board of Supervision of the VDB has a maximum of seven full-time members. The controller-general is appointed or dismissed by the Board of Management, and other members of the Board of Supervision are appointed or dismissed by the chairperson of the Board of Management based on the proposal of the controller-general. The Board of Supervision of the VDB is empowered to accomplish the following:

- Examine the abidance of guidelines, policies, laws, and resolutions of the Board of Management.
- Examine the financial activities and abidance of accounting mechanisms, the operation of internal inspections, and the audit system of the VDB.
- Review the annual financial statement and, if necessary, examine in detail each item related to the VDB's financial activities in order to report to the Board of Management, the MOF, and other relevant agencies.
- Report to the Board of Management about the accuracy, honesty, and legality of recording and filing of accounting records, as well as preparation of accounting books and financial statements; and about the operation of the internal inspection and audit system of the VDB.
- Approve controlling tasks and proposals submitted to the Board of Management for measures to amend, supplement, and improve the VDB's operation in accordance with the laws.
- Use the VDB's internal inspection and audit system for implementing its missions.
- Fulfill other assigned missions and use designated powers.
- The general director of the VDB is the legal representative of the VDB, responsible before the Board of Management, the prime minister, and the law for all management of the VDB's operation with the assistance of deputy general directors and the chief accountant. The general director has the following powers:
- Organize and execute the missions that the government and the prime minister assigned to the VDB.
- Manage the VDB's activities, decide issues related to the VDB's activities in compliance with the laws and resolutions of the Board of Management, and be responsible for performance of the VDB.

- Regulate the decentralization to the VDB's affiliates in carrying out operations of state investment and export credit, postinvestment support, guarantee, and the other operations in compliance with the laws.
- Decide the lending interest rate and deposit interest rate of the VDB in accordance with the regulations of the state development investment credit and export credit.
- Receive capital and other resources given by the government.
- Approve an independent audit institution to audit the VDB's activities.
- Decide the appointment and dismissal of the directors of departments at the head office, and directors of branches, operations center, and representative offices domestic and abroad (after getting approval of the Board of Management).
- Decide on the appointment and dismissal of the other positions of the VDB, including (a) deputy director of the operations center, branches, and representative offices; (b) managers and deputy managers of divisions, and director and deputy director of head office departments; and (c) other positions under the general director's authority as stipulated by the Board of Management.
- Issue documents on (a) general regulations on the operation and activity of the operations center, branches, and representative offices and (b) regulations on the organization and operation of internal inspection and audit in compliance with the laws.
- Submit to the Board of Management documentation for (a) approval of the VDB's yearly business plan; (b) reporting to the minister of finance to submit to the prime minister for decisions on the amendment or supplementation to the charter on organization and operation of the VDB and general regulations on the financial regime; (c) establishment, division, separation, mergence, or dissolution of the branches and representative offices of operations centers and branches and representative offices of the VDB; (d) appointment and dismissal of the deputy general directors and chief accountant; and (e) deciding of commission rate, fee, and fines applicable to customers in compliance with the laws.
- Be the legal representative of the VDB before the law in procedure, dispute, liquidation, dissolution, and international relations related to the VDB's activities.
- Exert authority in case of emergency (such as natural calamities, enemy-inflicted destruction, fire, breakdown) to decide on measures, to be responsible for such decisions, and to report immediately afterward to the Board of Management.
- Sign documents, agreements, contracts, and certificates of the VDB in the activities of internal affairs and foreign affairs in compliance with the laws.
- Be responsible before the Board of Management and state competency authority for the implementation of the authority's executive missions in accordance with the laws.
- Report to the Board of Management and other state competency agencies as stipulated in the charter and other regulations related to the VDB's operations.
- Exercise other rights and missions according to the regulations of the law and the Board of Management.

Eligible borrowers

Decision 44/2007 (Article 7) states that the VDB could use its operating capital for implementing the state policy on development investment credit and export credit in accordance with the regulation of the government. In this regard, the government issued Decree 75/2011 on state investment credit and export credit (as amended by Decree 54/2013/ND and Decree 133/2013), according to which (Article 5) eligible borrowers are investors having investment projects on the list of projects eligible for investment credit attached to Decree 75/2011. Examples include the investment projects on building works to treat wastewater and garbage in urban areas, industrial parks, economic zones, export-processing zones, high-tech parks, hospitals, and craft-village industrial complexes, all of which fall under groups A and B projects according to the laws on construction. Taking into account the definition of *investors* in Article 1.2 of Decree 75/2011, in which investors are enterprises, economic organizations, and self-accounting and revenue-generating state agencies, the researchers found that a provincial government and its subordinate departments (via their PMUs) could not be eligible borrowers of VDB loans, except in the case of the programs and projects approved by the prime minister, as further noted in the next section.

Tasks of the Vietnam Development Bank

According to Decision 108/2006 (Article 4), the VDB has the following tasks:

- Mobilize and receive capital of domestic and overseas organizations to provide state credits for development investment and export under the regulations of the government.
- Implement policies on development investment credit, including (a) granting of loans for development investment, (b) postinvestment support, and (c) investment credit guarantee.
- Implement policies on export credit, including (a) granting of loans for export, (b) export credit guarantee, and (c) guarantee for bidding participation and for implementation of export contracts.
- Accept entrusted management of ODA capital on-lent by the government and accept entrusted provision of loans for investment and collection of debts for domestic and overseas organizations through entrustment contracts between the VDB and entrusting organizations.
- Entrust financial and credit institutions to carry out credit transactions of the VDB.
- Provide payment services for clients and join domestic and international payment systems to serve the VDB's operations under the provisions of law.
- Perform international cooperation tasks concerning development investment credit and export credit.
- Carry out other tasks assigned by the prime minister, from time to time.

With regard to carrying out prime minister's assigned tasks, it is worth noting an example of Decision 13/2009 of the prime minister[37]: assigning the VDB to provide loans to provincial governments for solidifying the canals and developing rural transport roads, infrastructure for aquaculture, and infrastructure for craft villages in rural areas for the period 2009–15, as mentioned earlier.

The study team has noted that (a) the VDB has no function to provide on-lending loans to commercial banks for lending to provincial governments and (b) the VDB could provide eligible investors with guarantee services (that is, a type of credit enhancement), although they are not provincial governments (via a PMU or sectoral department). In other words, the VDB seems not to have a wholesale and credit enhancement function as the CIFF does.

Risk mitigation methods

The VDB may set up risk provision funds for dealing with risks caused by insolvency of investors, exporters, or overseas importers. The VDB's debt classification must follow regulations of the SBV. The prime minister decides on levels of deduction for setting up and using risk provision funds in the financial mechanism of the VDB. According to Decision 44/2007 of the prime minister (Article 8), the annual fund extraction rate of the risk provision fund will be equal to 0.5 percent of the average balance of loans for investment, export credit loans, investment credit, export guarantee, tender bond, and performance bond.

Taxation regime

According to Decision 108/2006 of the prime minister (Article 2), the VDB is exempt from taxes and state budget contributions applicable according to the provisions of law.

LEGAL ASSESSMENT AND RECOMMENDATIONS FOR SETTING UP A CITY INFRASTRUCTURE FINANCING FACILITY

Fundamental weaknesses constraining provincial borrowing

Vietnam currently has a weak enabling environment for providing subnational governments with access to debt finance for local public infrastructure. The existing regulations are incomplete, inconsistent, and scattered among different legal documents. Some regulations are established on a temporary basis for dealing with specific contexts without regard for the longer-term consequences of the regulations. Fundamental weaknesses in the current regime include the following:

Lack of legal clarity in borrowing authority. Generally, the regulation on the authority of subnational governments to incur debt has to be given by both the SBL and public debt management legislation. However, these regulations have not yet clearly specified the form of bank loan as one the sources of subnational debt, an omission that could lead to the interpretation that borrowing by provinces from commercial banks is not fully legally supported.

Restriction on debt terms/maturities. Currently there is no restriction on the maximum term of borrowing instruments. However, the maximum term of a bank loan to subnational governments is interpreted to be restricted to 24 months because of the provision of an official State Bank of Vietnam Letter (576/NHNN-CSTT). In practice, commercial banks strictly interpret the provision as applying to all types of lending so as to avoid any subsequent legal consequences.

Moral hazard of implicit guarantee of central government. Currently, the requirement that subnational borrowing must be approved by the MOF on a transactional basis may create the moral hazard of an implied central government guarantee.

Unspecified debt security. The presence of a mechanism that ties revenues of subnational entities pledged to creditors in case of debt insolvency is critical.

However, the current legal framework has not yet specified any means of debt security that provinces could use for their borrowing.

Inadequate standards of disclosure. Currently, formal principles and requirements on reporting and disclosure of subnational debt are not yet sufficiently in place, despite the existing provisions on disclosure of national public debt information. Potential lenders thus do not (a) have adequate information for credit evaluation, (b) feel confident in making decisions on credit provision, and (c) appear able to monitor and manage the loan uses and repayments by provinces.

Inadequate standards of default and insolvency. At present, no provisions in the current legal framework on the mechanisms and procedures are available in the event of default or insolvency of local governments.

Importantly, the government of Vietnam has already begun adopting regulatory reforms to improve the legal framework for subnational debt, including the new SBL of 2015. However, the legal and regulatory framework should be further upgraded to meet the government's financial objective, including setting up a financing facility to jumpstart the subnational debt market.

Specific legal considerations for setting up a city infrastructure financing facility pilot

The proposed CIFF with a wholesale function (which proposes to use the government's foreign loans) may not work without clarification or an appropriate amendment to Decree 78/2010.[38] That is because the interpretation of the provisions of Decree 78/2010 is that for on-lending of the government foreign loan to the provincial governments, the on-lending agency is always only the MOF itself. Thus, for a CIFF to be legally established, the government must (a) clarify or amend Decree 78/2010 to allow the establishment of a CIFF with wholesale function, (b) sign an international loan treaty with an international donor, such as the World Bank, that allows the establishment of a CIFF with credit enhancement function, or (c) combine the establishment of a CIFF with a wholesale function with a treaty that allows for a CIFF with a credit enhancement function.

It is assumed that a CIFF with wholesale and credit enhancement functions would be established. To avoid any unexpected conflict and overlap between these two functions, any reforms should establish two separate entities (or two separate units within one entity) for performing each of those functions separately. Subject to further discussion and determination by the stakeholders, such entities could be established within the MOF—such as a department or a PMU of the MOF—or outside the MOF—such as a new separate entity or unit outside the MOF—pursuant to a relevant decision of the MOF, a decision of the prime minister, or a decree of the government, respectively.

As discussed earlier in this chapter regarding the Law on Public Debt Management and Decree 78/2010, the MOF's DDMEF could provide on-lending of government foreign loans directly to provincial governments, such as by providing a retail function similar to that of the CIFF. However, that approach would not contribute much to the development of the debt market of the provincial governments, nor would it attract or mobilize the participation of the private sector in providing capital for the provincial governments for city infrastructure investment, as contemplated. Thus, subject to further determination by stakeholders, the CIFF with a wholesale function or credit enhancement function would likely meet the twin objectives of mobilizing more funds for provincial governments for infrastructure development while developing the debt market for provincial governments.

The SBL and all its guiding legislation are silent on a recourse mechanism, including detailed procedures to ensure that in the case of provincial government default, the lenders and financiers receiving loans from the CIFF with a wholesale function could recover the funds from the provincial budget. Therefore, subject to the further determination by the stakeholders, the government must stipulate a recourse mechanism when establishing the CIFF. The MOF and the SBV could guide the establishment of such a mechanism in accordance with their state management authority in a new circular (box 4.1).

Vietnam's laws currently have no specific regulations or guidance regarding the assessment of credit risks related to the loans to be provided by commercial banks to the provincial governments. In practice, commercial banks' own experience is in assessing credit risk of corporate or individual customers rather than of provincial governments. Thus, the SBV will need to provide specific guidance or regulations on the CIFF with a wholesale function, subject to the further determination by stakeholders. To some extent, such guidance will support the commercial banks' credit assessment process for providing loans to provincial governments.

BOX 4.1

City Infrastructure Financing Facility Recourse Mechanism

Purpose of a Recourse Mechanism

The purpose of the CIFF recourse mechanism is to encourage the commercial banks to provide loans to the PPCs. The mechanism would allow the commercial banks to secure the loans by requiring that the PPC set up a special account at a commercial bank for receiving part the annual revenue of the PPC. Such revenues might be from the provincial budget revenue sources or from a transfer from the central government and would belong to budget items used for repayment of borrowing by provincial governments. The lending commercial bank would have a senior right to intercept revenue if the debt service defaults.

Proposed Recourse Arrangement

The proposed CIFF recourse mechanism is shown in figure B4.1.1

Main Contents and Provisions of the Recourse Agreement

For the benefit of both the lending commercial bank and the PPC, the recourse agreement should contain the following main provisions:

- The recourse account is in the name of the PPC, as account holder, and is opened at the lending commercial bank.
- The recourse account is an interest-bearing account in which the earned interest belongs to the PPC.
- The money balance in the recourse account should be maintained at least at a level equal to the outstanding liability or debt (that is, the loan interest and partial principal) of the PPC to be paid or repaid in the payment period (for example, on a quarterly, semiannual, or annual basis) to the lending commercial bank.

continued

Box 4.1, *continued*

FIGURE B4.1.1
City Infrastructure Financing Facility Recourse Mechanism

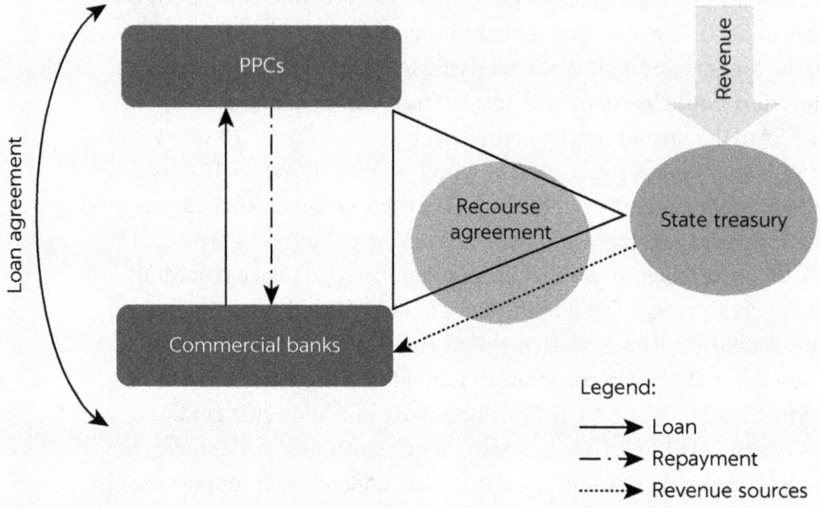

Note: PPCs = provincial People's Committees. The ***loan agreement*** is to be signed by and between a PPC and a commercial bank. The ***recourse agreement*** is a tripartite agreement among a PPC, a commercial bank, and the state treasury.

The lending commercial bank has an irrevocable right to deduct from the recourse account any interest and principal due if the PPC fails to pay or repay on the date payment is due. After such a deduction and upon receipt of a written request by the lending commercial bank, to ensure that the required balance is met, the state treasury will then transfer partial revenue of the PPC to the recourse account, using, for example, part of the provincial budget revenue or a transfer from the central government from a budget item assigned to repayment of borrowing by provincial governments.

As discussed earlier, the SBV Official Letter 576/NHNN-CSTT, dated June 10, 2005, guides lending by commercial banks to provincial governments. It stipulates a maximum loan term of 24 months, although infrastructure investments normally are medium to long term. Thus, subject to further determination by stakeholders, the SBV must issue a new circular that would facilitate the commercial banks' medium- and long-term lending to provincial governments and would invalidate the application of Official Letter 576/NHNN-CSTT.

RECOMMENDATIONS ON THE LEGAL STRUCTURE AND SETUP OF A CITY INFRASTRUCTURE FINANCING FACILITY

The recommendations on legal structures and preliminary roadmaps proposed for setup of the CIFF are provided in table 4.1.

TABLE 4.1 **Legal Structure and Considerations for a City Infrastructure Financing Facility**

ISSUES	RECOMMENDATIONS	NOTES, REMARKS, ASSUMPTIONS, AND LEGAL ADJUSTMENTS
Legal basis for establishment of a CIFF	CIFF may be set up under a decision of the MOF, a decision of the prime minister, or a decree of the government.	For a CIFF with wholesale function, it is necessary to have a clarification to or an appropriate amendment of Decree 78/2010, allowing the establishment of a CIFF with wholesale function. For a CIFF with credit enhancement function, or a CIFF with both wholesale and credit enhancement functions, it is necessary (a) to have a clarification to or an appropriate amendment of Decree 78/2010, allowing the establishment of a CIFF with wholesale function; and (b) to have in place an international loan treaty (to be signed by the government or the MOF, and an international donor, such as the World Bank), allowing the establishment of a CIFF with credit enhancement function. In this regard, the recommendation is to set up a CIFF in a pilot period (under a decision of the MOF or the prime minister, or a decree by the government), to be set on the basis of an international loan treaty (for example, between the World Bank and the government of Vietnam). The pilot period could be three to five years and would be aimed at investigating the market, the operation, and other matters. Some provincial governments and commercial banks would be selected.
Legal form	To be further discussed and determined.	Assuming that a CIFF with wholesale and credit enhancement functions would be established, in order to avoid any unexpected conflict and overlapping between these two functions and to assess the performance of each, one entity would be established with two separate units for performing each function of wholesale and credit enhancement. Subject to further decision by the government and the relevant international loan treaty to be signed by the government or the MOF, and an international donor, such entity could be established within the MOF (for example, as a department or project management unit of the MOF) or as a new separate entity outside the MOF, pursuant to a relevant decision of the MOF or prime minister, or decree of the government, depending on the entity to be created.
Functions of a CIFF: wholesale, credit enhancement, and retail	To be further discussed and determined.	From the legal perspective, the CIFF could be established with all three functions. However, now the MOF (via its DDMEF) could provide a retail function similar to the CIFF with retail function. That function would not contribute much to the development of the debt market of the provincial governments, nor would it attract or mobilize the participation of the private sector in providing capital for the provincial governments for city infrastructure investment, as contemplated. Thus, subject to further discussion and determination by the stakeholders, the CIFF with wholesale function, with credit enhancement function, or both would meet the twin objectives of mobilizing more funds for provincial governments for infrastructure development, while developing the debt market for provincial governments.
Financing period	To be further discussed and determined.	Generally, the CIFF should aim to provide medium- and long-term loans to commercial banks and provincial governments and/or provide credit enhancement for medium- and long-term loans provided by commercial banks to provincial governments. It is proposed that the SBV would issue a new circular that would facilitate the commercial banks' medium- and long-term lending to provincial governments and would invalidate the application of Official Letter 576/NHNN/CSTT. Such a circular could be issued by the SBV after or even before the establishment of the CIFF.
Potential roadblock	There may be such issues as the following: • No clear stipulations under the Vietnamese laws on the establishment of entities like a CIFF.	For a CIFF with wholesale function, it is necessary to have a clarification to or an appropriate amendment of Decree 78/2010, allowing the establishment of a CIFF with wholesale function. For a CIFF with credit enhancement function, or a CIFF with both wholesale function and credit enhancement function, it is necessary to (a) have a clarification to or an appropriate amendment of Decree 78/2010, allowing the establishment of a CIFF with wholesale function; and (b) have in place an international loan treaty to be signed by the government or the MOF, and an international donor (for example, the World Bank), allowing the establishment of a CIFF with credit enhancement function.

continued

TABLE 4.1, *continued*

ISSUES	RECOMMENDATIONS	NOTES, REMARKS, ASSUMPTIONS, AND LEGAL ADJUSTMENTS
	• No clear stipulations under the Vietnamese laws on a recourse mechanism, including its detailed procedures, which could ensure that in the case of a provincial government's default, the lenders or financiers could recover the funds from the provincial budget.	Subject to further discussion and determination by the stakeholders, the recourse mechanism should be mentioned and stipulated in the relevant decision of the MOF or the prime minister (or decree of the government) on establishment of the CIFF as noted previously. The mechanism would be further guided by the MOF and the SBV in accordance with their state management authority in the new circular.
	• No specific guidance or regulations under the Vietnamese laws regarding the assessment of credit risks relating to loans that would be provided by commercial banks to the provincial governments.	Subject to further discussion and determination by the stakeholders, regarding the CIFF with wholesale function, it is necessary to have specific guidance or regulations from the SBV on this matter, which will, to a certain extent, support the credit assessment process by the commercial banks for providing loans to the provincial governments.
	• Limitation on the maximum loan term of 24 months for loans provided by commercial banks to provincial governments.	Subject to the further discussion and determination by the stakeholders, in order to facilitate lending by the commercial banks to the provincial governments under the model of a CIFF with wholesale function and credit enhancement function, it is necessary to have the SBV's new circular, which would facilitate the commercial banks' medium- and long-term lending to provincial governments and would invalidate the application of Official Letter 576/NHNN-CSTT, dated June 10, 2005.
	• Lack of support from the key decision makers.	Key decision makers must be given information that explains and proves the positive impacts of the CIFF with wholesale and credit enhancement functions to enable them to make the decision to support the CIFF.

The following issues need to be further discussed and defined with all stakeholders in the potential project preparation:

- Financial and tax regime
- Charter of organization and operation of the CIFF
- Financial regulations of the CIFF
- Possible limitations to capital structure and financial instruments used to raise the capital of the CIFF
- Minimum capital requirement
- Reporting duties and accounting
- Relevant supervisory agency
- Requirements related to asset management
- Requirements related to risk management
- Possible limitations that could apply to sector financing or to types of clients. Wholesale facility: the eligible borrowers are commercial banks that directly borrow from the CIFF and then provide on-lending loans to provincial governments for infrastructure investment. Credit enhancement facility: the eligible clients are the provincial governments.
- Governance requirements and minimum staff requirements
- Average time needed to set up such entity

Notes: CIFF = city infrastructure financing facility; MOF = ministry of finance; DDMEF = Department of Debt Management and External Finance; SBV = State Bank of Vietnam.

NOTES

1. According to the Constitution and the Local Government Organization Law 2015 (which replaced the People's Councils and People's Committees Organization Law in 2016), in addition to the provincial, district, and commune-level councils, a "special administrative-economic unit" may be established by the National Assembly.
2. The former SBL was approved by the National Assembly on December 16, 2002. The current revised SBL was approved in 2015 and became effective in January 2017.

3. Under the SBL 2015, total borrowing of the provincial government budget comprises funds for (a) covering the deficit of the provincial government budget and (b) repaying the principal of the provincial government budget.
4. Under the SBL 2015, in addition to the deficit spending of the central budget, a deficit spending of the provincial budget is also allowed. Such deficit spending of the provincial budget is (a) used only for investment in projects under midterm public investment plans as decided by the PPCo and (b) aggregated with the state budget deficit and decided by the National Assembly. The deficit of the provincial budget could be covered by domestic borrowing sources (from the local government bonds issuance, on-lending loans from the government, and other domestic borrowings permissible by the laws).
5. Exceptions are stipulated in (a) Article 5.3 of Decree 123/2004 (for Hanoi), and (b) Article 5.3 of Decree 124/2004, which was amended by Decree 61/2014 (for Ho Chi Minh City).
6. Articles 26.1, 26.2, and 26.3 of Decree 60/2003 and Section II.1.3.4 of Circular 59/2003.
7. Article 7.6 of the SBL 2015. For Hanoi and Ho Chi Minh City, the limit is 60 percent. For localities that have an amount of revenue lower than recurrent expenditure of local budgets (third-tier provinces), the limit is 20 percent.
8. Article 7.5.c of the SBL 2015.
9. This book was prepared before the new Law on Public Debt Management (LPDM) was approved. The LPDM 2017 will be in effect in July, 2018; therefore, the main discussion is focused on LPDM 2009. Draft LPDM 2017 was reviewed in the preparation of this book, and did not substantially affect the discussion on the regulatory framework.
10. Article 39.2 of the Law on Public Debt Management 2009.
11. Article 18 of Decree 79/2010.
12. Resolution 10/2011 of the National Assembly and Decision 958/2012 of the prime minister.
13. Article 24.3 of the Law on Public Debt Management.
14. Article 2 of Decision 2328/2014 of the MOF on functions, duties, and powers of the Department of Debt Management and External Finance.
15. According to Article 19.5, Decree 78/2010 of the Law on Public Debt Management. Further advantages given to provincial governments under the decree are in Article 10, regarding lending fees; Article 7, on interest rates; and Article 12 on security requirements.
16. Article 94.1 of the Credit Institution Law.
17. Article 128 of the Credit Institution Law states that the total balance of loans made to a single client shall not exceed 15 percent of the equity of the commercial bank, and the total balance of loans made to a single client and related persons shall not exceed 25 percent of the equity of the commercial bank.
18. Article 130 of the Credit Institution Law relates to the prudential ratios: the solvency ratio, the minimum capital adequacy ratio of 8 percent or a higher ratio as stipulated by the SBV from time to time, the maximum ratio of short-term funds used to provide medium- and long-term loans, status of current foreign currency and gold over equity, the ratio of loan balance over total monies deposited, and the ratios of medium- and long-term deposits over total medium- and long-term loan balances.
19. Article 131 of the Credit Institution Law.
20. Article 17 of Circular 36/2014 of the SBV.
21. Decision 1627/2001. Amendments to SBV Decision 1627/2001 include Decision 688/2002, Decision 28/2002, Decision 127/2005, Decision 783/2005, and Circular 33/2011.
22. Article 2 of SBV Decision 1627/2001 (as amended from time to time).
23. Article 6 of SBV Decision 1627/2001 (as amended from time to time).
24. Article 7 of SBV Decision 1627/2001 (as amended from time to time).
25. Articles 8 and 10 of SBV Decision 1627/2001 (as amended from time to time).
26. Article 11 of SBV Decision 1627/2001 (as amended from time to time).
27. Article 16 of SBV Decision 1627/2001 (as amended from time to time).
28. In accordance with its Decision 1627/2001, the SBV issued Official Letter No. 1354/NHNN-CSTT, dated December 4, 2002. The MOF's Official Letter No. 4761/TC/TCNH dated April 21, 2005, requested the SBV to send an Official Letter 576/NHNN-CSTT, dated June 10, 2005.
29. Decision 13/2009 of the prime minister (as amended by Decision 56/2009 of the prime minister).
30. Decree 01/2011 consolidated and replaced the regulations contained in Decrees 141/2003 and 53/2009.
31. Article 4 of Decree 01/2011.

32. Contents must include (a) the purpose for bond issuance and other information on the project regarding the bond issuance capital source; (b) investment capital structuring of the project and the capital need from bond issuance; (c) expected volume, term, interest rate, form, and plan for bond issuance; (d) plan for allocation of payment source of principal and interest of bonds upon maturity; and (f) commitments of the issuing entity to bond buyers.
33. According to Circular 81/2012 (Article 8), within 30 working days from the date of receipt of the scheme of bond issuance (as approved by the PPCos) from the PPC, the MOF shall assess and notify in writing to the PPC requesting that it implement the bond issuance (if the conditions for bond issuance are satisfied).
34. The National Investment Support Fund was established under Decision 808-TTg, dated 09/12/1995, of the prime minister to raise funds and grant loans to the development investment projects in different branches and occupations under the preferential policy and in the areas with difficulties as defined by the government.
35. Decision 231/1999/QD-TTg dated 17/12/1999 of the prime minister on approval of the charter of the DAF.
36. Decision 231/1999 (Article 13) of the prime minister states that the eligible borrowers are stipulated in Decree 43/1999 on development investment credit. Article 8 of Decree 43/1999 stipulates those borrowers.
37. As amended by Decision 56/2009.
38. See descriptions of wholesale, retail, and credit enhancement functions in chapter 1 in the section, "Proposed CIFF Structures."

Appendix A
List of Key Legal Documents

CONSTITUTION

1. The Constitution of the Socialist Republic of Vietnam, dated November 28, 2013 ("Constitution").
2. Resolution No. 64/2013/QH13, dated November 28, 2013, of the National Assembly, on the implementation of the Constitution of the Socialist Republic of Vietnam.

GOVERNMENT, MINISTRY OF FINANCE, STATE BANK OF VIETNAM, AND LOCAL GOVERNMENTS

3. Law on government organization, dated December 25, 2001 ("Government Organization Law"), which was replaced by the Government Organization Law 2015, dated June 19, 2015 (effective January 1, 2016).
4. Law on the People's Councils and the People's Committees organization, dated November 26, 2003 ("People's Councils and the People's Committees Organization Law"), which was replaced by the Local Government Organization Law 2015, dated June 19, 2015 (effective January 1, 2016).
5. Law on State Bank of Vietnam, dated June 16, 2010 ("Law on State Bank of Vietnam").
6. Decree No. 36/2012/ND-CP, dated April 18, 2012, of the government, on defining the functions, tasks, and organizational structures of ministries and ministerial-level agencies ("Decree 36/2012"), as amended by Decree No. 48/2013/ND-CP, dated May 14, 2013, of the government, amending and supplementing a number of articles of decrees relating to control of administrative procedures ("Decree 48/2013").
7. Decree No.215/2013/ND-CP dated December 23, 2013, of the government stipulating function, task, power, and organizational structure of the Ministry of Finance ("Decree 215/2013").
8. Decision No.2328/QD-BTC dated September 9, 2014, of the MOF stipulating function, task, power and organizational structure of the Department of Debt Management and External Finance ("Decision 2328/2014").

9. Decision No.2338/QD-BTC dated September 9, 2014, of the Ministry of Finance stipulating function, task, power, and organizational structure of Department of Banking and Financial Institutions ("Decision 2338/2014").

LEGISLATION PROMULGATION

10. Law on legislation promulgation, dated June 3, 2008 ("Law on Legislation Promulgation"), which was replaced by the law on legislation promulgation, dated June 22, 2015 (effective July 1, 2016).

PUBLIC INVESTMENT AND PUBLIC DEBT MANAGEMENT

11. Law on public investment, dated June 18, 2014 ("Law on Public Investment").
12. Law on public debt management, dated June 17, 2009 ("Law on Public Debt Management").
13. (Amended) Law on public debt management, November 23, 2017. The law will be effective in July, 2018.
14. Resolution No.10/2011/QH13, dated November 8, 2011, of the National Assembly, on economic-social development plan for five years from 2011 to 2015 ("Resolution 10/2011").
15. Decision No.958/QD-TTg, dated July 27, 2012, of the prime minister, on approval of the public debt and national foreign debt strategy in the period of 2011–20 and the orientation toward 2030 ("Decision 958/2012").
16. Decree No.78/2010/ND-CP, dated July 14, 2010, of the government, on on-lending of government's foreign loans ("Decree 78/2010").
17. Decree No.79/2010/ND-CP, dated July 14, 2010, of the government, on public debt management operation ("Decree 79/2010").
18. Decree No.15/2011/ND-CP, dated February 16, 2011, of the government, on provision and management of government guarantee ("Decree 15/2011").
19. Decree No.01/2011/ND-CP, dated January 5, 2011, of the government, on issuance of government bonds, government-guaranteed bonds, and local government bonds ("Decree 01/2011").
20. Circular No.81/2012/TT-BTC, dated May 22, 2012, of the Ministry of Finance, guiding the issuance of local government bonds in local markets ("Circular 81/2012").

STATE BUDGET

21. Law on State Budget 2002, dated December 16, 2002.
22. Law on State Budget 2015, dated June 25, 2015, and effective from January 2017.
23. Law on Thrift Practice and Waste Combat, dated November 26, 2013 ("Law on Thrift Practice and Waste Combat").
24. Decree No.60/2003/ND-CP, dated June 6, 2004, of the government detailing and guiding the implementation of the State Budget Law ("Decree 60/2003").

25. Decree No.123/2004/ND-CP, dated May 18, 2004, of the government, stipulating a number of particular financial and budgetary mechanisms applicable to Hanoi capital ("Decree 123/2004).
26. Decree No.124/2004/ND-CP, dated May 18, 2004, of the government, stipulating a number of particular financial and budgetary mechanisms applicable to Ho Chi Minh City ("Decree 124/2004), as amended by Decree No.61/2014/ND-CP, dated June 19, 2014, of the government, on amendment and supplement of a number of articles of Decree 124/2004 ("Decree 61/2014").
27. Circular No.59/2003/TT-BTC, dated June 23, 2003, of the Ministry of Finance, guiding the implementation of Decree 60/2003 ("Circular 59/2003"), as corrected by Official Letter No.12725/TC-VP, dated December 4, 2003, of the Ministry of Finance, on correcting Circular 59/2003 ("Official Letter 12725/2003").
28. Circular No.51/2004/TT-BTC, dated June 9, 2004, of the Ministry of Finance, guiding the implementation of Decree No.123/2004 ("Circular 51/2004"), as corrected by Official Letter No.6616TC/NSNN, dated June 16, 2004, of the Ministry of Finance, on correcting Circular 51/2004 ("Official Letter 6616/2004").
29. Circular No.52/2004/TT-BTC, dated June 9, 2004, of the Ministry of Finance, guiding the implementation of Decree No.124/2004 ("Circular 52/2004"), as corrected by Official Letter No.6617TC/NSNN, dated June 16, 2004, of the MOF, on correcting Circular 52/2004 ("Official Letter 6617/2004").
30. Circular No.86/2004/TT-BTC, dated August 25, 2004, of the Ministry of Finance, guiding the management of mobilized capital for infrastructure investment of budget of provinces and municipalities within central authority ("Circular 86/2004").
31. Circular No.107/2008/TT-BTC, dated November 18, 2008, of the Ministry of Finance, providing supplemental guidance on a number of matters on management and operation of State Budget ("Circular 107/2008").
32. Circular No.128/2008/TT-BTC, dated December 24, 2008, of the Ministry of Finance, guiding collection and management of State Budget revenues through State Treasury ("Circular 128/2008").
33. Circular No.161/2012/TT-BTC, dated October 2, 2012, of the Ministry of Finance, stipulating the regime of control and payment of state budget expenditures through the state treasury ("Circular 161/2012").
34. Circular No.162/2012/TT-BTC, dated October 3, 2012, of the Ministry of Finance stipulating advanced payment fund from the state treasury ("Circular 162/2012"), as amended by Circular No.62/2015/TT-BTC, dated May 5, 2015, of the Ministry of Finance, on amendment and supplement of a number of articles of Circular 162/2012 ("Circular 62/2015").
35. Circular No.61/2014/TT-BTC, dated May 12, 2014, of the Ministry of Finance, guiding registration and usage of the account at the state treasury in the condition of applying budget and treasury management information systems ("Circular 61/2014").
36. Official letter No.576/NHNN-CSTT, dated June 10, 2005, of the State Bank of Vietnam, on lending to support the provincial budget for infrastructure works investment ("Official Letter 576/NHNN-CSTT").

37. Official letter No.1354/NHNN-CSTT, dated December 4, 2002, of the State Bank of Vietnam, guiding the lending to support provincial budget for infrastructure works investment ("Official letter 1354 /NHNN-CSTT").

CREDIT INSTITUTIONS

38. Law on Credit Institutions, dated June 16, 2010 ("Law on Credit Institutions").
39. Circular No.36/2014/TT-NHNN, dated November 20, 2014, of the State Bank of Vietnam, stipulating minimum safety limits and ratios in activities of credit institutions, branches of foreign banks ("Circular 36/2014").
40. Circular No.02/2013/TT-NHNN, dated January 21, 2013, of the State Bank of Vietnam, on providing on classification of assets, levels and method of setting up risk provisions, and use of provisions against credit risks in the banking activity of credit institutions, foreign banks' branches ("Circular 02/2013"), as amended by Circular No.09/2014/TT-NHNN, dated March 18, 2014, of the State Bank of Vietnam, on amending and supplementing a number of articles of Circular 02/2013 ("Circular 09/2014").
41. Circular No.43/2014/TT-NHNN, dated December 25, 2014, of the State Bank of Vietnam, on foreign currency loans provided by credit institutions and branches of foreign banks for clients being residents ("Circular 43/2014").
42. Circular No.28/2012/TT-NHNN, dated October 3, 2012, of the State Bank of Vietnam, on the bank guarantee ("Circular 28/2012").
43. Decision No.1627/2001/QD-NHNN, dated December 31, 2001, of the State Bank of Vietnam, issuing regulation on lending by credit institutions to customers ("Decision 1627/2001"), as amended by Decision No.688/2002/ QD-NHNN, dated July 1, 2002, of the State Bank of Vietnam, on overdue debt transfer of customers' loans at credit institutions ("Decision 688/2002"), Decision No.28/2002/QD-NHNN, dated January 11, 2002, of the State Bank of Vietnam, on amending Article 2 of Decision 1627/2001 ("Decision 28/2002"), Decision No.127/2005/QD-NHNN, dated February 3, 2005, of the State Bank of Vietnam, amending, supplementing a number of articles of Decision 1627/2001 ("Decision 127/2005") as amended by Decision No.783/2005/QD-NHNN, dated May 31, 2005, of the State Bank of Vietnam, on amendment and supplement of Article 1.6 of Decision 127/2005 ("Decision 783/2005"), amended by Circular No.33/2011/TT-NHNN, dated October 8, 2011, of the State Bank of Vietnam, on amendment and supplement of a number of articles of No. 13/2010/TT-NHNN dated May 20, 2010, of the State Bank of Vietnam issuing regulation on minimum safety ratio in activities of credit institution and regulations on lending of credit institutions to the clients promulgated by Decision 1627/2001 ("Circular 33/2011").

CIVIL CODE

44. Civil Code, dated June 14, 2005 ("Civil Code").
45. Decree No.163/2006/ND-CP, dated December 29, 2006, of the government, on secured transaction ("Decree 163/2006"), as amended by Decree

No.11/2012/ND-CP, dated February 22, 2012, of the government, on amendment and supplement of a number of articles of Decree 163/2006 ("Decree 11/2012").

INVESTMENTS AND ENTERPRISES

46. Law on investment, dated November 29, 2005 ("Investment Law of 2005"); replaced by Law No.67/2014/QH13, dated November 26, 2014, on investment ("Investment Law of 2014"), which was effective from July 1, 2015.
47. Law on enterprises, dated November 29, 2005 ("Enterprise Law of 2005"), as amended from time to time; replaced by Law No.68/2014/QH13, dated November 26, 2014, on enterprises ("Enterprise Law of 2014"), which was effective from July 1, 2015.

TAX

48. Law on corporate income tax, dated June 3, 2008 ("Corporate Income Tax Law"), as amended in 2013 and 2014.
49. Law on personal income tax, dated November 21, 2007 ("Personal Income Tax Law"), as amended in 2013 and 2014.

DEVELOPMENT INVESTMENT CREDIT AND POLICY CREDIT

50. Decree No.75/2011/ND-CP dated August 30, 2011 of the government on credit investment and export credit of the state ("Decree 75/2011"); as amended by Decree No.54/2013/ND-CP dated May 22, 2013, of the government supplementing Decree 75/2011 ("Decree 54/2013"); as amended by Decree No.133/2013/ND-CP dated October 17, 2013 of the government amending, supplementing Decree 54/2013 ("Decree 133/2013").
51. Circular No.35/2012/TT-BTC dated March 2, 2012, of the Ministry of Finance, guiding a number of articles of Decree 75/2011 ("Circular 35/2012").
52. Decision No.13/2009/QD-TTg dated January 21, 2009, of the prime minister on usage of the development investment credit fund of the state to continue the implementation of solidifying channels and canals, development of rural traffic road, infrastructure for raising and planting aquatic products and infrastructure of trade village in countryside in the period of 2009–15 ("Decision 13/2009"); as amended by Decision No.56/2009/QD-TTg of the prime minister amending, supplementing a number of articles of Decision 13/2009 ("Decision 56/2009").
53. Circular No.156/2009/TT-BTC, dated August 3, 2009, of the Ministry of Finance guiding mechanism of state development investment credit borrowing to the implementation of solidifying channels and canals, development of rural traffic road, infrastructure for raising and planting aquatic products, and infrastructure of trade village in countryside ("Circular 156/2009"), as corrected by Decision No.2326/QD-BTC, dated September 25, 2009, of the Ministry of Finance ("Decision 2326/2009").

54. Decision No.03/2011/QD-TTg, dated November 10, 2011, of the prime minister issuing regulation on guarantee for small- and medium-size enterprises borrowing loans from commercial banks ("Decision 03/2011").[1]

VIETNAM DEVELOPMENT BANK

55. Decision No.108/2006/QD-TTg, dated May 19, 2006, of the prime minister, on establishment of the Vietnam Development Bank ("Decision 108/2006").
56. Decision No.110/2006/QD-TTg, dated May 19, 2006, of the prime minister, approving the charter of Vietnam Development Bank's organization and operation ("Decision 110/2006").
57. Decision No.44/2007/QD-TTg, dated March 30 2007, of the prime minister, on issuance of regulation on financial management for the Vietnam Development Bank ("Decision 44/2007").
58. Circular No.111/2007/TT-BTC, dated September 12, 2007, of the Ministry of Finance guiding the implementation of financial management mechanism ("Circular 111/2007").

LOCAL DEVELOPMENT INVESTMENT FUNDS

59. Decree No.138/2007/ND-CP, dated August 28, 2007, of the government, on organization and operation of local development investment funds ("Decree 138/2007"), as amended by Decree No.37/2013/ND-CP, dated April 22, 2013, of the government, on amendment and supplement of a number of articles of Decree 138/2007 ("Decree 37/2013").
60. Circular No.28/2014/TT-BTC, dated February 25, 2014, of the Ministry of Finance, guiding the financial management mechanism of local development investment funds ("Circular 28/2014").
61. Circular No.42/2014/TT-BTC, dated April 8, 2014, of the Ministry of Finance, issuing standard charter of local development investment funds ("Circular 42/2014").

POLICY BANK

62. Decree No.78/2002/ND-CP, dated October 4, 2002, of the government, on credit for poor people and other policy beneficiaries ("Decree 78/2002").
63. Decision No.131/2002/QD-TTg, dated October 4, 2002, of the prime minister on establishment of social policy bank ("Decision 131/2002").

DEVELOPMENT ASSISTANCE FUND

64. Decree No.43/1999/ND-CP, dated June 29, 1999, of the government, on development of investment credit of the state ("Decree 43/1999") (*no longer applicable*).
65. Decree No.50/1999/ND-CP, dated July 8, 1999, of the government, on organization and operation of development supporting fund ("Decree 50/1999") (*no longer applicable*).

66. Decision No.231/1999/QD-TTg, dated December 17, 1999, of the prime minister, approving charter of organization and operation of development supporting fund ("Decision 231/1999") *(no longer applicable)*.
67. Decision No.232/1999/QD-TTg, dated December 17, 1999, of the prime minister, issuing regulation on financial management of development supporting fund ("Decision 232/1999") *(no longer applicable)*.
68. Decision No.59/2005/QD-TTg, dated March 23, 2005, of the prime minister, issuing regulation on financial management for development support fund ("Decision 59/2005") *(no longer applicable)*.

DRAFT LEGISLATION

69. Draft (amended) Law on State Budget.
70. Draft circular of the Ministry of Finance, guiding the capital mobilization of the local governments.
71. Draft (amended) Law on Public Debt Management.

NOTE

1. Replacement for the old ones being Decision No.14/2009/QD-TTg, dated January 21, 2009, of the prime minister, issuing regulations on guarantee for enterprises borrowing loans from commercial banks ("Decision 14/2009"), as amended by Decision No.60/2009/QD-TTg, dated April 17, 2009, of the prime minister, on amendment and supplement of a number of articles of Decision 14/2009 ("Decision 60/2009").

ECO-AUDIT

Environmental Benefits Statement

The World Bank Group is committed to reducing its environmental footprint. In support of this commitment, we leverage electronic publishing options and print-on-demand technology, which is located in regional hubs worldwide. Together, these initiatives enable print runs to be lowered and shipping distances decreased, resulting in reduced paper consumption, chemical use, greenhouse gas emissions, and waste.

We follow the recommended standards for paper use set by the Green Press Initiative. The majority of our books are printed on Forest Stewardship Council (FSC)–certified paper, with nearly all containing 50–100 percent recycled content. The recycled fiber in our book paper is either unbleached or bleached using totally chlorine-free (TCF), processed chlorine–free (PCF), or enhanced elemental chlorine–free (EECF) processes.

More information about the Bank's environmental philosophy can be found at http://www.worldbank.org/corporateresponsibility.

green press INITIATIVE

www.ingramcontent.com/pod-product-compliance
Lightning Source LLC
Chambersburg PA
CBHW080552220326
41599CB00032B/6452
9781464812873